Explorers and Exploration

Explorers and Exploration

The Best Resources for Grades 5 through 9

by Ann Welton

ORYX PRESS
1993

The rare Arabian Oryx is believed to have inspired the myth of the unicorn. This desert antelope became virtually extinct in the early 1960s. At that time several groups of international conservationists arranged to have 9 animals sent to the Phoenix Zoo to be the nucleus of a captive breeding herd. Today the Oryx population is nearly 800, and over 400 have been returned to reserves in the Middle East.

Copyright © 1993 by Ann Welton
Published by The Oryx Press
4041 North Central at Indian School Road
Phoenix, Arizona 85012-3397

Published simultaneously in Canada

Printed and Bound in the United States of America

∞ The paper used in this publication meets the minimum requirements of American National Standard for Information Science—Permanence of Paper for Printed Library Materials, ANSI Z39.48, 1984.

Library of Congress Cataloging-in-Publication Data
Welton, Ann
   Explorers and exploration: the best resources for grades 5 through 9 / Ann Welton.
      p.   cm.
   Includes index.
   Summary: Brief historical narratives on explorers and areas explored from the Vikings to Marco Polo, to the American West, to the polar regions and space. Includes an annotated bibliography.
   ISBN 0-89774-799-2
   1. Discoveries in geography—Juvenile literature.
   [1. Discoveries in geography.   2. Explorers.]   I. Title.
   G175.W45   1993
   910'.9—dc20
                                                    93-18190
                                                    CIP

To Kevin and Emily, for their great and consistent patience, and to the librarians of the King County (Washington) Library System for untiring assistance.

Contents

Preface

THE URGE TO EXPLORE

All exploration begins at home. In fact, the beginnings of exploration are more personal than that, starting in the head of the explorer as a drive that is finally expressed outwardly. Yet the outward expression remains a function of the inward drive, the internal motivation to push limits, look at new things, make something of oneself, achieve fame, find fortune, or construct a new life. The reasons are various and as individual as each person.

Not everyone will be seized by the urge to rise and go, but most of us will yearn at one time or another to push against our boundaries and see if they are actually as solid as they seem. The search for self and for self-expression that is common to all of us, at all ages, is perhaps the best reason to study what explorers have done, for their literal journeys provide a metaphor for our own inward travels. Today our physical frontiers may have diminished, but the human urge to move onward and outward from the personal center has not.

The lore of exploratory journeys can make history come alive. Far from being a dry recitation of facts, the story of Marco Polo's journey to Cathay,

---

*Eliot, T.S. (1973). "Little Gidding." *In The Norton Anthology of Modern Poetry*. Ellmann, Richard and O'Clair, Robert, eds. New York: W. W. Norton.

for example, provides adventure, exotic atmosphere, and drama. In the classroom it also provides a springboard for discussion of such varied topics as cross-cultural understanding, the difficulty people have accepting new ideas, and the changing Western view of Asian culture and geography over the last 800 years. Discussion can even be tied to present sociopolitical conditions in Mongolia and China, bringing Polo's experiences into a contemporary frame, and showing students that some things either don't change or change very slowly.

The importance of looking at past exploration and the men and women who engaged in it lies in this potential for addressing the exploratory urge in each student. Study of explorers and exploration pique interest not only in history but in other cultures and points of view as well.

CONTENT

This book divides the last 1,000 years into 10 periods, each characterized by either geographical location or time frame. The progression is not smoothly chronological, and the teacher or library media specialist is urged to fill in with his or her own materials whenever necessary. Each of the 10 chapters includes a brief narrative of the period as well as an annotated bibliography of fiction and nonfiction books on some aspect of the period. The narratives provide background for teachers and library media specialists and motivation for further study for students. The 10 bibliographies contain a total of 230 titles, over 200 of which have been published since 1986. Most of the books in the bibliographies are at a middle-school reading level, easily comprehended by fifth to ninth graders. When picture books, easy readers, or adult books are recommended, they are marked by **P**, **ER**, or **Ad.**

Books Selected

The books chosen for each section have been selected on the basis of their interest level for middle school readers, whether in text, formatting, or both. Picture books are included where they provide good introductory material or hooks for student interest. Most of the books are appropriate for reading, browsing, booktalking, or excerpting and can be used to form a base for high content, focused library programming units. These units can easily be tied in with library skills training on a literature-based, interdisciplinary model as well. Students involved in research or interested in one of the topics herein will find a wealth of resources. The book entries provide title, price*, presence of a bibliography or index, and ISBN. The annotations

---

*Although prices may change, they are listed here to give a general idea of the amount.

briefly describe the book's content, evaluate the book's style of writing and main features, and suggest ways to use the book with children.

Chapter Topics

The first four chapters look at European-based exploration to the eastward and the westward. Leif Eriksson (Chapter 1), Christopher Columbus (Chapter 4), and Ferdinand Magellan (Chapter 3), all sailed westward and discovered new lands and peoples. Marco Polo traveled eastward to Cathay and Vasco da Gama and the other Portuguese sailors from Prince Henry the Navigator's school of navigation (Chapter 3) also made pioneering voyages to the south and east. These Portuguese expeditions made possible later transoceanic voyages, and Marco Polo's travels brought a wealth of new (if contemporarily unaccepted) information back to Europe. Chapter 5 discusses European and American expansion westward across the North American continent, and Chapter 6 covers European exploration of Africa in the nineteenth century. As terrestrial territories were explored more and more thoroughly, the gaze of humankind turned first to the ends of the earth at the North Pole and the South Pole (Chapter 7), and then upward to the mountains (Chapter 8) and downward to the ocean bottoms (Chapter 9). Finally, human curiosity has reached beyond the earth to outer space (Chapter 10).

As you read through these chapters, consider open-ended questions that will aid your students in applying historical situations to their own lives. For example: What places that you have never visited do you feel curious about? How do you think Marco Polo felt when his father told him about Cathay? What do you think motivates mountaineers to extend themselves in potentially life-threatening situations?

AUDIENCE

This book is intended for use by both classroom teachers in the humanities and by library media specialists and librarians. It is also intended for students who want to research one of the explorational topics covered, or who want interesting reading on a particular explorer or time period. Since the following pages fit exploration into its historical and cultural contexts, this book is suited for use as enrichment and curriculum enhancement material for both history and the social sciences. Some chapters, such as Chapter 10 on space exploration, will have applications to science curricula.

"Mom! I found snakes out by the tomatoes. Can I take that little trail that goes into the field and look for more?" My seven-year-old announces at once a discovery and the urge to continue her explorations, a homely expression of the age-old drive to satisfy curiosity and expand horizons. Looking at exploration can open our own possibilities and help re-create the past. As you move through these units, may you find your own horizons broadened.

CHAPTER 1
Leif Eriksson and the Vikings

At home, the Vikings were quiet people who liked knitting, cheese tasting and boring things like that. But on tour they went wild. They put on their best horned hats and sailed across the sea, singing and shouting like mad. If you heard them coming, it was best to run away.—Martin Handford, *Find Waldo Now**

The version Handford's wild wanderer, Waldo, gives of the Vikings is a little different from the one we are used to, but it serves to warn us that the typical western European view of the Vikings may not be entirely accurate. To understand the Vikings as explorers, and not solely as marauders, it is necessary to look at their situation in the late eighth century A.D., when they began to sail both south and west from their northern waters.

The Vikings came from Scandinavia, an area that today comprises Denmark, Norway, and Sweden. In the eighth century, Scandinavia was an area of similar culture and a more or less shared language, though dialects varied. The stereotypical view of the Viking describes a person who is tall, blonde, and uncouth. However, Viking physiognomy varied considerably, enough for the Irish to distinguish between the *dubh ghall* (dark strangers) and the *fionn ghall* (fair strangers). The designation of "uncouth" must be seen as the product of a frightened populace subjected to brutal raiding.

---

*Handford, Martin. (1988). *Find Waldo Now*. Boston: Little, Brown.

Numerous theories try to explain why Norsemen left their homes to go "a-viking" or roving across the seas, but population pressure was probably the key factor. Mountains, heavy forests, and infertile soil made farming difficult in the Scandinavian homelands. The Norwegians settled in the Faroe, Orkney, and Shetland islands; Scotland; Ireland; and northwest England; while the Danes went to Germany, the Netherlands, France, and eastern England. The Swedes pushed through Russia to make trading contacts with Byzantium and the Arab world.

Certainly Vikings raided and pillaged in a lamentably destructive manner. Although later raids sought also to acquire land for settlement, the Vikings were undoubtedly concerned with quick gains, such as could be had from raiding monasteries, the repositories of much wealth in the eighth and ninth centuries. The attack on the monastery of Lindisfarne off the northeast coast of England in 793, for example, destroyed the monastery and laid the island to waste. If such pillage and destruction is not an understandable mode of operation to us today, it may be because the reasons for such behavior were unique to the conditions of eighth and ninth century Scandinavia. But the urge to move on, find more land, and stretch out is the same impulse that has fired explorational urges down the centuries, from the opening of the American West to the opening of the frontiers of space. It is a drive common to all and understood by all.

The Vikings were only able to carry out their raids and exploratory voyages because they possessed a ship-building technology that was unequaled at the time, both in terms of speed and efficiency. The Viking longship moved swiftly through oceans and up rivers, yet was lightweight enough to be carried. Constructed of overlapping planks, with the joints filled by rope, the longships were flexible and able to withstand high seas. These "dragon ships," so called because of their shape and the snake-like forms on their prows, plied waters as far south as the Black and Caspian Seas, and eventually touched the shores of North America.

While the ships themselves were an important factor in the Viking discoveries, the crew was more important still. Skilled mariners had to become adept at sailing through the gales so common in the northern seas. Ships were routinely swamped and the freezing winds could douse crews with wickedly cold spray. The troughs of waves were often incredibly deep, which made for a bumpy ride at best. In order to function at all in such conditions, not only did the ship have to be strong, flexible, and fast, but the crew had to perfect its sailing expertise.

Viking navigational abilities were based on observation of the positions of the sun and stars. Given this, the unpredictable nature of the ocean, winds, and weather caused not a few Viking ships to be blown off course. Such was the fate of the ship that came upon Iceland between 850 and 870 A.D. Living conditions on the island, though rough, were comfortingly similar to those in the rest of Scandinavia, and the Vikings stayed and thrived. Then, in 982 A.D., a Viking chieftain named Erik Thorvadsson killed two men in a quarrel. As a result, Erik the Red, as he is better known, was exiled from his home on Iceland. During the time of his exile, he heard stories of an island to the west and decided to look for it. He found a large island and spent three years there, discovering, he claimed, that both the land and the sea were fertile and the summers warm. He called the island Greenland. The name was chosen with forethought, for Erik wanted to induce people to settle there; and the ploy worked. Sometime in 985 or 986 about 400 people were enticed into leaving Iceland to voyage to the "greener" shores of the larger island. It was a rough crossing, with over half of the 25 boats turning back or sinking. Nor was Greenland what the settlers had been led to expect. The weather on the island today is no more unseasonable than that of Maine. One thousand years ago, however, Greenland was icier; the people found that eight months of intense cold each year would not allow crops to ripen. Also the island was often surrounded by pack ice, which made fishing difficult if not impossible. Erik may have sold his fellow Icelanders a bill of goods concerning Greenland, but his settling of the island marked the beginning of Viking voyages westward.

The year that Erik returned to Greenland, a fellow Icelander, Bjarni Herjolfsson, returned from a trip to Norway to find that his father had sold the family farm and gone with Erik as a settler. Bjarni was determined to join his father, and though it was autumn, the worst time for sailing the waters of the northern Atlantic, he formed a crew and set out. Fog was a besetting problem, obliterating any view of the sun and stars and effectively blocking the Vikings' ability to navigate. At one point, Bjarni's crew did not see the sun for four days. However, whenever the fog lifted, Bjarni set his course and sailed doggedly westward from wherever he happened to be at the time. So it was that when he sighted land it was not Greenland, but most likely the coast of Canada. However, once he realized he was not where he wanted to be, Bjarni, despite pleas from his crew to stop and investigate this strange land, exhibited the same single-mindedness that had brought him to a new shore and turned back.

Thus it was Leif Eriksson, the son of Erik the Red, who made the first landfall on the North American continent. Shortly after Bjarni Herjolfsson returned to Greenland with his tale, Leif set sail westward. Following a long ocean voyage, the crew arrived at an island they called Helluland, meaning "crag land" or "stone." This island and possibly another area they reached further south were most likely peninsulas of Baffin Island. Even further south they found a more hospitable land where they built grass huts and wintered. Leif called the land Vinland, which is usually translated "land of grapevines," but may have meant "pastureland." It was probably northern Newfoundland. When he returned to Greenland at the end of the winter, Leif carried trees and cattle fodder to prove that he had indeed been to a place where the climate was milder.

Several other Viking explorations to the New World are recorded in various sagas, or stories, but none of the settlements seem to have survived. Yet legends remain, and in Europe, far beyond Scandinavia, the traces of Viking culture have been blended into other cultures in melting pot fashion. Some even speculate that word of Viking discoveries to the west inspired Columbus, 500 years later, to try to reach the east by sailing into the setting sun. The Vikings' importance as explorers lies in the heritage they left us: their intrepid pushing of boundaries, and the willingness to endure hardship to discover new frontiers.

ANNOTATED BIBLIOGRAPHY

Nonfiction

Barden, Renardo. *The Discovery of America*. San Diego: Greenhaven Press, 1989. $12.95. 112p. index. bibliography. ISBN 0-89908-071-5.

Do we really know who discovered America, or is it a mystery? Many of us are aware that the Viking landfalls in North America predate Columbus's landing in the Caribbean, but were there others who arrived before 1492?

In six chapters, Barden examines how the existence of the New World was revealed. Calling upon evidence from archaeological finds, Barden begins with a chapter on Columbus and a chapter on the earlier explorations of Saint Brendan of Ireland and Madoc of Wales. Two chapters are devoted to Norse expeditions, and a fifth chapter treats the possibility of Polynesian explorations raised by Thor Heyerdahl's *Ra* expedition. The conclusion ties loose ends together and states the significance of the first contacts between New and Old Worlds.

Barden's interrogatory prose is lively and generally pulls the reader along, although he bogs down in the factual material at times. The type, running down the center of the book, leaves wide margins for quotes and sidebars. Numerous black-and-white illustrations and maps, a good index, and a short bibliography round out the volume. This thought-provoking entry in the Great Mysteries: Opposing Viewpoints series can be used to spark debate and engender discussion.

Bray, Warwick, et al. *The Ancient Americas*. New York: Peter Bedrick, 1989. $24.95. 151p. index. glossary. bibliography. ISBN 0-87226-303-7. **Ad.**

The Americas were a civilized land of complex, sophisticated cultures long before the Viking landfalls and millennia before Columbus. The arts flourished, as did agriculture, architecture, engineering, theology, and complex political systems. The Mayan civilization had developed place value numeration, the Hopewell a multi-layered trading economy. We usually consider the European civilization to have been more "advanced" than the "primitive" American cultures it encountered, but this is a misinterpretation that might be rectified by a closer look at those American societies and by a re-evaluation of what is meant by "primitive."

This volume in "The Making of the Past" series looks at the cultures of North, South, and Meso America over a long period of time. Beginning with a chronological table, chapters are devoted to "Man in the New World," "The Discovery of Ancient America," "North America," "Meso America," and "South America." Chapters 3-6 each include a "Visual Story," showing an archaeological site in each region and discussing its cultural ramifications.

The text, set in columns, is in a small face and is adult in vocabulary and phrasing. There are frequent illustrations, almost one to a page, either photos, paintings, or reconstructions, that make this a wonderful browsing book. The 12 maps are helpful in locating each culture. There is a solid adult bibliography, a good index, and an exemplary glossary with excellent definitions and explanatory drawings.

A draw for the casual viewer, this book provides excellent supplemental and background material for units that cover the state of American civilization as Columbus arrived on the Bahamian shore.

Gallant, Roy A. *Ancient Indians: The First Americans.* Hillside, NJ: Enslow Publishers, 1989. $13.95. 126p. index. bibliography. glossary. ISBN 0-89490-187-7.

People have lived in the Americas for about 40,000 years. What do we know about these early inhabitants, ancient people who left traces of their culture from the Arctic to the tip of South America?

Focusing on the archaeological record, Roy Gallant, a veteran writer of nonfiction for children, covers what is known about the ancient forerunners of North American Indian cultures. Beginning with a fictional account of a bison hunt 10,000 years ago, Gallant goes on to discuss the Clovis people and the arguments within the anthropological community over the age of various cultures. Succeeding chapters look at the spread of Paleo-Indian cultures and at the roots of the Eskimos and other North American tribes.

In a manner similar to that of Kathryn Lasky's *Traces of Life* (see Chapter 6), Gallant brings the processes of paleoarchaeology to the forefront, showing how use of the scientific method can help to reconstruct pre-history. A sound report source, this book could also provide interest reading for students investigating life in ancient America. A useful index and glossary are also included. The bibliography is largely adult, but is notable for its inclusion of an extensive periodical list. In terms of both format and content, *Ancient Indians* would serve library skills instructors well as an example of various types of bibliographic citation.

Krensky, Stephen. *Who Really Discovered America?* Illustrated by Steve Sullivan. New York: Hastings House, 1987. $12.95. 60p. index. ISBN 0-8038-9306-X.

In the lists of American firsts, Columbus is in some ways an also ran, but what he did definitively was to bring America into the sphere of European knowledge and influence. We know people came to America long before Columbus, people whose distant ancestors "discovered" America in much the same way that Cro-Magnon man "discovered" Europe.

There is much speculation as to who, aside from the indigenous inhabitants, discovered America. Krensky looks at a number of candidates for the honor he summarily denies Columbus. In four chapters he considers the Asian peoples who very likely crossed to North America via the Bering Straits 40,000 years ago; possible incursions from Asia and Polynesia; early Atlantic crossings, including the Viking voyages of exploration; and, finally, Columbus's and Cabot's expeditions. He produces facts to back his speculations, finding evidence of cultural exchanges in handicrafts and arts, games, toys, and the lowly sweet potato.

Krensky's style is lively and involving, reads aloud well, and will hold student interest. This ideal capsule treatment of the who-was-there-first debate works equally well for booktalking or classroom reading. There is no table of contents, but the index offers adequate access for report purposes. Steve Sullivan's iconic black-and-white acrylic paintings extend the text intriguingly.

Leon, George deLucenay. *Explorers of the Americas Before Columbus.* New York: Franklin Watts, 1989. $13.95. 64p. bibliography. index. ISBN 0-531-10667-5.

In eight brief chapters, Leon covers the explorers who visited the New World prior to Columbus's celebrated landing in the Caribbean in 1492. A brief introductory chapter is followed by chapters on the first Americans (which treats the crossing of the Bering Straits), archaeological evidence supporting the Bering Straits theory, the legend of St. Brendan, the Viking explorations, speculation regarding Phoenician influence on the civilizations of ancient Latin America, Heyerdahl's *Ra* expeditions, and the dawning of the age of exploration. The test is brief, but gives enough information for short reports. The layout is spacious, and the frequent use of excellent black-and-white maps makes the paths of the explorers easy to follow. Black-and-white photos and period drawings likewise extend the text.

The reportorial writing style is not inspired, but it is lively enough to hold the interest of even moderately inquisitive students. The frequent use of anecdotal material, from the Norse sagas to the economic conditions in Spain that allowed for Columbus's financing, add color to what could have been a lackluster narrative. This book would either booktalk well or read aloud to equally good effect, and might well be used to send eager readers to more lengthy and detailed works listed in the excellent two-page bibliography.

At 58 pages of text, this title is best used as an introduction to the subject or as a teaser to pique interest. The book's use is further extended by a thorough four-page index.

Livesey, Robert and A. J. Smith. *The Vikings.* Toronto: Stoddard, 1989. $17.95. 90p. index. ISBN 0-7737-5209-9.

In a unique approach, Livesey and Smith intersperse anecdotal and historical information on the Viking explorers of North America with ideas for supporting activities. The stories forms are as various as accounts of New World excavations and tales from *The Greenlander's Saga,* while the activities vary from conducting an archaeological dig in the backyard to trying your hand at composing a saga. There are patterns for creating three-dimensional dioramas as well as clear drawings of the Viking settlement at L'Anse aux Meadows, both in elevation and map form. Games, crossword puzzles, and instructions for making a *husnotra* (a Viking navigational tool) all make this book an excellent teaching tool for hands-on aspects of units on Norse explorers.

The book is open in format, illustrated with extremely clear, concise-looking black ink line drawings. Students may well pick this up to browse through and be caught by the conversational prose and interesting projects. An index that lists activities, illustrations, mini-facts, and personalities in separate categories gives welcome access to this unusual and excellent resource.

Maestro, Betsy and Giulio Maestro. *The Discovery of the Americas.* New York: Lothrop, 1991. $14.95. 48p. ISBN 0-688-06837-5.

A brief, factual text, large bright watercolor illustrations and clear maps make this book a fitting introduction to the opening of the Americas. It covers the crossing of the Bering Straits, the possible Phoenician influence on the New World, the voyage of St. Brendan, and the Vikings' explorations. It also gives background on numerous Indian tribes, and on exploratory voyages to the American shores from Columbus to Magellan.

The volume is oversized with a corresponding large type font and more illustration than narrative. The main text is followed by a table of dates, a listing of ancient American Indian tribes, and brief fact sheets on the Age of Discovery, the naming of the Americas, and other voyages not mentioned in the body of the book.

Since the book covers about 21,000 years in 43 pages, it is obviously too brief to be useful for reports. Nonetheless, it provides attractive browsing fare and is useful for opening units on topics from the Viking explorations to the exploitation of the native population in the New World. Because the format is juvenile, it will take a teacher's or librarian's promotion to encourage students to pick it up. However, the book's consummately visual format makes it a natural for group sharing and a wonderful opener for discussion. The maps, which are large and simplified to enhance clarity, are especially noteworthy and useful.

Martell, Hazel. *The Vikings.* Illustrated by David Salariya and Shirley Willis. London: Kingfisher Books, c1986. 38p. $12.95. bibliography. index. glossary. ISBN 0-86272-168-7.

The Viking lifestyle while on a raid differed from life at home. Martell's sensible approach mirrors these differences; she divides the book into two sections reflecting the dichotomy of lifestyle. The first section on Viking life deals with such mundane things as furniture and clothing and also with more important aspects of life, such as religion and the use of runes. From the day-to-day to the esoteric, the day-to-day life on a Viking homestead is brought to life. The second section, titled "The Vikings Abroad," looks at shipbuilding, raiding, trading practices, the Vikings of York, and considers Hedeby, a typical Viking trading town. Both the wilder aspects of Viking life and their success as traders come under inspection. The dual set-up of the book gives a lucid picture of Viking life.

The type font, which is clear but a bit cramped, is an accurate reflection of the prose style, which is long on information but dry. The text is helped out immensely by numerous earth-toned watercolor paintings and color photos. Enough information is included to write a short report on Viking life, and, by extension, to engender understanding of the Norse explorational impulse. Also, the slightly oversized appearance of the volume and the copious illustration make this a good choice for browsing.

The index, though only a page long, is adequate. However, the glossary is oddly selected and the bibliography is very brief. As well, the books listed are older, making this a poor source for references to other relevant works. This book is part of the History as Evidence series.

Matthews, Rupert. *Explorer*. New York: Knopf, 1991. $13.95. 64p. index. ISBN 0-679-81460-4.

The Eyewitness Book format is used here to excellent advantage. Double-page spreads show arresting photographs of people and artifacts that have to do with various eras or types of exploration. From Viking gold rings to a banjo from Shackleton's Antarctic expedition and Henry Stanley's hat, numerous visual treasures add depth to exploration units. Twenty-six different eras or locations of exploration are covered. Among these are such little-considered topics as Egyptian explorational expeditions, Arab explorers, and the role of missionaries in exploration.

Eyewitness Books are justly praised for their brilliance of conception and fine construction. There is certainly not enough information here for a report, but browsers will pick up countless tidbits of information. These bits and pieces come together to create a mosaic of exploration on our planet.

Units on any phase of exploration would benefit from the presence of this book, both as introductory and extension material. The index and table of contents are both specific and helpful, and a composite map of exploration routes is a real plus.

Mulvihill, Margaret. *Viking Longboats*. New York: Gloucester Press, c1989. $11.89. 32p. index. ISBN 0-531-17168-X.

Just who were the Vikings? How were their boats built, and where did they travel? What was their daily life like? Taking a simple, direct approach, this book is divided into 14 two-page sections, covering such areas of interest as the building of a longship, raiding, growing up in the Viking culture, government, religion, and feasting. Mulvihill asks what became of the Vikings (other countries grew stronger, raiding got more treacherous, and the Vikings became Christians and assimilated into local populations) and notes traces of Viking influence on present-day cultures. This last section, though extremely short, gives a good sense of the continuity of history.

The writing style falls just short of the sensationalistic, and while no real misinformation is given, the text is occasionally brief to a fault. There is almost more illustration than text, but this gives the book a tremendous advantage as a browsing book or a booktalking tool. Used as introductory material, this book can grab interest and generate questions. The illustrations range from full-page watercolor paintings to small inset photographs and rather rudimentary maps.

The 30-page text is followed by a date chart, which is useful to both teachers and students for quick reference and for comparing the Viking incursions with other world events of the same epoch. The index is too brief to be useful, but the table of contents is adequate. This book is part of the History Highlights series.

Odjik, Pamela. *The Ancient World: The Phoenicians.* New York: Silver Burdett, 1989. $14.98. 47p. index. glossary. ISBN 0-382-09891-9.

Long before the Vikings set out, whether in flight (as in Eric the Red's case) or to explore (like his son), the Phoenicians may have plied the seas westward from their towns in what is today Lebanon. The Phoenicians, the Canaanites of the Bible, sailed the Mediterranean between 1200 and 800 B.C., trading, colonizing, and building a merchant empire. This introductory volume focuses on the Phoenician civilization as it existed in the Mediterranean area in its heyday. While the book does not mention the possibility of Phoenician exploration of the New World, it does give a clear picture of this sea-faring society.

Highly pictorial one to two-page sections cover most aspects of Phoenician life: landform and climate; flora and fauna; livelihoods; family; food, medicine, and clothing; religion and rituals; the arts; transportation, exploration, and communication; recreation; military concerns; inventions; and the decline of the civilization. The illustrations are mostly photographs of Phoenician artifacts and ruins, or pictures of Lebanese wildlife.

The text is brief. In some areas, such as family life, historical data are almost nonexistent, thus the information given is speculative at best. The prose is stylistically blocky, plodding along in an uninspired fashion, so the book is carried largely on the merits of the illustrative material. A short report could be written from this, but there is not much more than could be found in an encyclopedia. Despite its deficiencies, this volume in the Ancient World series is an appealing browsing title and can be used as support material for classroom or library units.

Rosen, Mike. *The Journeys of Hannibal.* Illustrated by Tony Smith. New York: Bookwright, 1990. $11.40. 32p. index. glossary. bibliography. ISBN 0-531-18334-3.

Some explorations, unlike the Vikings' voyages to untamed shores, occurred in lands we think of as long settled. In 247 B.C. a son was born to the Carthaginian leader Hamilcar Barca. Sworn at an early age to despise and do battle against everything Roman, Hannibal, as the child was named, grew up to be a great leader. In 221 B.C.

young Hannibal launched an incredible assault on Rome, one that would take him overland 1,500 miles, through wild Spain, across the Pyrenees, and into France. The army would have to cross the flooded Rhone delta and then the high mountain passes of the Alps. This was thought impossible, but Hannibal did it.

Divided into two-page sections, Rosen's book gives the background on Carthage and Rome necessary to an understanding of the Punic Wars. Rosen chronicles Hannibal's bold attack on Rome and his ground-breaking journey, the eventual defeat of Hannibal, and his death. The end is extremely abrupt, giving the impression that the need to fit into the 32-page format of the "Great Journeys" series won out over literary considerations. Table of contents and index are both adequate. The extremely brief (12 entries) glossary might just as well have been left out. The bibliography is equally brief, but the titles are solid and current.

Photographs, rather bland-colored but action-filled paintings, and period drawings enhance the text. There are some very good maps, which could be used to compare Hannibal's crossing of the Alps with equally arduous crossings of the Rockies during the American westward expansion. This is good introductory and browsing material with potential for encouraging discussion and critical thinking.

Simon, Charnan. *Explorers of the Ancient World.* Chicago: Children's Press, 1990. $23.93. 128p. index. bibliography. glossary. timeline. ISBN 0-516-03053-2180.

In simple, direct prose, Simon introduces readers to some of the earliest explorers. Eight heavily illustrated chapters tell of the exploratory journeys of Himilco and Hanno of Carthage who traveled down the coast of Africa to Sierra Leone; of Egyptian sea voyages; of the Minoan explorations from Crete, which went as far as Spain; of the Phoenicians, who may have sailed around Africa some 2000 years ago; and of two Greek explorers—Alexander the Great and Pytheas—who sailed from present-day Marseilles perhaps as far north as Greenland. Also included are Chang Ch'ien of China who, beginning in 138 B.C., mapped what would become the Silk Road, Roman journeys, and a summarizing chapter mentioning Scylax and other Persian explorers.

A brief bibliography references other sources, mostly dated between 1950 and 1970. The dated nature of the sources is no problem in terms of informational accuracy, but many titles may be out of print. The index is serviceable, but the glossary reduces definitions to their lowest common denominator, resulting in misinformation at times. The visual element of the book is a strong attractive force. Many of the photos and period drawings are in color, and all are crisp and clear. The final section, showing maps from 226 B.C. to present Landsat photographs is fascinating. There is enough information here for short reports or for brief readings and booktalks.

Simon, Charnan. *Leif Eriksson and the Vikings.* Chicago: Children's Press, 1991. $23.93. 128p. index. bibliography. glossary. ISBN 0-516-03060-4.

Most of us have heard of Peregrine White, the Pilgrim baby born on the Mayflower. He is often considered North America's first citizen of European ancestry; he misses this distinction by over a half a millennium, losing out to Snorri Thorfinnson. This baby, the child of Thorfinn Karlsefni and his wife Gudred, was born in Newfoundland early in the eleventh century. The story of Thorfinn Karlsefni and the First Settlement is just one of the tales that veteran author Charnan Simon weaves into her fascinating factual account of the Viking explorations of the New World.

Divided into nine chapters, the narrative relates the adventures of Leif Eriksson and the explorers who followed him west into uncharted waters in search of new land. The first four chapters cover the early sightings of the northern land mass and the history of Erik the Red's quarrelsome brood. Chapters 5 and 6 look at voyages to Vinland and the journey of Thorfinn Karlsefni. The last three chapters cover the Norse sagas and their sources and archaeological digs and what they have shown. These chapters further discuss what became of the Viking voyagers once Vinland was definitively abandoned. The copious illustrations enhance the text. The book's usefulness is further increased by a serviceable index. An excellent report source, this book also makes good interest or group reading, given Simon's clear, lucid style.

Triggs, Tony D. *Viking Warriors.* Illustrated by John James. New York: Bookwright Press, 1990. $10.40. 24p. glossary. bibliography. index. ISBN 0-531-18356-4.

Very brief, printed in large type, and extended by ample illustrations, Trigg's book is introductory material of the most rudimentary kind.

Two-page sections cover the origin of the Vikings, Viking seafaring abilities, weapons, battle dress, forts, settlers, religion, and social life. The prose is simple, the information direct, and the illustrations clear if undignified. In addition to the painted illustrations, there are numerous photographs showing pertinent artifacts or archaeological ruins.

The index, glossary, and bibliography are so brief as to be of limited use.

An excellent beginning research tool for slower readers, this book will give most middle schoolers just enough brief information on the Vikings to fuel interest and have them looking for more detailed sources.

Voices from Our Nation. Austin, TX: Steck-Vaughn, 1991. $11.97. 124p. index. ISBN 0-8114-2771-4.

There are few better ways to give a sense of history to our children than to expose them to primary source material. Though none exists from the landing of Leif Eriksson in Vinland, this book describes Eriksson's voyage and landing in good saga style: " ...they came first to that land which Bjarni had sighted last. Leif was at the tiller and he brought the ship close up to the shore...Great glaciers rose before them...and...the land was like one great slab of rock...A worthless country they all agreed, barren and useless."

The 14-page unit presented here includes maps, reproductions, and a six-page timeline for the Viking explorations. The same is given for Columbus's exploration of the Bahamas, and DeSoto's exploration of the Mississippi River. Thus, this volume can be extended for use in units on later expeditions to the Americas. For a focus on Vikings, however, this book provides and excellent point of departure and a springboard to more detailed books and to the saga form of narrative. For details on format, see the annotation for *Voices from America's Past* in Chapter 4.

Wahlgren, Eric. *The Vikings and America.* New York: Thames and Hudson, 1986. $22.50. 192p. index. bibliography. notes. ISBN 0-580-02109-0. **Ad.**

For many, many years both lay people and academics have argued about whether Leif Eriksson reached Vinland, the mysterious "land of grapevines" of Icelandic saga; and if he did reach it, just where was it? Excavations of L'Anse aux Meadows in Newfoundland indicate the Vikings did indeed reach the North American continent around A.D. 1000, but was L'Anse aux Meadows Vinland? The author, after 50 years of studying not only saga but archaeology and history, has come to believe the Viking landfall was further south, perhaps Grand Manan near the Maine/Nova Scotia border. He discusses various purported Viking discoveries that proved to be frauds, such as the Kensington Stone, and gives evidence supporting the belief that the Vikings did explore Arctic Canada far to the north.

This is an adult book, a piece of adult scholarly research. Middle school students would be hard pressed to wade through it. There are over 100 illustrations, all rather small black-and-white photos and drawings, so there is little to attract middle grade browsers. However, for the middle school teacher preparing a unit on Viking exploration this is hard to beat as a source of both information and story. The index is detailed and the bibliography is divided into subject groupings and contains over 150 titles although many are not in English. This formidable and authoritative reference work has considerable strengths as a teaching or library reference tool.

Fiction

Haugaard, Erik Christian. *Leif the Unlucky.* Boston : Houghton Mifflin, 1982. $9.95. 206p. ISBN 0-395-32156-5.

In the last days of the Greenland colony, Leif Magnusson, the son of a landholder, tries to deal with the problems besetting his home farm of Brattahlid. The year is 1406, and the colony is 400 years old. The climate, harsh at the best of times, has taken a turn for the worse, and the settlers watch a slow, downward spiral in their hopes and aspirations for a better life. While the elders are lost in their dreams of the past and wait for a supply ship from their native Norway, Leif and some of the other children attempt to confront the practical problems of life on a barren, icebound outpost. Leif's plans are challenged, however, by the ambitious Egil Sigurdson, who wants to restore the worship of the old gods, Thor and Odin, and become master of Greenland.

Haugaard has based this story in part on the last recorded visit of Norwegians to Greenland in 1406. Though we will never know precisely what happened to this colony, which eventually came to an undoubtedly tragic end, the author has given us a vividly imagined story of its last years, peopled with believable characters in extreme circumstances. Both the ethos of the Viking nations and the urge that led them to explore and settle in strange lands are well in evidence, as are the all too human needs for home, love, and stability.

Hendry, Frances Mary. *Quest for a Maid.* New York: Farrar Straus Giroux, 1988. $13.95. 288p. ISBN 0-374-36162-2.

When she was nine years old, Meg Wright hid under her table and heard her sister kill a king. The king in question is Alexander, the beloved King of Scots, and her sister Inge's tool is sorcery. So begins a whacking good story about love, intrigue, sailing, relations between Scotland and Norway, and the rise to power of Robert de Brus (better known as Robert the Bruce) over the young bones of the Maid of Norway, the rightful heir to the Scottish throne. Along the way a great deal of history is painlessly imparted, painting a picture of the Viking culture as it blends with the other cultures of northern Europe, influencing them and being influenced in turn. Lively characterizations, a compelling plot, and a lovingly drawn setting all combine to create a three-dimensional picture of life in twelfth-century Scotland and Norway. The Scottish dialect might cause readers some trouble. However, the author has included a good glossary that effectively prevents confusion. This is a well-crafted, laudable performance, sure to draw readers of all ages.

Jones, Terry. *The Saga of Erik the Viking.* Illustrated by Michael Foreman. New York: Puffin Books, 1985. $7.95. unpaged. ISBN 0-14-03-1713-9.

"This is the tale of a Viking warrior who lived hundreds and hundreds of years ago. His name was Erik." What a perfect way to introduce a unit on the Vikings! Each of these stories, most no more than six pages long, tells a tale about Erik the Red. These fictional tales catch the imagination and talk about adventure, exploration, Viking life, and Norse mythology in such a natural and integrated way that students will absorb the information inadvertently.

Each of the 27 yarns is illustrated in pen and ink and luminous full palette watercolors by Michael Foreman. Here are hideous giants and snakes, sensuous mermaids, comical dwarfs, and great snarling wolves. Students will pour over the pictures and ask for the stories again and again. These tales can be used as library period fillers or classroom sponges; readers or listeners will be anxious to learn more about the nonfictional Viking expeditions after meeting Jones's Eric.

Manson, Christopher. *Two Travelers.* New York: Henry Holt, 1990. $14.95. unpaged. ISBN 0-8050-1214-1. **P.**

Taking a few fictional liberties in a picture book that bears tangentially on the Vikings, Manson recreates the story of two unusual travelers who journey from Baghdad, presumably to the court of Charlemagne. An author's note tells us that the story originates in the Royal Frankish Annals of Eginhard of Franconia, secretary and biographer of Charlemagne.

In 787 A.D., Charlemagne sent a delegation to Harain-al-Rashid, caliph of Baghdad. Included was an interpreter referred to as Isaac the Jew who returned to France with a goodwill gift from the caliph—an elephant named Abulabaz, "Father of Wisdom" in Arabic. Abulabaz lived in France until 810 when he was killed in a battle with the Vikings.

Manson's account tells of the friendship that develops between Isaac and his pachyderm buddy as they ply the long road from Baghdad. It's humorous and touching, extended reasonably well by ceremonious yet tongue-in-cheek pastels in earth tones and clayey blues, with a lush spring green denoting France.

Why use a book that is tangential to the topic of Viking exploration? Although the book must be told or shown because the juvenile format will not appeal to middle schoolers who are not introduced to it, the book's strengths are considerable. It provides a comic interlude and is a wonderful question generating tool: How far south is Charlemagne's capital from the Island of Cormac in Mary Stolz's *Pangur Ban* (see below)? What can be deduced from this in terms of Viking raiding patterns? What does their willingness to attack an elephant say about Viking courage (or foolhardiness)? Manson's book offers opportunities to make cultural contrasts and rich prospects for student thought and involvement.

Stolz, Mary. *Pangur Ban.* New York: Harper and Row, 1988. $13.95. 182p. ISBN 0-06-025861-6.

Cormac, son of Liam Brudair, is destined, it seems, to become a farmer like his father, for this is the way of life in ninth-century Ireland. He could also become a soldier, for there is always a need for men to protect the land from the savage Viking raiders who periodically lay the coast to waste. But Cormac is too gentle to fight and has no feel for farmer's work. What he wants to do is draw. Alone in the woods with Pangur Ban, his cat, he draws birds and animals. He feels filled with the wonder of God's creation and comes to realize that he has found his calling. Cormac's father is torn. He wants his son to follow tradition but finally, with dismay, he allows Cormac to enter a monastery where he exercises his gift by illuminating manuscripts. Years later, as Cormac is finishing his masterpiece—the life of St. Patrick—an alarm sounds. Viking raiders have been sighted off the coast. Cormac must save his work from destruction and so comes to made a choice that has far-reaching consequences, affecting the life of another young man centuries later.

Divided into three parts, Stolz's narrative is clear and contemplative, her lucid prose a delight. Characterization is deep, and one comes to care for the people in this story. More important is the tapestry of Irish life in the ninth century that is created in these pages. The effect of Viking raids had on surrounding countries is brought to life here. The typeface is clean and open, and chapter illuminations enhance the character of the narrative.

This is an excellent book for better readers who wish to explore the broader world in which the Vikings lived. Too contemplative and slow-paced for group reading, this book is best savored as an individual experience.

Wisniewski, David. *Elfwyn's Saga.* New York: Lothrop, Lee & Shepard, 1990. $13.95. unpaged. ISBN 0-688-09589-5. **P.**

The Hidden Folk, ghostly creatures of mist, have favored Anlaf Haraldson by helping him to safe harbor in the greenest valley in the North. Gorm the Grim, a competitor for this land, is outraged and lays a curse, carved upon a stone, on Anlaf and all his line. As a result, Anlaf's daughter, Elfwyn, is born blind. But the Hidden

Folk befriend her, enabling Elfwyn to see without sight. When Gorm returns with a gift even more dire than his curse, Elfwyn is able to turn the dangerous gift against him and so save her people.

Based on Icelandic history and incorporating not only narrative elements but symbolic cultural forms from Viking lore, this slightly oversized picture book can provide an excellent introduction to the Norse culture. Implicit in the tale are several reasons for Viking exploration, which could serve as discussion starters. The best use of this book with middle schoolers would be to tell the tale and then show the gorgeous, intricate cut paper illustrations. A teacher or librarian can use this book to present Norse saga, lifestyle, and mores, as well as modern art techniques, at the same time.

CHAPTER 2
Marco Polo: The Eastward Pull

When I was a child in southern California, we played a water game called Marco Polo. To the best of my recollection, it was a kind of tag, and even then it was fraught with imagery for me. When I was seven my mother had read me a book entitled *He Went with Marco Polo*. It told about the adventures of Marco Polo as he traveled along the Silk Road into the Orient. My mind's eye produced camels ambling with ungainly grace across open, swept sands in oven-like heat, and Marco arriving at last in the fantastic land of Cathay, a place of inexplicable splendor and mystery. It was very much at odds with the splashy chlorinated California pool but seemed every bit as real.

Marco Polo traveled to China at a time when this had seldom been done by Europeans. China must have seemed strange to him at first, a different world entirely in those days when the concept of a global community did not exist. The globe, in fact, did not exist, for the earth was considered to be as flat as the sands across which the camels, laden with trade goods, made their stolid way.

Marco was the son of Nicolo Polo, a merchant who around 1254, the year of his son's birth, made his way with his brother from his home city of Venice to China. He did not return for 15 years, leaving Marco, whose mother died during his infancy, in the care of an aunt and uncle. The boy was undeniably intelligent and energetic, and applied himself vigorously to his books, learning reading, writing, philosophy, and mathematics. Then, one morning in the spring of 1269, a large ship from the city of Acre, in Palestine, dropped anchor. Along with the cargo, two men in unusual garb disembarked and went at once to the Polos' house. There they identified themselves as Nicolo and Matteo Polo. Their relatives were understandably relieved and pleased, but Marco was transported. He hung on every word his newly returned father uttered.

Nicolo reported that he and Matteo had made their way first to Asia, then sought to return to Venice, but the outbreak of a war prevented them from doing so. Instead, they fled eastward to Bukhara in Turkestan. They spent three years there engaged in trade before accepting with alacrity an opportunity to travel to China. The journey was lengthy and difficult, but the Polos were rewarded by arriving in a land of spectacular strangeness and riches. Kublai Khan, the ruler of China (or Cathay, as it was then known) was in turn fascinated with the Polos' tales of their journeys. Intrigued by the idea of converting the Mongols to Christianity, the Khan sent the Polos back to ask the pope to send 100 priests to China to aid in this project.

Marco was fired by his father's stories of the Orient, stories other citizens of Venice frankly doubted. This mocking disbelief would also plague Marco upon the later publication of his book detailing his own travels. The Venetian lifestyle in the eleventh century was, despite the city's cosmopolitan trading orientation, that of any insular community cut off from a larger world. Reports from distant lands were scoffed at as being impossible, and the teller roundly condemned as a monger of tales. The fact that so few people traveled beyond the confines of the European continent added to the general climate of skepticism.

Nicolo and Matteo left Venice in the spring of 1271 to return to China, taking the seventeen-year-old Marco with them. Marco was desperate to travel with them, and his pleadings must have been convincing. The pope could spare only two friars, so the traveling party was small.

The trip was rigorous, and physical toughness was required. From Venice one traveled by boat across the Mediterranean to Jerusalem. A short overland trip to Acre was followed by an equally short sea voyage to Layas. On the outward journey, the Polos thought to save time by sailing to China from the Persian Gulf port of Hormuz. However, the vessels at Hormuz were completely inadequate—"death traps" in Marco's words—so they elected the overland route instead. The overland trip began with a great deal of bartering for horses, pack animals (often camels), and guides, not unlike the process that contemporary Himalayan mountaineers engage in today. Once the animals were secured and the trade goods loaded onto the smelly, cantankerous beasts, the journey began.

All this was new to Marco; nothing seemed an inconvenience. Alive to and engaged in all he saw, he kept a diary, which allowed him to record his impressions while they were fresh. He proved to have an amazingly photographic memory as well as an unusually high level of retention. He picked up foreign languages with tremendous speed and this, along with what seem to have been great charm and wit, quickly make him a valued member of the party.

From Hormuz, the Polos traveled northeast through Afghanistan, finally reaching the lush foothills of the Pamir range, which teemed with exotic birds and other fauna. Crossing the Pamirs, the Polos made their way briskly until they reached the Gobi desert. The Gobi took 30 days to cross at its narrowest point. Because the waterholes were widely spaced, travelers had to carry their own water if they hoped to survive. Once across the Gobi, no major obstacles, except sheer distance, stood between the weary travelers and Shang-Tu (Xanadu), the Khan's summer palace. They arrived nearly three years after setting out from Venice.

Kublai Khan welcomed the Polos warmly. He had feared them dead and was delighted at their return. He was particularly taken with young Marco, who within a short time became one of the Khan's trusted diplomats due to his linguistic ability and native charm. He was especially good, because of his capacities for observation and retention, in reporting back to the Khan on what he had seen in various cities of the realm. The Polos stayed in China for nearly 20 years, but at last they asked to return home and were allowed to do so, accompanying a young Chinese woman who was being sent as a bride to a Turkish ruler.

The return trip, made mostly by sea, was just as arduous as the trip to China had been two decades earlier. Shortly after Marco Polo's return to Venice, war broke out with Genoa. This conflict, the strife between the Guelfs and the Ghibelines, which birthed Dante Alighieri's *Divine Comedy*, allowed the production of *The Travels of Marco Polo*. Incarcerated in a Genoese prison, Polo dictated his adventures to a scribe, Rusichello of Pisa, with whom he shared a cell. The tales were extremely popular, but the people of Venice treated his adventures as imaginary stories, causing Marco some bitterness in his otherwise prosperous and peaceful later years. He found himself taken seriously only by those with considerable education, scholars and doctors. Yet time would show that he had truly opened Europe to the world of the East.

Today the roads that one must take from Italy to Beijing are much the same. One can fly, of course, but going overland would still expose the traveler to stretches of open desert, poor and perilous roads, and little recourse to modern conveniences. Marco's adventures come brilliantly to life when one looks across the rugged Afghan terrain, or observes Mongolian shepherds still living in their yurts. If Marco was disbelieved in his day, he has been vindicated in ours.

ANNOTATED BIBLIOGRAPHY

Nonfiction

The Age of Exploration. Freeport, Long Island, New York: Marshall Cavendish, 1989. $19.95. 64p. bibliography. index. (Exploring the Past: Four). ISBN 0-86307-997-0.

This 64-page overview describes the life and times of Marco Polo, Christopher Columbus, and Hernando Cortez. Each chapter is divided into a "portrait" section, giving a succinct but detailed overview of the subject's life; a "History in the Making" section, which gives an account of the high points of each explorer's voyages; and "The Way We Were," a generally first-person narrative detailing contemporary life in China, among the Aztecs, or on the high seas. These narratives are lightly to heavily fictionalized. Although they achieved their purpose of imparting information, the first-person point of view gives the narrative a fabricated sense. One particular frustration is the double-page illustration of the Aztec Volador ceremony, which lacks any accompanying explanation of the ceremony. There is a brief glossary, detailed chronology, reasonably good bibliography, and merely functional index.

In a style typical of many series books, a lot of information is literally crammed in. There are numerous full-page and double-page color paintings, inset reproductions, photographs, and maps. If a student wants to know what Marco Polo's birthplace looks like or what route he took to China, or if a student wants to see an ancient Chinese seismograph or magnetic compass, this book will answer nicely.

The highly pictorial aspects of this book and its relatively short chapters make it useful in several contexts. It is an excellent browsing book, sure to pique the interest of students who pick it up. Because of its nonthreatening look, the high ratio of pictures to text, poorer readers may be less intimidated by it and able to use it as a starting place for reports. It is a natural for excerpting in reading sessions, and lends itself well to telling.

Berrill, Margaret. *Mummies, Masks, and Mourners.* Illustrated by Chris Molan. New York: Lodestar/Dutton, 1989. $14.95. 48p. index. glossary. ISBN 0-525-67282-6.

While in China Marco Polo observed the impressive mass burials of the Chinese nobility. Yet even without his accounting of this phenomenon, we would know about it today. Scientific researchers have helped archaeological experts reconstruct the way of life of ancient people from burials. Mummies can give us much information on the civilization that produced them as well as on typical causes of death. Burials give us clues as to what people thought about life in the next world, giving insight into ancient cosmologies.

Beginning with a four-page introductory section on the advent of burial grounds and customs, the text of this book goes on to consider stone age burials; the burial at Haddenham, Great Britain; Egyptian mummies; Sumerian burial customs; Siberia and Lindow man; the burial of Lady Dai (Han China, c.100 B.C.); Roman memorials; New World mummies; Norse and African burial customs; and modern day customs. The text is lively and engaging and suits the absorbing subject matter. The large, clean typeface is open and inviting. The index and glossary are both adequate, but the information here is good only for very general reports.

Illustrated with numerous paintings and photographs, this book is an excellent introduction to a number of exploratory units. A discussion of Lady Dai's last day and a photograph of her mummy will certainly spark interest in Marco Polo's later trip to China. Pictures of Viking ship burials or Inuit mummies can introduce units on Viking and Polar exploration equally well. This book and the others in the Time Detectives series are perfect examples of what browsing books should be.

Beshore, George. *Science in Early Islamic Culture.* New York: Watts, 1988. $11.90. 69p. index. glossary. bibliography. ISBN 0-531-10596-2.

For over 500 years Islamic science evinced an eagerness to experiment and find new truths about the natural world. Tremendous advances were made in astronomy, mathematics, medicine, and botany, among other areas of scientific endeavor.

Beshore is informative, but dry. Still, he gets across the history of scientific achievements as well as giving information on the men who pioneered advances in their fields. Seven fairly brief chapters give background on Islamic culture, and cover mathematics, astronomy, vision and sight, meteorology, biology, and the scientific method. There is sound report material here, the accessibility enhanced by a good table of contents and comprehensive index. A short glossary does a good job of defining unusual words, and black-and-white illustrations are in keeping with the objective nature of the text.

This book enhances units on Marco Polo because Polo frequently noted the primacy of Eastern over Western science. How the eastern cultures attained this scientific primary, by what methods, and with what vocabulary, are all questions that supply fertile ground for thought. In integrating a unit on Polo with a science unit, this book is a natural bridge.

Ceserani, Gian Paolo. *Marco Polo.* Illustrated by Piero Ventura. Translation of *Il viaggio di Marco Polo.* New York: G.P. Putnam's Sons, 1977. $12.95. unpaged. ISBN 0-399-20843-7.

Two-page entries on aspects of Marco Polo's life and journeys follow a basically chronological order. Beginning with a section on Venice, the text covers merchants, Chinese trade goods, and Polo's trip to China. The latter topic is divided into a section each on the trip to Hormuz, the Gobi Desert, the Mongols, the great Buddha, and Kublai Khan. The book also discusses the years in China, Chinese inventions, and travelling within the Mongol Empire. Polo's return trip and declining years are covered in four pages. The prose is lucid and the bones of the story are there. As an introduction, this book is hard to beat, partly because of the watercolor illustrations.

Piero Ventura's hallmark style—clear, incredibly detailed watercolors that make excellent use of negative space, is very much in evidence here. These paintings are made for pouring over, and indeed they yield a wealth of information on sailing ships, merchants' overland journeying, thirteenth century China and Venice, and Chinese inventions. Occasionally the illustrations display things not discussed in the text, which may cause some frustration. Also, the only map, which is placed on the boards of the book, is too general.

Perhaps the best use of this book is as browsing material to back up more specific information on Polo. The illustrations are informative and, if the book is left available, almost irresistible. There is no index or bibliography.

Greene, Carol. *Marco Polo: Voyager to the Orient.* Chicago: Childrens Press, 1987. $13.95. 108p. index. timeline. ISBN 0-516-03229-1.

In 13 short chapters, the life and times of Marco Polo are set out in approachable prose. The chapters cover Marco's early years in Venice, his father's sudden reappearance, the wait for a return to China, and the eventual journey. The next six chapters treat the Polos' years in China and a trip they took to Persia. The last three chapters deal with homecoming, the years in prison which produced *The Travels of Marco Polo,* and Marco's later years. The volume ends with an excellent map of Marco's journeys, detailed timeline, and excellent, comprehensive index.

The illustrations, while not fascinating, are informative. Including the frontispiece and map, there are 18 black-and-white reproductions of period drawings, paintings, and etchings. These give a feel for the era, both in Venice and China, as well as showing reasonably contemporary portraits of all the Polos. It satisfies curiosity to see what Marco looked like, both in his prime and during old age.

There is easily enough information here for a detailed report. The excellence of the index and the table of contents makes this a solid research tool. It is, as well, a sound biography, paced well and interesting enough to hold readers' attention. Whether used for research or reference, this book certainly can lead students on to Polo's own book.

Humble, Richard. *The Travels of Marco Polo.* Illustrated by Richard Hook. New York: Watts, 1990. $11.90. 32p. index. glossary. ISBN 0-531-14022-9.

The Mongol conquests changed the Far East in almost every way. When the original conqueror, Genghis Khan, died in 1227, the conquest continued under his sons. The greatest of the Mongol Khans, Kublai Khan, was Genghis's grandson. Ruling until his death in 1294, Kublai was a wise head of state and spent much of his energy preserving the art and learning of his favored Chinese civilization. That we know as much about Kublai Khan as we do is the result of the writing of another thoroughly unusual man, the Venetian merchant, Marco Polo.

In this brief pictorial book, Richard Humble gives an overview of Polo's experience in prose that is sufficiently brisk to hold interest. Divided into double-page sections, the book covers the Mongol Empire, the trip to China, the years spent in "Cathay," the return trip, and the writing of the *Travels.* The glossary is brief (10 terms) and the definitions oddly digressive. The reader finds the meaning of the word and a little story about it, too. A brief time chart and acceptable index are also included.

Richard Hook's illustrations appear to be in watercolor on dry paper. They are large and attractive, though the colors are a bit muddy. This is definitely Hollywood

Marco: very attractive in a smooth, leading man sort of way. The contemporary illustrations are occasionally augmented by the insertion of period paintings.

The basic facts are here, perhaps the beginning for a report, but this title in the Exploration through the Ages series is best used as either a browsing book or a teaser to whet the intellectual appetite for more in-depth treatments.

Kranz, Irene and David M. Brownstone. *Across Asia by Land.* Adapted by Rachel Kranz from *To the Ends of the Earth.* New York: Facts on File, 1991. $17.95. 112p. index. bibliography. ISBN 0-8160-1874-X.

Trade routes today are largely traced upon our sky. Airplanes carrying cargo, whether humans or inanimate commodities, whisk through the atmosphere and make deliveries, if not overnight, at least within a very short time. However, the first trade routes, predating even the early sea routes, were overland roads like the Silk Road, the Ambassador's Road, or the Eurasian Steppe Route. The Silk Road, the route that Marco Polo took, is perhaps the best known, but certainly not the only overland road to cross Asia.

This informative volume covers the history of the Silk Road in great detail from the Greco-Roman period, through its heyday, to early modern times. Also discussed are the Ambassador's Road and the Burma Road, the Eurasian Steppe route, and the Russian River routes. Each of these is considered in the context of the time in which the road saw the most intense use. Two and a half chapters are devoted to the Silk Road, one to the Ambassador's Road and the Burma Road, one to the main Chinese routes in early modern times, one to the Russian River routes, and half a chapter to the Eurasian Steppe route. The prose is readable, if unexciting, but the detailed maps are more valuable. Looking very much like Rand McNally road maps, these show the lay of the land though which the travellers passed. Another particularly worthwhile feature is the detailed coverage given to the ethnic groups populating each area. Not only does this coverage explain history, it gives students insight into some of the ethnic conflicts that continue today.

A better source for reports is hard to imagine. The information is easy to locate through the excellent table of contents and index. Annotated bibliographies at the end of each chapter point students to more challenging and detailed works.

Although students will most likely use this book solely for reports, it is an excellent teachers' information and reference source.

Lim, John. *Merchants of the Mysterious East.* Montreal: Tundra Books, 1981, o.p. 32p. ISBN 0-88776-130-5. **P.**

The picture book format may make this a difficult book to sell to middle schoolers, but it is worth the effort. John Lim was born in 1932 and was raised in Singapore. Emigrating to the United States in 1959, he took a degree and worked as an accountant until his artwork proved so successful that he was able to devote himself to it on a full-time basis.

Singapore, the city, is on the island of the same name, located in Southeast Asia. Seventy-five percent of the population is Chinese and the various merchants Lim discusses and portrays here represent elements of Chinese culture that might well have been familiar to Marco Polo. Divided into sections on fortune tellers and story tellers, sellers of novelties and necessities, vendors of herbs and spices (included among the herbs are frogs), kites, firecrackers, and open air opera, Lim describes each merchant's wares and methods of sales as he observed them in the Singapore of his childhood. There is a wealth of fascinating information here, and a sense of color and proportion.

The illustrations are bright, busy, and primitive. The people look like painted Chinese dolls with round heads, black laquered-looking hair, and uniformly blue eyes, certainly an oddity. Since Lim is an internationally known artist, this could be used as an art awareness resource even as it functions as an enrichment tool for exploring Oriental culture.

Major, John S. *The Land and People of China.* New York: Lippincott, 1989. $14.95. 298p. index. bibliography. ISBN 0-397-32336-0.

As in his *The Land and People of Mongolia* (see below), Major presents a comprehensive, composite picture of China as a product of its cultural and historical heritage. Despite tremendous changes, Marco Polo would still recognize in today's China a number of aspects of the Mongol Empire that he knew 700 years ago.

Thirteen detailed chapters provide information on Chinese culture, land, early history (chapters 3–6), art and literature, religion and philosophy, science and technology, and modern history from 1800 (chapters 10–13). Boxes, graphs, and black-and-white photographs add information and extend the text. Major is certainly accurate, but his prose and presentation style are too dry for interest reading. This is, however, a definitive report source on China in any period, and a good vehicle for tracing the persistence of cultural values through political upheaval. The index and bibliography are both helpful and detailed.

Major, John S. *The Land and People of Mongolia.* New York: Lippincott, 1990. $15.89. 200p. index. bibliography. ISBN 0-397-32387-5.

For most students, the only image conjured up when Mongolia is mentioned is that of Genghis Khan and the Mongol Horde riding out of the north to conquor China. Few would connect Mongolia with Marco Polo's fantastic Kublai Khan, Genghis Khan's grandson. Yet is was from these Mongolian roots that the Yuan Dynasty of Chinese monarchs sprang. Major gives a comprehensive study of Mongolia. Eleven chapters cover the Mongolian heritage, land, culture, history (five chapters), arts and religion, daily life, and the status of the nation today.

The picture produced is of a country with a complex history matched by an equally complex set of problems as an emergent third world nation. The prose is painfully dry. The lengthy historical section is better, but the geographical and cultural sections stick to a monotone droning of facts. The book is attractively formatted, with an open, spacious look to the page. Boxed inserts on specific events or areas of Mongolian history or life provide breaks. The inclusion of Coleridge's "Kublai Khan" is a lovely touch. Frequent black-and-white photographs and reproductions add interest and some browsing appeal, but this book will be used mainly as a teacher reference or report source.

As a report source, it is clearly superior, having an excellent table of contents and index and an extensive, though mostly adult, bibliography. This is a solid source of background information on Kublai Khan and the culture that formed him.

McKillop, Beth. *China: 1400 B.C.–A D. 1911.* New York: Watts, 1987. $10.90. 32p. index. ISBN 0-531-10536-9.

Somehow we still regard the East as mysterious, even 720 years after Marco Polo set out on his historic trip to Cathay. This may be due to the long course of civilization there, undisturbed by influence from the West. The Asian civilizations achieved high levels of sophistication well before those of Europe. While Europeans still huddled around outdoor fires in tribal units, the Chinese were predicting earthquakes with scientific accuracy.

McKillop's overview gives a whirlwind view of Chinese civilization. Divided into four sections containing four double-page spreads each, the book covers The Age of Conflict (1400–221 B.C.), The First Empire (221 B. C.–A.D. 618), The Golden Age (A.D. 618–1368), and Imperial Splendor (A.D. 1368–1911). Within these sections religion, court life, technology, the arts, economics, and politics are all covered in a surface manner. There is less text than illustration, which is a combination of bright watercolor sketches and color photos. The maps inserted at the beginning of each section are useful for noting border changes. The index is rudimentary but functional.

With so little information, not enough for a report on any one era, what is the use for this book? There are several. It gives enough background to add context to Polo's trip. The pictures will invite browsers, and the low key text will appeal to less able readers. Perhaps best of all, the scant information will create interest by provoking questions. Used as a point of departure, this can send students on to books like Carol Greene's *Marco Polo: Voyager to the Orient* (see above).

Roth, Susan J. *Marco Polo: His Notebook.* New York: Doubleday, 1990. $14.95. unpaged. ISBN 0-385-26555-7.

Roth notes in her opening pages that while the story she tells is not entirely true, it certainly could have been. Roth has filtered through Polo's writings and eliminated the passages on Madagascar and Japan, places he did not truly visit. The rest she has condensed into 24 journal entires which range in length from one-third of a page (two to three sentences) to one page. The book ends with two pages of "Notes on Marco Polo's Travels."

Each page is matched by a full-page illustration; the illustrations are reproductions, maps, or photographs of places Polo travelled to or things he might have seen. The brief journal entries are a bit gushy and exclamatory. However, when pieced together they give a lovely, immediate picture of the effect his travels had on Marco over the 20-year duration of his journey. The book is beautifully crafted, lovingly put together on parchment-colored paper; the text is bordered by what appears to be torn or burnt paper. Some of the illustrations are beautifully tinted in pastel colors. This is a book to inspire art projects even as it introduces history. Aside from providing superlative read-aloud introductory material, this book could be used to inspire creative writing projects, providing students with a model for writing journal entries for other explorers. Despite its picture book appearance, this book is a winner for middle school history/exploration units.

Rowell, Galen. *Mountains of the Middle Kingdom: Exploring the High Peaks of China and Tibet.* San Francisco, CA: Sierra Club Books, 1983. $40.00. 208p. index. chronology of exploration. bibliography. ISBN 0-87156-339-8. **Ad.**

In 1980, after 30 years of closure, the Peoples Republic of China opened parts of their mountain provinces to outsiders. Galen Rowell, a photojournalist and mountaineer, travelled through eight provinces, producing the most extensive exploration of Chinese mountain territory by any American since World War II.

This gorgeous pictorial volume is a thorough documentation of this territory in China's remote and mountainous west. The people, landscape, flora, and fauna all appear in vital, engrossing color photographs. The text recapitulates the journeys of past explorers, giving detailed coverage to Marco Polo, George Leigh-Mallory, Eric Shipton, Heinrich Harrer, and Terris Moore. Looking at the changes that have taken place in each region since the explorers mentioned above were there, and providing detailed portraits of the fiercely independent mountain tribes, Rowell's text gives insight into present day China. The prose style and presentation are adult, and for middle schoolers the visual aspects must carry the reader along.

A good index aids in location of specifics, and the table of contents in locating geographic areas. A 12-page chronology of exploration gives excellent capsule histories. Despite the good text, *Mountains of the Middle Kingdom* is best used as a kindler of interest and a browsing book. Most students who pick it up will find it hard to put down, and when they do, they may well want to read something more about the 8,000-meter peaks of the Himalayas.

Sancha, Sheila. *Walter Dragun's Town: Crafts and Trade in the Middle Ages.* New York: T.Y. Crowell, 1987, 1989. $13.89. 64p. glossary. ISBN 0-690-04806-8.

Walter is a cloth merchant in the town of Stanford, England. In the summer of 1274, Walter and Hugh, another cloth merchant, are awaiting a visit from a wealthy Florentine merchant, Fulk Clarissimus. They hope to sell the merchant their hometown goods. Interspersed with this story is a look at a "greedy and corrupt" seneschal, Walter Dragun, who has a gang of bailiffs and underbailiffs to see that Walter gets what he wants.

The author does a creditable job of recreating the hustle and bustle of a town contemporary with Marco Polo. Numerous black-and-white ink sketches illustrate each slice of life, and the information imparted, in a deceptively readable way, helps deepen understanding of the way life was lived in medieval England. Town structure varied some from country to country, but the rudiments were the same for England as they were for Polo's Italy.

There is no index, but the detailed, thorough glossary is excellent. This book is a good starting place for units on the Middle Ages, employing a slice of life approach that will attract readers.

Stefoff, Rebecca. *Marco Polo and the Medieval Explorers.* New York: Chelsea House, 1992. $18.95. 112p. index. chronology. bibliography. ISBN 0-7910-1294-8.

Stefoff's readable prose presents Marco Polo's journey to Beijing in great detail. The book covers the various roads east, the Khan's court, and the civilization described by Polo, and concludes with a chapter on subsequent European travellers to China. The wealth of information combined with a somewhat dry style make this a better source for reports than pleasure reading. The text is interspersed with black-and-white reproductions and maps. The open type face and good leading give the page an approachable look. A nine-page color center section of period paintings gives an idea of the contemporary European conception of the East. The index is serviceable and the chronology puts Polo's journey into perspective. The bibliography, though quite lengthy, consists mostly of adult books, and is thus of more use to the teacher than the student.

Ventura, Piero. *Venice: Birth of a City.* New York: G. P. Putnam's Sons, 1987. Translation of *Venezia, nacita de una citta.* Translated and adapted by John Grisewood. $13.95. unpaged. ISBN 0-399-21531-X.

Highly illustrated and relatively light on text, this fine volume details the growth of Venice from 300 B.C. until the present day. The text of one to five paragraphs per double-page spread is both readable and informative. Students will come to comprehend why there are all those canals (the city is built on an archipelago of over 110 islets in the Lagoon of Venice), what began its rise (the salt trade), and what sustained it (diversified trading). Polo's journey receives coverage, and the detailed pictures show a clear view of Venice and the kind of ship in which Marco would have sailed south and east.

Government and the arts receive coverage, and the final three-page fold-out of Venice today gives a clear picture of the city in present times, though certainly the effects of pollution are not much in evidence.

Ventura is a master in the use of negative space, and his Venice should both capture and hold attention whether booktalked or made available for browsing. This book provides a natural opening, or a natural extension, to the story of Marco Polo.

Fiction

Norton, Andre and Susan Schwartz. *Imperial Lady: A Fantasy of Han China.* New York: Tor, 1991. $17.95. 293p. ISBN 0-312-93128-X.

The Han dynasty ruled China more than 12 centuries before Marco Polo, but during that period many of the cultural traits that the youngest Polo observed in Kublai Khan's court were formed and set in place. Sometimes this information can be better imparted and better assimilated in fictional form than in a straight history.

Silver Snow, lovely and capable, is the daughter of a disgraced general of the Imperial Army. Her exile is abruptly ended when the emperor sends for her as a new concubine. Between court politics and a frustrated and vicious eunuch, Silver Snow finds herself first confined to her quarters and then summarily adopted by the Emperor and sent to Mongolia to marry the leader of the Hsuing-Mu.

This well-written fantasy will engage young fans while giving them a lesson on Chinese history and culture that will prepare them for units on China.

CHAPTER 3
Prince Henry and the Circumnavigation of the Globe

Navigation: the science of getting ships, aircraft, or space craft from place to place; esp: the method of determining position, course, and distance traveled.—Webster's Ninth New Collegiate Dictionary

Navigation is nothing new to us. In hours we travel the globe, airborne, using computers to plot and set our courses, serene in the calm conviction that we know where we are. The world in the twentieth century is a vastly smaller place than it was 500 years ago when the first concerted attempts were being made to develop navigation into the art and science that it now is. It is easy to romanticize the development of navigational arts as being motivated entirely by curiosity. In fact, the primary motive was profit.

The development of oceanic navigation began in the fifteenth century, when Europe, self-sufficient in some respects, needed and desired some products that were available only from the Orient. Silk and gem stones were alluring, but of much greater value were spices, a blanket term referring to such products of non-European plants as sugar, incense, waxes, or the true spices—nutmeg, mace, cinnamon, cloves, and pepper. These latter had particular value, because farmers could not feed their livestock through the winters and had to slaughter most of their animals each fall. The smoked or pickled meat could be stored longer and enhanced in flavor by the use of spices, especially pepper. Beyond the practical considerations, the use of spices denoted high status. The wealthy demonstrated this by sprinkling both sugar and pepper on their toast.

The route spices followed prior to their arrival in Europe was long and circuitous. Chinese junks plied the seas around the Spice Islands (known as the Moluccas) buying mace, cinnamon, or cloves—whatever happened to be available. These spices were then traded to Indian traders at the port of Malacca on the Maylasian peninsula. From there, the Indians shipped the goods to western India, or the Malabar Coast, as it was then called. Arab brokers loaded spices into dhows and sent them either via the Arabian Sea, the Persian Gulf, or across the Indian Ocean to the Red Sea and up to Suez. Finally, the spices arrived in the eastern Mediterranean, where they were at last available to Europeans. The shipping families of Genoa and especially Venice held a virtual monopoly on the spice trade. As these two cities grew richer, other European nations began to consider bypassing the Italian shipping cities entirely and finding alternate routes to the Spice Islands. Land routes to Asia were closed to Christian nations during the last years of the fifteenth century by the Ottoman Turks in western Asia and the isolationist Ming Dynasty in China. For those countries seeking competing routes to the Spice Islands, the only logical alternative was the sea.

In 1480 Portugal was the same small country that it is today. Although its natural resources were limited, Portugal had, by that year, taken the lead in the exploration of sea routes to Asia. The Portuguese, therefore, were able to benefit from the trade their explorations generated to a greater degree than any other nation plying the sea at the time. That Portugal had managed to attain such an hegemony was largely the doing of one man.

Prince Henry of Portugal was a calm-looking, prepossessing man, long of face and nose, with a firm chin, set mouth, and eyes that seemed to gaze perpetually into the middle distance. By virtue of his passionate interest in oceanic navigation, he is known to us today as Prince Henry the Navigator, though he himself never set to sea. In 1419 he was granted governance of the Algarve, the southernmost province of Portugal. In the Algarve, Prince Henry turned himself over to his all-absorbing interest: the study of geography. On a cliff overlooking the Atlantic near the village of Sagres, he built a small fort. Here he set about creating the best known navigational school of its time. All schools need informational resources, and the type of information Henry needed concerned climactic conditions and topography. When compiled, this data took the form of a map.

In the fifteenth century, maps were rare commodities. Henry went about constructing them in the only way available to him: brain-picking. He invited merchants, sailors, and other travellers to Sagres and made detailed notes of recollections of their travels. He undoubtedly got some wild stories, but he also received sound information on winds, currents, and the shapes of coastlines. The more he talked, the more he filled his observatory with newly constructed maps and books, and the more convinced he became that the rich Asian spice lands could be reached by sailing south around Africa and then east toward India. Today we can picture this easily and clearly. In Prince Henry's time, such ideas were frightening and even heretical. It was akin to thinking about colonizing distant planets of which we have not yet heard.

Besides constructing maps, Henry turned his fertile mind to the daily needs of navigation. The most pressing of these needs was precise positional knowledge. How were sailors to set courses? Through his concern with this conundrum, he initiated pioneering work on basic tools like the quadrant, cross-staff, and compass. The other tool the Portuguese explorers needed was a suitable expeditionary vessel. Henry's patronage was largely responsible for the development of such a ship, one that combined cargo-carrying capacity with fluid maneuverability. The caravel, an example of early research and development, was beautifully suited for exploratory voyages.

In a Portuguese manuscript from the middle of the thirteenth century, the word *caravela* occurs describing fishing vessels. On the Tagus River and the waters outside Lisbon one can still see small vessels called *frigatas*, which are believed to be relics of the caravel. The original caravels were all lateen rigged. This means they sported three-cornered sails that allowed the ships to move windward. Prince Henry would have needed this capability, for his captains sailed home from their African explorations against the northeast trade winds. Later caravels, Columbus's "Pinta" for example, were square rigged. Typically, caravels were "[l]ong, relatively light so that they could ride the waves of the Atlantic, of shallow draught so that they could be used for coastal reconnaissance, swifter than . . . other round-bellied vessels" (Landstrom, 1961).

Though Henry did not live to see the Portuguese round the southern-most point of the African continent, his navigators got far enough along the coast and returned with enough profitable trade goods—including, in 1444, Africans to be sold as slaves—that when he died in 1460 the kings of Portugal continued to finance expeditions. Prior to Henry's death, Nuno Tristao, one of Henry's notable navigators, made three voyages along the coast of Africa. Sailing between 1441 and 1446, Tristao mapped the western bulge of Africa as far south as the mouth of the Saloum River in what is today Senegal. When one of his navigators rounded Cape Verde, the westernmost point of Africa in 1444, Henry was sure that his navigators were over the hump and would soon sail around the continent. However, he underestimated the extent of the land mass.

Between 1460 and 1473, Portuguese navigators inched their way down the African coast until they finally crossed the equator. In 1483, Diogo Cao passed the mouth of the Congo River, and year later a Genoese navigator, Christopher Columbus, tried to interest the Portuguese king in a plan to reach Asia by sailing west across the Atlantic. King Joao II, however, was committed to continuing the search to the south and east around Africa. Like many before him, and many since, he had spent so much time and money on a particular project that he felt his reputation was on the line. It simply had to succeed. He turned Columbus down and continued to send expeditions southward.

In 1488 it seemed that Bartolomeu Dias had justified the king's efforts. Dias rounded the southern tip of Africa and entered the Indian Ocean. It was a rough voyage, and Dias, listening to the heartfelt pleas of his crew, turned around and returned to Portugal without reaching India. However, he had proven that it was indeed possible to sail around Africa, even if it wasn't much fun. He gave the promontory at the bottom of the continent the altogether apt name of the Cape of Storms, but the enthusiastic (and perhaps relieved) king renamed it the Cape of Good Hope to immortalize his expectations that Portugal had finally found its route to the Indies. Once again, however, it would be 10 years before those expectations came to fruit.

Columbus's triumphant return to Spain in 1493 instantly provoked disputes between Spain and Portugal, neither of which wanted competition from the other over their respective routes to the Orient. Since both countries were Catholic, they applied to the newly installed pope, Alexander VI, father of the infamous Borgias, to settle the matter. The result was the Treaty of Tordesillas, proclaimed in 1494, by virtue of which Alexander decreed that everything to the east of an imaginary line drawn down the middle of the Atlantic Ocean would be explored and could be claimed by Portugal, and everything to the west by Spain. This gave Portugal the control of the eastern route to Asia along with, as it turned out, Brazil.

Competition with Spain spurred the Portuguese on. Acting on information on the contours of the east coast of Africa supplied by an adventurer named Pero da Covilha, Duke Manoel, who had succeeded King Joao in 1495, sent an expedition that was to follow Dias' route around the Cape of Good Hope and then use Covilha's data to head north along Africa's nether coast. This fleet of four ships was led by Vasco da Gama. It set off in 1497 and took 13 weeks to reach and round the cape. This entire leg of the voyage was made in the open sea, out of sight of land; it was the longest such voyage ventured by Europeans to that time. It took da Gama nearly five additional months to reach India, but he did so and returned triumphantly to Lisbon in 1499 with a load of spices, thus confirming in a way the hapless Columbus could not that he had indeed been to the Indies. Da Gama's delivery had almost instantaneous effects. By 1503 pepper purchased in Lisbon cost one-fifth what it did in Venice. The shift in power had been made from those who controlled the Mediterranean to those who controlled the open seas.

When Da Gama returned, a 19-year-old squire was working in the Casa de India, a government office that organized maritime expeditions and regulated eastern trade. His name was Fernao de Magalhaes, better known to us today by the French version of his name, Ferdinand Magellan. When trouble broke out in 1505 between the Portuguese and the Arabs, who did not want to share their monopoly on the Indian Ocean trade routes, King Manoel sent a 22-ship military fleet under Franciso de Almeida to put the Arabs in their place. Magellan received the king's permission to enlist. This was the beginning of a sea-going career that ended with his death on a remote island in the Philippines. But Magellan had begun the first circum-navigation of the globe, and part of his crew would finish it.

What is astonishing about Magellan, in common with Columbus and Sir Francis Drake, was his ability to find his way across uncharted tracts of water, depending upon a few rudimentary instruments and his own innate sense of position. He also had the ability to hold a crew together under the most trying circumstances and to inspire in them a sense of vision and purpose. Whether it was their devout belief in God and country, the need for glory, or just that human itch to see what no one had seen before, these men carried on, in their restless searching and mapping of the globe, the vision of the quiet scholarly Prince Henry of Portugal (Stefoff, 1990).

References

Landstrom, Bjorn. (1961). *The Ship: An Illustrated History.* Garden City, NY: Doubleday. o.p.
Stefoff, Rebecca. (1990). *Ferdinand Magellan and the Discovery of the World Ocean.* New York: Chelsea House.

ANNOTATED BIBLIOGRAPHY

Nonfiction

Alper, Ann Fitzpatrick. *Forgotten Voyager: The Story of Amerigo Vespucci.* Minneapolis: Carolrhoda, 1991. $11.95. 80p. index. bibliography. ISBN 0-87614-442-3.

The Florentine explorer Amerigo Vespucci was only about three years younger than Columbus, but his temperament seems to have been less obsessive and more measured than the Genoese explorer's. It is precisely because of his superior powers as an observer that Vespucci, rather than Columbus, gave his name to the continents of the New World.

This brief but fairly comprehensive book, well bound and attractively laid out in a generous type font, is interspersed with numerous black-and-white reproductions and attractive maps. Eight chapters cover Florence in the mid-fifteenth century, Vespucci's education, his early travels, and his voyages to the New World. An afterword discusses the naming of America, and a two-page index is adequate for accessing information lodged in the text. Alper's style is straightforward and clear, less condescending than Dennis Fradin's in *Amerigo Vespucci* (see below). Alper's chronicle of Vespucci's life and his impact on world history provides a sound and attractive report source.

Blumberg, Rhoda. *The Remarkable Voyages of Captain Cook.* New York: Bradbury Press, 1991. $18.95. 137p. source notes. bibliography. index. ISBN 0-02-711682-4.

Captain James Cook was killed in an altercation with Hawaiian Islanders in February 1779. Somehow, this violent death has left him indelibly associated with the tropics, but in fact Cook's explorations were far-ranging. His presence in Hawaii was part of a search for the ever-elusive Northwest Passage. Cook was also one of the early and significant explorers of Antarctica, leaving countless new areas explored and mapped.

Blumberg recapitulates a remarkable life in lively prose. Beginning with a chapter on Cook's rise through the naval ranks, which also sets the scene for his first voyage, the text is then divided into three sections, each covering one of Cook's three voyages in detail. The first section details the South Sea journey of 1768–1771, the second the Antarctic and South Sea quest of 1772–1775, and the third Cook's final voyage in search of the Northwest Passage, 1776–1780.

The volume is oversized with a spacious page layout. Numerous fascinating period drawings extend the text intriguingly. Double-page line maps of each voyage are immensely helpful in following the narrative. Whether for pleasure reading, browsing, or report writing, Blumberg's book is a fitting introduction to an intrepid and humane explorer. Excellent notes, bibliography, and index round out an outstanding piece of nonfiction writing.

Fisher, Leonard Everett. *Prince Henry the Navigator.* New York: Macmillan, 1990. $14.95. unpaged. ISBN 0-02-735231-5.

The explorers who actually plied the waters around the European and African coasts in the fifteenth century were the glory boys. When we think of early explorations in the eastern Atlantic, the names that come to mind are Dias, da Gama, and of course Columbus; yet none of these men could have made the voyages they did, much less made them successfully, without the attention the art of navigation received from Prince Henry of Portugal.

Beginning with the defeat of the Moors in Ceuta in North Africa in 1415, Fisher describes the rise of Portuguese sea power. His subject is not so much Prince Henry himself as the school of navigation he founded at Sagres, the most southwesterly point on the Iberian Peninsula. Henry's underwriting of voyages of exploration and his inspiration in helping to create the caravel are discussed in prose that is absorbing enough to hold attention. Fisher's illustrations, done in black, white, and grey acrylic on paper, are riveting, dramatic, and integral to the text. This book is an impressive visual introduction to the Age of Exploration and a fitting tribute to Prince Henry's vision.

Too brief for reports, this is an ideal booktalking, introductory, and browsing book. It could easily arouse interest in Prince Henry on the basis of Fisher's reworkings of portraits of the dour Portuguese nobleman. The brief text raises other issues, notably the interrelationship between exploration and slavery. This is an ideal starting point for discussion not only of exploration but of the social issues surrounding it.

Fradin, Dennis Brindell. *Amerigo Vespucci.* New York: Watts, 1991. $11.90. 64p. index. bibliography. glossary. ISBN 0-531-20035-3.

Christopher Columbus was born in 1451 and is said to have discovered the New World. However, the man whose name was bequeathed to the new continents was born in 1454. Although Amerigo Vespucci did not set to sea until his forty-fifth year, his understanding of just what Columbus had stumbled upon—two new continents and not the outer edge of Asia nor the Garden of Eden—made him one of the most renowned geographers of his time.

Fradin does his best to trace Vespussi's life in five brief chapters with an added postscript. But Fradin runs into a problem that other biographers have encountered as well: Vespucci is elusive. Columbus, the Admiral of the Ocean Sea, may have been half crazy and definitely megalomaniacal at times, but he can be grasped. For all his mapping activities and level-headedness, one comes away feeling that Vespucci was just not very interesting. The writing style is chattily familiar, peppered with "Amerigo this" and "Amerigo that," but it does recount the facts. Period reproductions enhance the attractively set text. (*One caveat:* A third of the text on page 43 is inexplicably missing.) The index is decent, the bibliography three-fifths out of print, and the glossary no more than a token. However, there's not much out there on Vespucci for this age group and Fradin's coverage is solid report fodder.

Hook, Jason. *The Voyages of Captain Cook.* Illustrated by Richard Hook. New York: Bookwright, 1990. $11.40. 32p. index. glossary. bibliography. ISBN 0-531-18359-1.

Hunter, Nigel. *The Expedition of Cortez.* Illustrated by Peter Bull. New York: Bookwright, 1990. $11.40. 32p. index. glossary. bibliography. ISBN 0-531-18335-1.

Similar in format, these two volumes in the Great Journeys series will pique a reader's interest in the conquest of Mexico and the exploration of Polynesia. Each book consists of 12 two-page sections covering varying aspects of their subjects' explorations. The prose in both is lively and interest catching as are the illustrations. Both contain reasonably good glossaries, brief bibliographies, and minimal indices.

Captain James Cook made numerous voyages throughout Polynesia until his tragic death in a tribal war on Hawaii in 1779. Hook's prose is engaging if not stylish, and Richard Hook's soft-looking, muted paintings extend the text nicely. The judicious use of period reproductions is another plus. The book is divided into sections entitled "A Secret Task," "The Endeavour," "Tahiti," "The Maoris," "Shipwreck," "The Seagoing Clock," "Islands of Ice, " "The Farthest South," "The Death of a God," and "The Legacy of Cook." These sections may well spur browsers on to more complex books. As this overview so amply illustrates, Cook had an abundance of the raw skill that counted for everything in the days before computer navigation.

The life of Hernan Cortez, who almost single-handedly destroyed an entire culture, makes vivid if depressing reading. Hunter tends a bit toward the prolix and sensational, but he does hold readers' attention. He discusses Cortez's life as an adventurer, the conquest of Mexico, and Cortez's later years, as well as his legacy, which includes the mestizo ethnic mix. Though extended by good maps, photos, and period drawings, the text relies too heavily on Peter Bull's rather lurid and awkward watercolor paintings for illustrative extension—though given their subject matter, they may actually provide a draw of sorts.

Browsers, report writers, instructors, and librarians looking for snappy introductory material to explorations made possible by the mapping of sea routes will find it here.

Humble, Richard. *The Explorers: The Seafarers.* Alexandria, VA: Time-Life Books, 1978, o.p. 176p. index. bibliography. ISBN 0-8094-2659-5. **Ad.**

Most Time-Life series books tend to be comprehensive, and this is no exception. The focus of this volume in The Explorers series is on the exploration of the oceans. The format pairs each of five chapters with an essay and a lush pictorial extension that excites interest as it instructs. A cogent opening essay, preceding Chapter 1, gives background on humankind's expanding view of its planet. It sets the stage appropriately for the succeeding chapters, which open with the fourteenth-century Portuguese explorational voyages. The real strength of the book, however well-phrased and informative it may be, is in its illustration. Several double-page spreads show a myriad of early maps, portraying the evolution of people's view of the earth's face.

Following the account of Henry the Navigator's incursions along the coast of Africa and Marco Polo's reports from China—voyages that irrevocably altered the fate of the world and shifted political balances in influential and long-ranging ways—further chapters cover Columbus's voyages, da Gama's rounding of the Cape of Good Hope, and Magellan. Biographical information is abundant, as is technical, seafaring material.

The prose is well wrought, but clearly adult. However, the quality of the illustrations will attract browsers, and the road from caption to text is a short one. Some pictorial segments are lengthy enough to be used almost as picture books with the captions read as text. This is an excellent tool for reinforcing units on any aspect of early Age of Exploration sea voyages.

Poole, Frederick King. *Early Exploration of North America.* New York: Watts, 1989. $11.90. 64p. index. bibliography. ISBN 0-531-10683-7.

Both before and after Columbus explorers ventured to the shores of the New World. Many of them came during a period called the Age of Discovery, running roughly from 1415 to around 1620. Though none of the early explorers left permanent colonies on what would become the United States and Canada, they opened the way for later colonization.

This Watts "First Book" has the standard format—large, clean typeface, good leading, numerous black-and-white and color reproductions. The chapters are short and conversational, easy to read, and informational enough to be a source for reports. The seven chapters cover Viking exploration, Henry the Navigator, Columbus, Cabot, early French explorers, and the British search for the Northwest Passage, with the final chapter discussing the explorers' accomplishments.

Teachers can use this book as supplemental material for general explorational units or for units on any one of the explorers mentioned in these pages. Reasonably accessed through either the table of contents or index, this source for short reports may well appeal to remedial students since the reading level is rated for upper elementary.

Stefoff, Rebecca. *Ferdinand Magellan and the Discovery of the World Ocean.* New York: Chelsea House, 1990. $18.95. 127p. index. chronology. bibliography. ISBN 0-7910-1291-3.

Small and unprepossessing in appearance, Ferdinand Magellan did not look like the sort of man who would undertake to circumnavigate the globe. Yet he not only began this ambitious project, but held to it despite the open contempt of his officers. The crew, however, recognized in the slight, dark, grim Portuguese a natural and fair leader. Brooking bad weather, starvation, and mutiny before his death in the Philippines in 1521, Magellan did not live to see one of his ships, the "Victoria," limp into port three years after he set out. However, it would hardly have surprised him, so unswerving was he in the execution of his duty.

This is more than a biography of Fernao de Magalhaes, known to us by the French version of his name. In seven chapters, the well-written and involving text gives background on Magellan and his voyages, but it also covers the history of westward exploration and navigation, including the influence of Prince Henry the Navigator, Vasco da Gama, Columbus, and Balboa, among others. Cultural and political background is given in both micro- and macrocosmic terms, offering a context for Magellan's drive. Given the primitive nature of the still infant art of navigation, Magellan's feats were, as this title shows, all the more amazing.

The text is gathered toward the gutter of the book, leaving lots of marginal space for copiously captioned illustrations. There is an eight-page color insert at the middle of the book, but the black-and-white period reproductions and maps peppered throughout the text are far more useful and informative. A chronology and reasonable index increase utility as a report source. The bibliography is not terribly current, but may help both teachers and readers to find additional information. Good for browsing and research, this book can be excerpted and booktalked with fair success as well.

Sugden, John. *Sir Francis Drake.* New York: Henry Holt, 1990. $29.95. 353p. index. bibliography. glossary. ISBN 0-8050-1489-6. **Ad.**

Francis Drake, circumnavigator of the globe and nemesis of the Spanish Armada, receives mixed reviews from historians. He is described as fearless, canny, and enterprising, or as ruthless and self-interested. A man of many contradictions, both a product of and a mystery to his times, Drake's boldness marked the emergence of England as a maritime power. In contrast to Roy Gerrard's picture book version of the intrepid navigator (see below), Sugden's tome is encyclopedic and painstakingly researched.

Divided into a preface, 22 lengthy chapters, and an afterword, Drake's approximately 56 years are covered in detail, giving information on his historical, geographical, and sociopolitical milieu. There is hardly a stone left unturned in this exhaustive exploration of the elusive Englishman who gave his name to New World landmarks and left his footprints on the history of Europe.

A center section containing black-and-white reproductions of paintings and drawings of the individuals involved in Drake's life, as well as the events that marked turning points, make fascinating viewing. The four maps are clear and enhance understanding. A glossary of sixteenth-century general and naval terms is helpful in clarifying the text, and the index and bibliography are detailed beyond belief. The dust jacket, showing a larger-than-lifesize close-up of Drake's face is arresting.

Who will read this book? Teachers, if they are intrepid, and the rare gifted middle schooler with a burning interest in the biography's subject. As a teacher reference, it is hard to beat. Anything one wants to know about this diminutive, ginger-haired maker of history is in these pages.

Weiss, Harvey. *Maps: Getting from Here to There.* Boston: Houghton Mifflin, 1991. $14.95. 64p. ISBN 0-395-56264-3.

As people began to ply the seas further from home, they charted the places they had been. The charts were then refined and improved until they became maps like those we see today. But how many of us have trouble drawing a map? Even with the clear vision of the *Rand McNally Road Atlas* or National Geographic maps in our minds, our sense of scale gets off, directions grow muddy, and the finished product may be more hindrance than help.

Weiss's clear introductory text, peppered with explanatory line drawings and cartoon illustrations, will help even the least map-and-chart inclined to feel familiar, even competent, with maps. His introductory discussion of various aspects of maps includes direction, distance, symbols, latitude and longitude, how maps are made, and special purpose maps and charts. Chapters are brief, most being only six pages long, and offer clear and explanatory examples of types of maps, from ocean charts, to hikers topographic maps, to maps used by airplane pilots. Students will enjoy browsing, be amused by Weiss's prose (which always retains a light touch), and want to try their own hands at mapping. An excellent classroom tool, adjunct to units on explorers from the Portuguese navigators to Lewis and Clark, this book can flesh out curricula from art to geography.

Wolfe, Cheri. *Lt. Charles Wilkes and the Great U.S. Exploring Expedition.* New York: Chelsea House, 1991. $18.95. 111p. index. bibliography. ISBN 0-7910-1320-0.

Few people have heard of Lt. Charles Wilkes, and fewer yet will connect this obscure name with the creation of the august Smithsonian Institution. Yet it was Wilkes's voyage as commander of the United States South Seas Exploring Expedition, from 1838 to 1842, which brought back the seed collection of "scientifics" that led to the Smithsonian collection.

The lucid text paints a portrait of a difficult, occasionally tyrannical man, determined to carry out his charge to an extreme of punctilio. Wilkes succeeded in exploring not only the South Seas, but Antarctica as well, establishing it as our seventh continent, and more or less continuing the work of circumnavigator James Cook. The use of drawings made during the course of the expedition by artist Alfred Agate, among others, extend the text well and add a sense of freshness and immediacy. The eight chapters paint a clear picture of a period in American history and the voyage's impact on native populations in the South Pacific.

The bibliography is mostly adult titles and therefore limited in utility. The index is excellent, however, enhancing the book's use as a report source. The book could be used as an introduction to science units, tied as it is to the founding of the Smithsonian.

Fiction

Gerrard, Roy. *Sir Francis Drake: His Daring Deeds.* New York: Farrar, Straus, & Giroux, 1988. $13.95. unpaged. LC 87-047847. **P.**

This luminously illustrated picture book relates the life of Sir Francis Drake from the age of 10 until the defeat of the Spanish Armada in 1588. The text, brief and to the point, is in quatrains composed of two sets of rhymed couplets in iambic pentameter. Given a sure, dramatic delivery, the wit and humor Gerrard put into his poem will resound to great effect. The illustrations are amazing in their detail. If all the people look squashed and dwarfish (Gerrard seems to have a complimentary and opposite visual distortion to that of El Greco), they are certainly piquantly interesting. The landscapes, however, whether urban London, the Panamanian jungle, or the open seas are glorious, richly displayed in patterned watercolors, and almost palpable.

Read out loud as an introduction to the era, this book will amuse and intrigue middle schoolers who may well go on to more detailed books on Drake. Students interested in the Elizabethan era will get an eyeful of court dress and building and ship design. All listeners will get some basic, easily swallowed background on a fascinating and intrepid explorer.

CHAPTER 4

The Admiral of the Ocean Sea: Columbus and the New World

He was more than middling tall; face long and giving an air of authority; aquiline nose, blue eyes, complexion light and tending to bright red; beard and hair red when young, but very soon turned gray from his labors; he was affable and cheerful in speaking ... and so could easily incite those who saw him to love him. ...

Without doubt he was Catholic and of great devotion ... he desired and was eager for the conversion of [the indigenous American populations], and that in every region the faith of Jesus Christ be planted and enhanced. —Bartolome de Las Casas.*

★ ★ ★ ★ ★

The Scriptures tell us that in the Earthly Paradise grows the tree of life, and that from it flows the source that gives rise to the four great rivers, the Ganges, the Tigris, the Euphrates, and the Nile. The Earthly Paradise, which no one can reach except by the will of God, lies at the end of the Orient. And that is where we are.
—Christopher Columbus, 1498

---

*De Las Casas, Bartolome. (1971).*The History of the Indies.* New York: Harper & Row.

Christopher Columbus cannot truly be said to have discovered the New World. There were already large populations inhabiting the Caribbean islands when he landed in 1492, populations which, thanks to the contact with Europeans that he initiated, would be all but exterminated in less than a hundred years.

Five hundred years later the American continents still reel under the impact of Columbus's fateful landfall. Whether we look upon the Admiral of the Ocean Sea with distaste or adulation, we cannot deny the great echoing force of his will. It was only that which eventually washed this complex man up on American shores.

There are myths. In my grade school in the 1950s, Columbus was a sort of wildly garbed Caspar Milquetoast figure who, smarter than the rest of the world, had figured out that the earth was not flat. I was suitably shocked a few years further into my education to find that Leif Eriksson might more appropriately be credited with the first American landfall by a European. That the New World was new only to people from Europe and Asia and might not have needed discovering at all never crossed by mind.

The South American continent deals with this on a much more daily basis than do we in the north. Zealous though the conquistadors were in their efforts to obliterate native culture, they nonetheless intermarried and mingled their actual and cultural DNA with that of their new land. In North America this was not so. The Native American populations were often subjected to attempted genocide, the feelings of Americans of Northern European descent about Columbus (fair-skinned, blue-eyed, redheaded) are much less equivocal. It still seems that he did this group a favor.

Who was this man? No one has been able to ascertain for certain just where and when Christopher Columbus was born. The great navigator himself kept some facts about his past even from his sons. Though scholars suggest either political or religious reasons for this, there is no certain attribution. It appears, based on notarial and municipal evidence, that he was born into an obscure family in the Italian port city of Genoa in 1451. The family was in the business of woolen weaving and had been for at least two generations. All members of his family worked hard, and there are no records indicating that Columbus had any kind of formal schooling during his childhood or youth. He was functionally illiterate in Italian, speaking the common Genoese dialect, a spoken, not written, language. As an adult he taught himself to read and write Castilian, the language of the educated on the Iberian Peninsula. Having lived a decade in Lisbon, he had learned to speak Portuguese, and had somehow learned to use Latin as well. Obviously, he had a fairly high degree of intelligence, and a ready ability to assimilate information.

When Columbus was 19 his father moved his business and his family to Savona, a coastal port west of Genoa. A year later, in 1471, Columbus, who had been seafaring for perhaps nine years, went on his first extended voyage. Sent as a business agent for a Genoese firm on an expedition to the island of Chios, off the coast of Asia Minor, Columbus found himself on a ship that did not hug the coastline but moved out boldly into the open sea. He watched how the helmsman navigated by the art of dead reckoning. This method requires the navigator to keep meticulous account of direction by compass, speed through the water, direction and strength of the wind, and the effects of wind pressure on the ship. One difficulty with dead reckoning is that once out of sight of land, one cannot gauge with any certainty the effect of currents. Apparently navigation was another area in which Columbus had ability, for in his transatlantic voyages he would demonstrate an almost uncanny skill for arriving where he intended to arrive, even though he employed what were really very approximate methods. His internal compass and innate sense of position must have been acute and accurate.

In 1476, in the aftermath of a shipwreck, Columbus made his way to Lisbon, where the Genoese firm he had worked for had offices. Portugal was the foremost seafaring power in Europe at the time, and an ideal place for the gangling, redheaded Columbus to pick up more expertise in his chosen field. Instead of seeking employment with his former bosses, Columbus ventured into a partnership with his younger brother, Bartholomew. They set up a shop that made and sold mariner's charts. How they had managed to pick up enough training in cartography and calligraphy to bring old charts up to date by adding new information supplied by homecoming seafarers is unknown, but their business was a success.

Not long after settling in Lisbon, Columbus shipped out to the North Atlantic. Myth tells us that he got as far as Iceland where he may have heard stories about the Norse voyages to the coasts of Greenland and Labrador. Whether or not this was the beginning of his obsession with sailing west to get to the east, we don't know, but certainly he began to inquire about it increasingly. He also began to associate himself with prophetic passages from Seneca, among others, that proclaimed the coming of a great discoverer.

Columbus's increased curiosity was well timed, for it coincided with the publication of the first European navigational and nautical almanac. This almanac aided him in learning how to sail by latitude and pole star observations. In addition, he avidly read everything about exploration he could get his hands on. To him, the most important books were *The Travels of Marco Polo*, Pliny's *Natural History*, Zacuto's *Perpetual Almanac*, Cardinal d'Ailly's *Imago Mundi*, and Cardinal Piccolomini's *Historia Rerum*. He jotted down lines from other works that seemed significant to him, and stretched his imagination to produce a significantly changed global perspective. In one respect our myths are true: Columbus did not fear falling off the edge of a flat earth, though he was certainly not alone in believing the earth was round. As far back as Aristotle the idea of a spherical planet had been in circulation.

Columbus married a wealthy young woman named Dona Felipa Perestrello e Moniz. They lived briefly with her mother in Lisbon and then moved to Porto Santo, an island near Madiera where her brother was governor. When Dona Felipa died around 1484, Columbus left Portugal with his five-year-old son, Diego, to begin a seven-year quest for patronage. He invested this time in Portugal in concerted investigation, devoting himself to the study of maps and pilot books, and noting his own observations on winds, tides, and currents. Additionally, he participated in a long voyage down the coast of Africa to the equator in 1482 or 1483. By this time his certainty that there was a better way to the Indies had grown; it seemed to him simple and obvious that all one had to do was sail west. This belief became the ruling passion of his life.

Since there was no real struggle in convincing potential backers that the world was spherical, what did Columbus have to sway them to accept? When he presented his Great Enterprise of the Indies to King Joao II of Portugal in 1484, his main selling point, besides the obvious one of profit, was his calculation that the distance between Iberia and the Indies was not great and would allow for a relatively quick voyage. We know now that Columbus had greatly underestimated the size of the globe, but even then he was unable to convince the Portuguese monarch. Columbus doggedly hawked his idea across Europe, finally dancing tireless, persistent, and no doubt slightly aggravating attendance on Isabella of Spain until at last in 1492 she agreed to give him his chance.

What we need to do in studying Columbus is look more critically at our own reading of this history. Columbus did not want to find new lands, but to discover a new sea route to something very old—Asia. His need to believe that he had done this was great; he insisted on seeing the Caribbean and South America, as Cipango (Japan) and China, even when it became obvious that they were not. He oppressed the natives trying to make them what they were not; he forced his men to sign papers saying that they believed he had found the Indies; and, in the end, he tortured himself. He was so intent on being right that he could not take the full measure of what he had done.

Columbus brought the Old World to the New, and in so doing changed both beyond recognition. We can fairly say that he did this solely on the force of his personality and his belief in his venture. Certainly if he had not made his historic voyage someone else would have, but that would have been a different discovery creating a different history. All we need do is imagine Sir Francis Drake claiming South America for the English Crown to see what a drastic alternative history would have been produced: though the native peoples would no doubt have been similarly exploited, a British colonial South America would have produced different traditions, attitudes, and certainly a different power balance in Europe. Whether we like it or not, Christopher Columbus, a gifted, determined man from Genoa has made our history what it was, and our problems as nations what they are. His cultural prejudices and personal judgments helped give the Americas their historical base.

Reference

Fuson, Robert A. (1988). *The Log of Christopher Columbus*. New York: International Maritime.

ANNOTATED BIBLIOGRAPHY

Nonfiction

Brenner, Barbara. *If You Were There in 1492.* New York: Bradbury Press, 1991. $13.95. 106p. index. bibliography. ISBN 0-02-712321-9.

If you had been alive in 1492, what would it have been like? Would you have known that great things were afoot? New ideas? Big changes? In this easy-to-read exploration of the world of Columbus, Barbara Brenner looks at many aspects of life in late fifteenth-century Europe, with a focus on Spain.

    After a concise introduction, 16 chapters cover the following: general European geography and politics of the time, Spanish life, food and clothing, sickness and health, education, kings and queens, arts and entertainment, books and printing, the penal system, map making, the expulsion of the Jews, ships and sailors, life in the Americas before Columbus, and a brief summation of life after 1492. The information is set out in an easy-to-extract smorgasbord fashion. The consistent use of the word "you" (e.g., "When you saw the queen, you would have noticed . . . " or "There's a good chance you might not have been able to read or write . . . ") can be grating, but it does add immediacy. This good source for reports is enhanced by a respectable index. The bibliography, though lengthy, is over half adult works, which reduces its utility. Page layout and use of black-and-white photographs and reproductions are all attractive and well placed. The bright, appealing cover gears this toward the lower elementary grades, thus it may have to be pushed to middle schoolers. The text is adaptable for both dramatic use and discussion starting.

Burch, Joann J. *Isabella of Castile: Queen on Horseback.* New York: Watts, 1991. $11.90. 63p. index. bibliography. ISBN 0-531-20033-7.

A lot gets written about Isabella of Castile, but most of it is in books about Christopher Columbus, whose stormy relationship with his patron has provided fertile ground for speculation. Joann Burch's book about Isabella for upper elementary and middle school students is, unfortunately, better in conception than in execution.

Heavily fictionalized with lots of "she thought," "she prayed," "she cried with relief," etc., the book sounds like a soap opera. Isabella, for instance, has a "pale face [that] was round and plain," but what she lacks in looks she predictably makes up for in spirit. We see her on horseback in 1490, urging her army onward through slippery November mud, even though she is expecting a baby—a real warrior queen. The Jewish expulsion and the Inquisition are discussed, and the suffering created by both is treated frankly, but Burch distances Isabella from this. The Queen, she seems to say, was after all a devout Christian and just got carried away. Everyone, she assures us, makes mistakes.

A chapter on Columbus's first voyage pulls the focus off Isabella almost entirely and does nothing for the narrative flow. Very little of this demanding, assertive, cantankerous woman comes through, and Burch makes Ferdinand (whose portraits look like Jimmy Carter) sound a lot less devious than he was. Still, the flavor of the time slips through in small doses.

The period reproductions and clear, large, well-leaded typeface give the book an approachable appearance. The index is sound but the bibliography brief and mostly out of print. There's not much else out there on Isabella, so until something more penetrating is published, this is the title of choice.

Dodge, Stephen C. *Christopher Columbus and the First Voyages to the New World.* New York: Chelsea House, 1991. $17.95. 127p. index. bibliography. ISBN 0-7910-1299-9.

Born in 1451 in Genoa, Christopher Columbus rose from humble beginnings to change the fate of the world in ways he himself would never fathom. A complex and troubled man who was tireless in his wooing of the Spanish monarchs to his cause, he came, over the many years of their association, to "love [Ferdinand and Isabella] with a passionate hatred," and he went to his deathbed angry and embittered.

Dodge's book in the World Explorers series does a superb job of reporting on this involved and fascinating life; but he does so in a style that is best suited for report writing, lacking the narrative flair of Milton Meltzer's treatment in *Columbus and the World Around Him* (see below). Despite the intermittent dryness of the text, Dodge gives detailed information on Columbus and his times. Beginning with 1492 and the first voyage, Dodge returns in the following chapters to trace Columbus's life from birth until his Enterprise of the Indies was finally accepted. Succeeding chapters discuss the four voyages to the New World and Columbus's death.

Embellished with frequent black-and-white reproductions of maps and period art, this book also contains an eight-page color section showing maps, paintings, and Columbus's coat of arms. The format is attractive though, given the density of the typeface, a little forbidding. A good index and bibliography enhance the book's usefulness as a report source. There is also enough anecdotal or tellable material to make the book a good source for booktalking or classroom reading.

Dolan, Sean J. *Christopher Columbus: The Intrepid Mariner.* New York: Fawcett Columbine, 1989. $3.95. 117p. ISBN 0-44990393-1.

"He's mad, you know," says one of Columbus's crewmen depicted in Dolan's book. Was Columbus crazy? Information on the life of this most documented of sailors indicates that he was at least obsessed. But did his crew speculate on their captain general's madness? We don't know, but this fictionalized biography uses an eavesdropping technique to present background information and contemporary views regarding Columbus's expedition to what he so firmly believed was Asia. While this is certainly not a technique that receives widespread approval among critics, it does liven up the narrative.

Dolan writes blocky, constructionist prose that rarely rises above the strictly earthbound. However, the story is all here. Though the author glosses over some of Columbus's less admirable actions and attitudes, the picture, especially of the first voyage, is relatively accurate and complete. This volume in the Great Lives series has a particular role to play in appealing to students who are threatened by large or scholarly looking books. This slim paperback may induce nonreaders to pick it up. Sound as a backup source for units on Columbus, this book is illustrated with infrequent black-and-white period reproductions. Though out of register, they do enhance the text.

Dor-Ner, Zvi. *Columbus and the Age of Discovery.* Written with William D. Scheller. New York: Morrow, 1991. $40.00. 370p. bibliography. index. ISBN 0-688-08545-8.

If a comprehensive treatment of Columbus's landfall and its effects is what you have in mind, then this 370-page, oversized tome is just right. A companion volume to the PBS series that aired in the falls of both 1991 and 1992, this book is not merely a biographical treatment. The scope is broad and inclusive, viewing not only the individual man but the repercussions of his actions, and his symbolic function—in short, the whole amalgam of social, cultural, and political considerations that his name evokes.

The book is divided into seven lengthy chapters, each considering various aspects of the interactions of Europe (as embodied by Columbus) and the New World. Historical/political milieus, the conception of sailing west to reach the East, navigating the crossing, the clash between the Europeans and the Native Americans, the intermingling of peoples and cultures, and the "Columbian Exchange"— the wholesale transfer of peoples, flora, fauna, and diseases between two formerly unconnected land masses—are all covered in an open, readable manner that is occasionally wryly humorous. Information on the recreation of Columbus's voyage using facsimiles of the "Nina," the "Pinta," and the "Santa Maria" is also included.

The format guarantees continual use. Highly pictorial, it is packed with beautiful high-resolution color photographs, period reproductions, and excellent maps, both contemporary and from Columbus's time. It will easily draw browsers and is sturdily enough constructed to withstand constant use. The index is thorough, but the bibliography is in narrative form, making citations hard to extract. Certainly there is material here for reports. Dor-Ner has put Columbus in an historical and social context, thus creating an objective portrait of the enigmatic Admiral of the Ocean Sea. (John Dyson's *Columbus: For Gold, God, and Glory: In Search of the Real Christopher Columbus* is similar in format and content. See below.)

Dyson, John. *Columbus: For Gold, God, and Glory. In Search of the Real Christopher Columbus.* Photographs by Peter Christopher. New York: Simon & Schuster, 1991. $35.00. 228p. bibliography. index. ISBN 0-671-68791-3.

John Dyson uses a large, highly pictorial format similar to Zvi Dor-Ner's book (see above), but his basic premise is quite different from Dor-Ner's. Dyson believes that Columbus owned a map which showed him a route across the Atlantic. In order to test this theory, Dyson and a largely Spanish crew sailed a facsimile of the *Nina* from Palos, Spain, to St. Bartholomew in the Virgin Islands. A detailed historical text covering Columbus's explorations is interspersed with the narrative of the modern voyage.

The clearly written text makes riveting reading, either aloud or alone. While Dyson's premise (which assumes that Columbus knew exactly where he was headed, knew it wasn't the Indies of the Far East, and was in fact hunting for gold) is not nailed down to everyone's satisfaction, his arguments are persuasive. This book is potent fuel for discussion.

The illustrations, ranging from well composed modern photographs of the voyage of the contemporary *Nina* to period reproductions, are all beautifully reproduced. The book will draw plenty of browsers, controversial theory or no, and many of those who are just looking at the pictures will be encouraged to read the text in search of explanation or elaboration. A detailed chronology and excellent index round out an attractive and debate-provoking volume.

Finkelstein, Norman H. *The Other 1492: Jewish Settlement in the New World.* New York: Scribners, 1989. $12.95. 100p. index. bibliography. ISBN 0-684-18913-5.

We think of 1492 as the year Columbus happened upon the Bahamas, but for the Jewish citizens of Spain the year had a much more sinister and earth-shaking connotation. In 1492 Ferdinand and Isabella of Spain signed the Edict of Expulsion, formally exiling all Jews from Spanish lands. Only a few months later, Christopher Columbus set sail from Palos, on a journey that would open new lands and give the Jews of Europe a new place of refuge.

This lucid and absorbing account of the lot of the Jews in Spain and their eventual settlement in both North and South America adds a dimension to New World history that is often ignored. The first six chapters cover the Jewish experience in Spain and the beginning of their exile, while the last three chapters look at Jewish settlement in the New World.

The format is very attractive, with clear type and good leading on creamy paper. Black-and-white reproductions break up the text and the index is quite good, but does not do well for accessing illustrations. Illustrations do occasionally appear with unrelated text, but this is not a major flaw.

A reading from the section on the auto-da-fe ought to perk up student interest and attention to this fine report source and information bank on a little examined portion of our history.

First Encounters: Spanish Explorations in the Caribbean and the United States, 1492-1570. Edited by Jerald T. Milanich and Susan Melbrath. Gainesville, FL: University of Florida Press, 1990. $12.95. paper. 222p. index. references. ISBN 0-8130-0947-2. **Ad.**

That Florida was part of Spain for 300 years, longer than it has been part of the United States, is a little considered fact. The Spanish heritage of the Caribbean and the southern United States tends to be thought of in terms of relatively recent influxes of new immigrants or in terms of a long and almost forgotten influence. In fact, we still see and live with the effects of Spain's attempts to explore and settle these areas.

First Encounters is a collection of essays reporting on original archaeological and historical research findings over the last 10 years. These essays give information that has resulted in an increase in understanding of the cultural depth of the events that followed Columbus's historic landfall in 1492. There are 13 essays in all, including four on Columbus, several on Florida, two on De Soto, and some dealing with the effects the European influx had on the native populations. The use of archaeological evidence and the archaeological reconstructive method is striking. Along with clear maps and period pictures (most in black-and-white), there are numerous color photos of archaeological finds that support the explorers' presence in a given place at a given time, and that confirm the causes of death among members of the native tribes.

These essays are aimed at adult readers. The vocabulary is occasionally complex and technical. Students will be interested in the illustrations, especially the archaeological photos, and may well dip into the text to see exactly what the illustrations are depicting. A good index and comprehensive reference list round out an excellent browsing book, supplemental reference, and report source.

Fradin, Dennis Brindell. *The Nina, the Pinta, and the Santa Maria.* New York: Watts, 1991. $11.90. 64p. index. bibliography. glossary. ISBN 0-531-20034-5.

The *Santa Maria*, the nao, sank off the coast of Hispaniola on Christmas 1492. The *Pinta*, a caravel, returned to Palos, Spain, in 1493 and became lost to history. But the sturdy little *Nina* made three voyages with Columbus and was last known to have set sail for Africa in 1501.

Focusing on Columbus's ships, this large print, copiously illustrated book tells the story of Columbus's pursuit of his great Enterprise of the Indies and his first voyage to the west. Later voyages are briefly summarized, and the histories of the *Nina* and *Pinta* given. Fradin's prose is straightforward and definitely beats the encyclopedia. Unfortunately, it is marred by misleading generalizations ("Uneducated but bright, Christopher learned . . . " Self-educated would be accurate.) and an occasionally too-chatty style. Nonetheless, the spotlight on the ships and the crews' lives on board make this a good report source and fitting nonfiction backup to Olga Litowinsky's *The High Voyage* (see below), which is a fictional treatment of these aspects of sixteenth-century navigation.

An excellent index and brief bibliography add to this book's usefulness as a report source. The glossary unfortunately gives definitions that are vague and useless. The frequent full-to half-page period reproductions and photographs add browsing appeal. If not the best book to introduce a unit on Columbus, it is solid support material.

Fritz, Jean. *Where Do You Think You're Going, Christopher Columbus?* Pictures by Margaret Tomes, New York: G.P. Putnam's Sons, 1980. $8.95. 80p. notes. index. ISBN 0-399-20723-6.

In brisk, simple prose, Fritz covers Columbus's four voyages to the New World. The text is fast paced and easy to read. The numerous black-and-white or pink, gold, brown, and red tinted illustrations, generally one to a page, provide breaks that serve to maintain interest and support the narrative. Tomes's Columbus is obviously based on observation of contemporary portraits; although her style sometimes verges on the cartoonlike, Columbus retains his distinctive appearance and is entirely recognizable.

Fritz gives some indications of Columbus's sometimes less than honorable nature and incredible stubborness, though she is not explicit. She rather glosses over his reprehensible treatment of the native population. However, all the basics are here and in an engaging form.

The book is a single 80-page narrative, undivided into chapters. The typeface is large, clear, and well leaded. There are three pages of notes, but no references. The one-page index is adequate.

This book provides excellent high interest, low vocabulary reading and contains enough solid information for a report. Perhaps one of its most effective uses, however, would be as the subject of a booktalk or as a classroom read-aloud. Even if the lily is slightly gilded, this idiosyncratic man and his times come through clearly.

Hills, Ken. *The Voyages of Columbus.* Illustrated by Paul Wright and others. New York: Random House, 1991. $7.00. 32p. index. ISBN 0-679-82185-6.

Humble, Richard. *The Voyages of Columbus.* Illustrated by Richard Hook. New York: Watts, 1991. $11.90. 32p. index. glossary. ISBN 0-531-14189-6.

These books by different publishers have the same title, length, and format. Both are slightly oversized, heavily illustrated in similar murky watercolors with added maps, photos, and period reproductions. Both are divided into two-page sections covering Columbus's life and the history of the exploration of the spice routes previous to 1492. Both present the heroic version of Columbus, wondering why the Admiral was shipped back to Spain in chains after his third voyage. (Today, we would say it was for human rights violations.) Hills's book gives more information on the peoples of the Americas but has a smaller typeface than Humble's book, giving the text a slightly more difficult look.

Hills's book is divided into 14 sections covering Columbus's childhood, his marketing of the Enterprise of the Indies, his four voyages (including a map of all four routes), and includes interpolated sections on ships and sailing as well as on the Arawak and Carib peoples of the Caribbean islands. Humble's 14 sections take a less structured and more narrative approach, but cover much the same ground. Both books are written in workmanlike prose that goes along at a brisk plod. Humble's book contains a helpful glossary, and both have time charts and basic minimum indices.

Why buy these books? Both have a high degree of browsing appeal (lots of nifty drawings of skeletons, fierce dogs, and shipwrecks) and introduce students to the topic. There are definitely better books for more able readers, but these can serve to generate questions and move the less able, or initially less interested,toward more challenging books.

I, Columbus. Edited by Peter and Connie Roop. Illustrated by Peter E. Hanson. New York: Walker, 1990. $13.95. 57p. ISBN 0-8027-6978-0.

In a slim but valuable volume, the editors' present excerpts from Christopher Columbus's ship's log. The entries begin on Friday, August 3, 1492, as the *Santa Maria* sets sail from Palos, Spain, and end on Friday, March 15, 1493, upon Columbus's return to Palos from the New World. Through these excerpts, young readers or listeners can gain a picture of the arduous nature of the voyage, the constant bickering between Columbus and his men, and, most importantly, insight into Columbus himself. His amazement at the wonders of the lands he encountered is palpable, as is his obdurate insistence that he had found the Indies.

The format is exceedingly attractive, with a large, open type font and one inset watercolor illustration for every two pages. While making the book inviting, the format also results in an unwontedly juvenile look. This is unfortunate, for the language is complex and the subject matter of considerable depth.

Given these considerations, the book will be best used if introduced by the teacher or librarian. A short reading of a few entries should hook students. Furthermore, this is a natural tool for introducing a journal keeping approach to history and could be used to encourage students to write their own journals.

Katz, William Loren. *Breaking the Chains: African-American Slave Resistance.* New York: Atheneum, 1990. $14.95. 194p. index. bibliography. ISBN 0-689-431493-0.

One of the first things Columbus brought to the New World was slavery. Today millions of black and white Americans live with the effects of his legacy. This exhaustive account of African-American resistance to slavery from its inception until the end of the Civil War will prove enlightening for those upper middle school students who can plow through it.

Thirteen chapters are divided into four sections covering fighting slavery on land and sea, daily toil and struggle, flight and revolt, and the urge toward freedom during the Civil War. Katz certainly covers his ground, and his painstaking research shows in his liberal use of first person accounts. However, his style makes the encyclopedia seem exciting, dooming the book to use exclusively as a report source. This is a pity, because a judicious reading sheds light not only on our own history but on current events. The southern justifications for slavery were frighteningly similar to more recent justifications for apartheid, suggesting that racism wears the same false face across cultures.

Period photographs and drawings break up the text and add needed interest. An excellent index and three-page bibliography complete a volume that is just a bit too scholarly and detached in tone to circulate as interest reading. Teacher highlighting or library booktalking may serve to draw attention to a much neglected area of our national history.

Levinson, Nancy Smiler. *Christopher Columbus: Voyager to the Unknown.* New York: Lodestar/Dutton, 1990. $16.95. 118p. index. bibliography. ISBN 0-525-67292-3.

Among the many books on Columbus, this is one of the better ones, giving background on Columbus's times and their influence on him. The four voyages to the New World are covered, taking into account the frenzy of Columbus's insistence that he had discovered a way to Asia.

Although Columbus is whitewashed at times, the plight of the Native American populations is not glossed over. Lively, readable prose in a large, clear type font, ample white space, and numerous well-placed black-and-white period illustrations make this book a pleasure for both browsing and reading.

A chronology is given as are reproductions of the original Articles of Capitulation and Letter of Introduction written by Ferdinand and Isabella before the first voyage. A roster of the crew for the first voyage is appended. The index is good, but the bibliography is composed mostly of adult titles. This is a solid choice as a report source, as well as for interest reading.

Lowe, Steve, ed. *The Log of Christopher Columbus.* Illustrated by Robert Sabuda. New York: Philomel, 1992. $15.95. unpaged ISBN 0-399-22139-5. **P.**

A consideration that often lurks in the minds of middle school teachers and students is that middle schoolers are too old for picture books. This may be true in general, but once in a while along comes a picture book that is perfectly suited for introducing a unit, or extending one, or just inducing thought and discussion. Lowe's selections from Columbus's log accompanied by Sabuda's woodcuts create such a book.

Short, boxed excerpts from the Admiral's log are coupled with arresting tinted woodcuts. The large size of the pictures makes them perfect for sharing, and their evocative nature gives added depth to Columbus's words. The listener will understand just how uncertain was this undertaking, just what a risk Columbus was taking. Changes in perspective, use of both silhouette and white highlights heighten the dramatic intensity of picture and word.

This book is an ideal introduction to units on exploration generally and Columbus in particular; as it demonstrates the force and propulsion that both Admiral and crew felt, as well as the terrible uncertainties they faced.

Matthews, Rupert. *The Voyage of Columbus.* Illustrated by Tony Smith. New York: Bookwright Press, 1987. 32p. index. bibliography. glossary. ISBN 0-531-18101-7. $11.40.

This account from the Great Journeys series of Columbus's first two voyages, in the course of which he reached hitherto unknown islands and the South American continent, is a typical series book presentation. Thirteen double-page spreads comprise the chapters which give a brief history of navigation and exploration prior to Columbus, cover the first voyage in detail, and the later voyages is passing. Given the brevity of the text, a surprising amount of information is conveyed, and the basic lineaments of Columbus's life and times are clearly outlined. There is enough information for brief reports, and, as is generally the case with this sort of format, there is a strong draw for browsers.

The illustrations are copious—photographs, watercolors, and period reproductions. Maps are included and are generally clear and accurate, though an omitted comma on a map of "The Bahamas Cuba" makes the reader pause in a bit of confusion. The watercolors are of indifferent quality, representative but unremarkable, and tending to be dark. They do show the dramatic moments of Columbus's life from roughly 1490 to 1505. One painting, showing a savage Arawak Indian exulting over the body of a dead Spaniard is questionable; its caption, although true, might lead readers to believe that the Spanish casualties in the New World were heavier than those of the indigenous people. This is simply not so. Still, this is an acceptable introduction to the exploits of one of Europe's greatest navigators.

Meltzer, Milton. *Columbus and the World Around Him.* New York: Watts, 1990. $14.90. 192p. index. source notes. ISBN 0-531-10899-6.

This detailed account of Columbus's four voyages provides not only historical data but a psychological profile of the explorer. It also gives an analysis of the effects of his discoveries on his era. Information on the Renaissance, navigation, late medieval politics, and mapmaking is seamlessly incorporated. Columbus emerges as a complex product of complex times.

Sixteen chapters of lively, direct prose give an in-depth look at the newly extended world of the late fifteenth and early sixteenth centuries. One of the real strengths of Meltzer's book is his unsparing look at the destruction of the Native American populations. His view of Columbus's responsibility for this is shrewd, penetrating, and indeed necessary. Five hundred years later we are still dealing with the effects of Columbus's exploitation.

Black-and-white maps and reproductions of period paintings and drawings extend the text well. Excellent for reports, this book may also draw some students for interest reading. The extensive notes and comprehensive index are added plusses, as is this thoughtful book's tremendous potential as a discussion starter.

Pawonsky, Michael. *Conquest of Eden, 1493-1515: Other Voyages of Columbus; Guadeloupe, Puerto Rico, Hispaniola, Virgin Islands.* Rome: MAPes MONDe Editore, 1991. $34.95. 176 p. ISBN 0-926330-03-9. **Ad.**

In his preface the author notes that his book begins where most books on Columbus end, on the voyage home. The main section of the book traces the second, third, and fourth voyages and considers the evolving Spanish community and its impact on the Indians. Four documents follow, brief surviving records of the Indians as they faced the Spanish holocaust. An afterword contains two "second thoughts" by contemporary settlers of the New World.

The book is pricey; yet if one were to choose a single book on Columbus for middle schoolers, this is surely it. Beautifully laid out and printed in 14-point type, the book is exquisitely illustrated with prints and maps, all contemporary, from the publisher's archives. There are also a number of modern color photographs of the islands, which do much to set the scene and flesh out what is described in the text. The text itself is remarkable in two respects: it consists, with brief connecting explanations, almost entirely of primary source material; it gives a balanced representation of both Spaniards and Indians, as close to an objective accounting as one can come.

The book is useful for browsing, reading aloud, discussing, pondering, and writing reports. In 176 heavily illustrated, large print pages, *Conquest of Eden* gives a comprehensive view of clashing cultures.

Pelta, Kathy. *Discovering Christopher Columbus: How History Is Invented.* Minneapolis, MN: Lerner, 1991. $15.95. 112p. index. bibliography. ISBN 0-8225-4899-2.

In this profusely illustrated, clearly written book, Kathy Pelta recounts the life of Christopher Columbus by discussing the way in which the information we have on him was discovered. Her highlighting of the historical sources and the research process yields an original and uniquely useful approach for incorporation into classroom curricula.

The cogent introduction is followed by nine chapters which follow a chronological progression. After the first chapter, which tells the story of the first voyage, the chronological divisions are 1493-1506 (Chapter 2), 1506-1599 (Chapter 3), 1600-1699 (Chapter 4), 1700-1799 (Chapter 5), 1800-1899 (Chapter 6), 1900-1992 (Chapter 7), and 1992 and the Quincentennial Celebration (Chapter 8). Chapter 9, entitled "You, the Historian," discusses the uses of bibliographies and gives tips on how to weigh information in order to judge is correctness. The note on "Sources of Information" is a good narrative bibliography, and the index is excellent.

A fine work for instructing both on Columbus and the way in which historical information is unearthed and verified, this is a tool not only for the Quincentennial year but for any middle school history class at any time.

Soule, Gardner. *Christopher Columbus on the Green Sea of Darkness.* New York: Watts, 1988. $13.95. 128p. index. bibliography. ISBN 0-531-10577-6.

Five centuries ago two caravels and one nao, wooden sailing vessels of small size and little durability, set sail on a journey that would irrevocably alter the shape of the known world. Cutting into unexplored waters, the Captain General of the fleet sailed either fearlessly or foolishly into what the apprehensive Muslims of North Africa termed The Green Sea of Darkness. While the story of his successful, if not triumphant, voyage is well known, the incredible volume of scientific information his voyages produced is less comprehensively examined.

Soule's book is an extended look at this wealth of information about the natural world of the Americas that Columbus brought back. The indefatigable Admiral of the Ocean Sea observed weather patterns and ocean currents, brought Europe the hammock and the canoe, popcorn, pineapple, and tobacco. Through Columbus's voyages westward, the New World experienced the introduction of such things as sugar cane, horses, and longhorn cattle, all of which irrevocably altered the economic base of the western hemisphere.

The book is divided into 19 short chapters. Information on scientific angles is interspersed with the tale of Columbus's voyages, thus keeping a narrative sense to the whole. The prose is a little blunt and choppy, but does not detract significantly from the overall appeal of this title. The book takes a mildly revisionist view of Columbus, but its main accent is scientific. Excellent maps and clear black-and-white reproductions extend the text. A good index and table of contents add accessibility to a sound report source for both history teachers and for those who find an integrated curriculum attractive.

Ventura, Piero. *1492: The Year of the New World.* New York, Putnam's Sons, 1992. $19.95. 93p. index. ISBN 0-399-22332-0.

Reminiscent of Barbara Brenner's *If You Were There in 1492* (see above), Ventura's book takes a look at the Old and New Worlds in the year of Columbus's landing in the Florida Keys. His writing style is light and readable, moving from present to past tense depending upon the nature of the entry. The accessibility of the text makes this book good for excerpting or for informational reading. In addition, Ventura's hallmark watercolor illustrations abound. Busy scenes of cities in the Old World contrast with those of cities and activities in the New World. There's a lot to look at in every picture, with numerous accurate and well-placed inset maps giving readers an idea of just where each civilization is located on its continent.

The first nine sections, covering 41 pages, look at various sections of the Old World, from Flanders to the Ottoman Empire. The following 14 pages focus on Columbus and his first voyage, with emphasis on geographic theories of the time. The next 30 pages are concerned with New World civilizations and the effects Columbus's landing had on them. The last eight pages briefly bring the reader up to date on changes produced by the Columbian exchange. The index is complete and gives good access to the text.

Middle schoolers may feel that the book is too juvenile in appearance to pick up. The best ploy for getting this pleasurable source of information into their hands is to leave it laying open about the classroom where students can browse through it. Booktalking or reading sections from it may also serve to move it. This is a fine tool for adding breadth and depth to units on Columbus and the New World.

Voices from America's Past. Austin, TX: Steck-Vaughn, 1991. $11.97. 124p. index. ISBN 0-8114-2770-6.

There are few things as useful as the primary source, the eyes and voices of the observers present at the time an event took place. In their words we can still taste the events, fresh and immediate. We can share emotions—shock, outrage, love, homesickness. We begin to put history into a human context.

While only three chapters (termed "units") of this book—the first, the second, and the fourth—apply directly to the exploration of the North American continent, the use of primary sources makes this an invaluable aid. Each unit runs from eight to ten pages and includes background material, a timeline, and reproductions of written communications of people in the focus period. Terms in the letters that may be unfamiliar are noted in bold in the text and defined in the margins, which eliminates flipping back and forth to find word meanings. Unit One covers the years 1492–1541 and contains letters from Columbus and Amerigo Vespucci to their respective patrons, and journal excerpts from the account of Pedro de Castaneda, a soldier who rode with Francisco de Coronado. Unit Two quotes Edward Winslow, a member of the Plymouth colony, the diaries of Mary Osgood Sujmer, an excerpt on colonial Sabbath Laws from Joseph Bennett's *History of New England*, and a German's account of the life of indentured servants in the colonies. Unit Four is perhaps less useful, being largely concerned with the Underground Railroad. However, it does contain two account of cross country treks, one to the Gold Country in 1849, and Amelia Stewart Knight's diaries recounting her journey on the Oregon Trail in 1858.

A natural for reader's theater, these letters and diaries will pique interest. The format, though attractive, is a bit cluttered, but the period illustrations may draw browsers. This is a good source for provoking debate and controversy, thought and empathy.

Fiction

Litowinsky, Olga. *The High Voyage: The Final Crossing of Christopher Columbus.* New York: Delacorte, 1991. $14.95. 147p. ISBN 0-385-30304-1.

Originally published in 1977, Litowinsky's version of Columbus's final voyage has been reissued for the quincentennial year. Told from the viewpoint of Columbus's younger son, Fernando, the narrative flows smoothly and believably.

Fernando is a likeable protagonist accustomed to life at court and shocked by the squalor of life aboard a caravel. The poor food, close quarters, lack of places to sleep, short tempers, and stench all take him aback. The sailors' rough talk, frequently mutinous, is surprising and distressing. Still, among them he finds friends who are staunch and loyal, including the cabin boy, Paco, who chooses to remain in the New World as a settler.

Historical characters abound, and a detailed recording of Columbus's last voyage is made available in a breezy, easy to read form. It must be kept in mind that this is an idealized Columbus, very concerned with good treatment of the Indians, wise and generous, and loving to his son. Based on Fernando Columbus's *The Life of the Admiral Christopher Columbus*, written sometime before Fernando's death in

July 1539, it is not surprising that Columbus's greed and cruelty to the Indians are glossed over. What the book loses in objectivity, it more than makes up for in period flavor. This is a good choice for interest reading or for reading aloud in class.

Schlein, Miriam. *I Sailed with Columbus.* Illustrated by Tom Newsom. New York: HarperCollins, 1991. $13.89. 136p. ISBN 0-06-022514-9.

Twelve-year-old Julio has led a quiet, sheltered life until one day in 1492 when he helps load a ship. Offered a place on the nao, he cannot refuse the call of adventure. Thus it is that he sets off on a voyage that will leave an imprint on history: Columbus's first voyage to the New World.

Written in journal entry form, the prose has a remarkable freshness and credibility. Indeed, the entries are based in part on Columbus's own journals. Three sections cover "The Voyage West," the exploration of the islands of the Caribbean, and "The Voyage Home." Clear maps and full-page pencil sketches augment the text.

This book is suitable for independent reading and the good leading makes this appealing for HiLo readers (high interest/low vocabulary readers who are reading well below grade level); the book is also an ideal classroom read aloud, and can also be used to model journal writing.

CHAPTER 5
Westward Expansion on the North American Continent

My grandparents met each other during childhood. They grew up in the same small Minnesota town. The families, both large, were friendly with each other, and eventually my grandfather fell in love with my grandmother's older sister, Anne. She didn't return his sentiments. Grandpa was only about 18, but that was old enough to nurse a broken heart. His anodyne was to move west. He spent a number of years herding cattle, an archetypal cowboy, before returning to Minnesota to find that the object of his affection had, in the interim, likewise moved west to Montana. Attempting to find her, he found her younger sister instead, teaching in a one-room schoolhouse on the Montana plains. Though glad, no doubt, to see a face from home, Grandma had only sad news: Anne had married and subsequently died in childbirth. At least mildly grief stricken, Grandpa nonetheless noticed that the sister wasn't half bad. They got married and moved still further west, to California, where he made a good living working in the oil fields and singing in a barbershop quartet.

This quiet story contains within it, as grounding and context, the end of the North American westward expansion. Grandpa was a cowboy; Grandma taught in a school that would have been familiar to Laura Ingalls. The pioneering spirit had brought Grandma's family from Sweden and Grandpa's from New England to settle the Minnesota farmlands. This is what most citizens of the United States would recognize as the familiar story of the settlement of the West.

I was raised with Annie Oakley as a role model. Children today may pretend that they are turtles mutated into something powerful by the contents of a sewer. We, however, looked to the cowboys and cowgirls of the not-too-distant past to give us heroes and heroines, to give us that American ethos of going up against "the bad guys" (anyone different from us) and overcoming tremendous odds—hordes of Native Americans, dry deserts, cold, hunger, bandits, and evil cattle barons. The legacy of the European movement across the Northern American continent yielded up a number of myths that were part of the upbringing of my generation. Obviously, I identified with the cowboys, the "good guys."

Here was a part of my family's history that I did not discover until I was in my twenties. My father's side of the family had come from Minnesota. My mother's side had come from New York City—German on her father's side and from the South on her mother's. Her maternal great-grandmother had been a full-blooded Choctaw, raised by missionaries and light enough of skin to "pass." When Nancy Brown, as she was called, chanced to catch the fancy of a young Confederate soldier, David Walker, she obscured her origins, married him, and never looked back. He was killed in the Civil War, and she moved with her sons (one of them my great-grandfather) to Texas. The boys knew that she was Native American, but seeing the treatment accorded the indigenous tribes, knew better than to speak a word about it.

Somewhere on the Oklahoma reservations, my sisters and I have relatives whom we will never know. In us, the blood lines of the Native Americans and the European encroachers sit uneasily together. For how many people this is the case we will likely never know, but the truth is that the course of European expansion on both the North and South American continents bore both in its cutting edge and in its wake the attempt to permanently eradicate any trace of native culture. As we look at the westward expansion, we must consider the human cost on all fronts, to settlers and original inhabitants alike.

Conestoga wagons rolling westward, poke bonnets, plows, buffalo: Many symbols of the westward movement originated in the late eighteenth and early-to-mid nineteenth centuries. The westward expansion, however, began much earlier than that. The images we associate with it are images from the settlement stage, when the land was mapped well enough to plat off and administer from government offices. The actual exploration began centuries before with Columbus's first settlement at Navidad in the Bahamas. Much of the comprehensive exploration and mapping was done between 1500 and 1682, though it would be completed only much later by men like Meriwether Lewis, William Clark, and John C. Fremont. These mapmakers were the ones who drew the shape of the land, marveled at the mountains, whether Rockies or Andes, and opened the way west for the settlers of later years.

LA SALLE

Rene-Robert Cavelier, Sieur de la Salle, was born in Rouen in 1643. An elegant and educated man, he was bitten by the travelling bug early on and eventually became an explorer of the sourthern part of the North American continent. At the age of 29, the bright, educated young man emigrated to Montreal in La Canada, as the colony was known in France at the time. When, on April 9, 1682, he planted the flag of France alongside a wooden cross at the mouth of the Mississippi River, he laid claim to the vast territories that would be explored 121 years later by Meriwether Lewis and William Clark. La Salle and his tired band had made it as far as the Louisiana territory only by dint of the explorer's determination to perform great deeds. Almost alone of the early explorers of the Americas, La Salle was not motivated by greed or the desire for financial gain. His arduous explorations were made as tests of his will and for the greater glory of France.

On his pioneering voyage down the Mississippi, La Salle had conceived the plan of securing the mouth of the river by building a fort and establishing a colony there. "La Salle returned to Canada and then went home to France. But in 1684 he was back in the Gulf of Mexico with three boat loads of prospective settlers, many of them former residents of French jails and waterfronts. The venture was ill-fated from the start" (Lawrence, 1991, p. 188). Finding the mouth of the mighty "Father of Waters" would seem a simple matter, but La Salle's ships overshot the Mississippi delta and landed at Matagorda Bay in Texas. Deciding to settle his people there for a time and search for the Mississippi later, La Salle built a stockade at the site and stayed at the fort for some time before beginning again to search for the Mississippi. After his first two attempts at locating the river failed, La Salle set out on his third and final journey in 1687. It had been raining for weeks, streams were swollen, and the men with La Salle were uncomfortable, restive, and dissatisfied with his dictatorial leadership. The dissatisfaction turned murderous, and La Salle was shot by conspirators among his party on March 18, 1687, along the Trinity River in what is now East Texas. He never realized his goal of exploring the entire North American continent and claiming it all for France. However, if his grand aspirations were never realized, he had certainly, in his 44 years, left a legacy on the continent.

DE SOTO

La Salle's exploratory motivation contrasts markedly with that of an earlier explorer who covered some of the same ground. Hernando De Soto was born around 1500 in Jerez de los Caballeros in central Spain. He, like La Salle, died in his early forties, at the age of 42, along the banks of the Mississippi River. A man of his time, he was possessed of the typical conquest mentality of the Spanish conquistadores. This orientation allowed for incredible abuse of the native population, but De Soto was cruel beyond the norm. When he succumbed to the effects of a fever in 1542, his own men were relieved, sick of "his merciless, endless journey of destruction" (Whitman, 1991). He had pushed out from Tampa Bay in Florida where he had landed in 1539 with " the largest force yet assembled on the North American continent: about six hundred men, some two hundred horses, a pack of vicious blood hounds, and thirteen pigs" (Whitman, 1991). He journeyed through the American South, leaving in his wake brutalized and hostile Native American tribes. De Soto's inhumanity, even allowing for the prevailing Spanish mind-set, was excessive. "The bloodhounds [he brought with him] were for ferreting out the natives, for De Soto delighted in 'the sport of hunting Indians.' Sometimes he set dogs on them just to watch the mongrels tear the poor victim to shreds" (Lawrence, 1991, p. 45). Marching through Florida, Georgia, the South Carolina Piedmont, North Carolina, Tennessee, northern Alabama, Mississippi, and Arkansas, De Soto covered much of the territory La Salle would later stake for France. Since De Soto's interest was only in himself and not nationalistic, he left the land unclaimed. However, if he did not mark out the territory for Spain, he set a precedent for the way relations were to continue between Europeans and Native Americans for centuries to come.

LEWIS AND CLARK

In 1803 Napoleon Bonaparte, in need of ready cash, sold to the United States the Louisiana Territory that La Salle had so triumphantly and lovingly claimed for France. Thomas Jefferson, the third president of a fledgling republic now about doubled in size, quite naturally wondered just what he had purchased for the price of three cents an acre. The natural reaction was to send someone to find out, which is exactly what Jefferson did. "To head an exploring expedition Jefferson picked his protege Meriwether Lewis, the young army officer he had recently made his private secretary. To share the burden of command, Lewis chose his good friend William Clark, younger brother of the Revolutionary War hero George Rogers Clark" (Lawrence, 1991, p. 195). Lewis, the younger man, was a charming, dashing, slightly hot-headed hypochondriac. The more impetuous of the two, he tended to make a stronger and more immediate impression. Though appearing sober and a bit plodding in his journals, Clark, 33 at the beginning of the expedition, was of an optimistic, personable bent. He was an accomplished boatman and incisive observer, saving the company from severe difficulties on several occasions. They made an excellent team, for their differing temperaments were well balanced.

Congregating in Pittsburgh in late 1803, the expedition proceeded to Camp Wood near St. Louis at the confluence of the Mississippi and Missouri Rivers. From here, at about 60 strong, the Corps of Volunteers for North Western Discovery set out in the spring of 1804. Proceeding up the Missouri River, the Corps spent its first winter among the Mandan Indians in central South Dakota, there building a stockade which they called Fort Mandan. It was at Fort Mandan that "the corps picked up two new members: Toussaint Charbonneau and his wife Sacagawea, who was about fifteen years old . . . . Lewis and Clark thought the Frenchman would be valuable as an interpreter and that Sacagawea, a captured Shoshone, would know the Rocky Mountain country" (Lawrence, 1991, p. 204).

Having with some difficulty repaired their boats during the winter, the Corps of Discovery set out again in April of 1805. Following the rivers as best they could, carrying their vessels when they had to, they came, with some help from Sacagawea (though she by no means guided them across the country), to the source of the Missouri. It was there that Lewis found a "'handsome bold running creek of clear cold water.' It was running handsome and bold to the west—he had reached the Continental Divide" (Lawrence, 1991, p. 218). It was just such a trickle of a stream that the Corps followed until it linked them through a series of tributaries to the mighty Columbia River and thence to the west coast of the continent. Though all travelled together on the outward trip, on the return both Lewis and Clark left the main body of the expedition at times to explore differing areas. Clark left for quite some time to follow the Yellowstone River through some of the United States' most spectacular scenery. They arrived back in St. Louis on September 23, 1806.

Did Jefferson get what he wanted out of the expedition? Apparently so, for he gave both Lewis and Clark political appointments. Clark did brilliantly, but Lewis proved unstable and unequal to his job as governor of the Louisiana Territory. He died, an apparent suicide, in 1809, just three years after returning from his great adventure. We may speculate that he suffered from some sort of manic/depressive illness, which would have accounted for his mercurial personality and his inability to cope with a less stressful life after the expedition ended. (There is some evidence that situations of extreme hardship and challenge alleviate manic/depressive symptoms.)

With the return of Lewis and Clark, an era of exploration ended. The way was now open for pioneers, like my great-grandparents, to make their ways west to fertile lands and new lives. While we may idolize the intrepid explorers who made this possible, it is well to remember that both their way and their wake was not bloodless and that this expansion rolled over countless Native American lives and involved a great cultural loss. At the very outset of the westward expansion, on his deathbed in Santo Domingo in the early sixteenth century, Domenico de Betanzoes, a priest, sounded both a warning and a knell:

> "I say that I, Domenico de Betanzoes, friar of Santo Domingo, have frequently, in discussing matters relating to the Indians, spoken of their defects, and I have submitted to His Majesty's Council of the Indies a signed memorial dealing with these defects, on which I said that the Indians were beasts, that they had sinned, that God had condemned them, and that they would all perish.
>
> "Great scandal may have resulted from this and the Spaniards may have taken advantage of it to commit more evils and injury on the Indians and kill more of them than they might have if they had not known of this memorial.
>
> "I swear and beseech the Royal Council of the Indies . . . and all others . . . not to give credence to anything I have spoken or written against the Indians and to their detriment . . . . I believe that I erred through not knowing their language or because of some other ignorance . . . . It grieves me I can not retract my statements in person . . . ." (Paiewonsky, 1991)

The story of the exploration of the North American continent is a wonderful one, full of great deeds and survival at incredible odds. While we laud the men and women who performed these feats, we may also wish for a more contemporary sense of balance, and a greater respect for both the land and for human life, be it European or Native American.

References

Jacobs, W.J. (1975). *Robert Cavelier de La Salle*. New York: Watts.

Lawrence, Bill. (1991). *The Early American Wilderness As the Explorers Saw It*. New York: Paragon House.

Paiewonsky, Michael. (1991). *Conquest of Eden, 1493–1515: Other Voyages of Columbus*. Rome: MAPes MONDe Editore.

Whitman, Sylvia. (1991). *Hernando de Soto and the Explorers of the American South*. New York: Chelsea House.

ANNOTATED BIBLIOGRAPHY

Nonfiction

Anderson, Joan. *Pioneer Settlers of New France.* Photos by George Ancona. New York: Lodestar/Dutton, 1990. $15.95. unpaged. ISBN 0-525-67291-5.

We often consider our country's relations to Great Britain, but seldom to France. In this evocative pictorial work, Anderson and Ancona look at the French settlement of North America through the eyes of two boys, Pierre Andre and Jean Francois Lelarge. Set in Louisburg, a French settlement in what is today Nova Scotia, the book offers a combination of text and pictures that shows what life was like in 1744 as France and Great Britain struggled for control of North America.

Matching one page of text to each full-page picture, this large format book practically reads itself. The story of two boys turning point in their settlement's history is fairly involving and provides a good vehicle for a soft sell history lesson that is nonetheless effective.

Ballinger, James K. *Frederic Remington.* New York: Harry N. Abrams (in association with the National Museum of Art, Smithsonian Institution), 1991. $39.95. 160p. index. bibliography. ISBN 0-8109-1573-1. **Ad.**

This oversized volume printed on heavy paper contains over 100 reproductions, 58 in color, of Remington's paintings of the west. The text provides a detailed and well researched biography of this painter who first came to the attention of the public as an illustrator for Harper's.

By the time Remington began to paint, he knew that the characters and scenes he depicted represented a passing way of life, so there is a sense of poignancy and loss in his almost photographic representations of the life of the frontier.

Though the narrative, index, and bibliography provide excellent information, this book is recommended solely on the basis of its pictorial merit. Students may move on to the text after looking at the paintings and reading the captions, but the book best serves as enrichment and browsing fare to extend students' ideas about the closing phases of the westward expansion and the "classic" west while introducing some ideas about artistic composition and technique.

Brown, Marion Marsh. *Sacagawea: Indian Interpreter to Lewis and Clark.* Chicago: Childrens Press, 1988. $11.95. 119p. index. timeline. ISBN 0-516-03262-3.

Sacagawea was 16 and the common-law wife of a French trapper named Charbonneau when the Lewis and Clark expedition happened through her neck of the Montana frontier. Though expecting her first child, the young Shoshone was determined to accompany the white explorers on their trek to the Pacific. Taken on as an interpreter, "Janie," as the eastern expedition leaders called her, made it to the Pacific, all the while caring for her infant.

This fictionalized biography is based closely enough on the historical facts to offer sound insight into the life of a cheerful and adventurous young woman who, almost by accident, earned a place in history. The book is divided into 16 chapters,

10 of which are devoted to her tenure with the Lewis and Clark expedition. The book is a sound report source, enhanced by a good index and narrative timeline that place "The Bird Woman" into the larger historical context. The text is a bit leaden, but the fictionalization helps to personalize it. Despite its less than lyric quality, the book is easy to read, either aloud or silently. The format is clean and open, illustrated with photos, maps, and period reproductions, making the title attractive for use with younger middle schoolers.

Cavan, Seamus. *Daniel Boone and the Opening of the Ohio Country.* New York: Chelsea House, 1991. $18.95. 112p. index. bibliography. ISBN 0-7910-1309-X.

"I can't say as I was ever lost, but I was bewildered once for three days." Daniel Boone is an American legend, the ultimate self-made man and patriot, the spirit of independence. From his birth in 1734 to his death in 1820, Boone's life mirrors that of the United States as a nation. During his 86 years, Boone helped to open what was termed the "Ohio Country" to white settlement. What we now view as an easterly portion of our country—the Appalachian area, Kentucky, and Missiouri—then demarcated the far western reaches of the United States.

Typical of the World Explorers series, this book is a detailed, intelligently written account not only of Boone's life but of a chapter in American history. Unlike survey treatments, this title deals with historical complexities, specifically the hostile relationship between the settlers and the native population. Boone had, besides his reputation as a trail blazer, a prodigious reputation as an Indian fighter. His concerns were of a personal nature at times. One of his daughters was abducted and one son killed in disputes with the native tribes. The presentation is objective and at times sympathetic to the plight of the Native Americans of the Ohio territory.

An excellent index and bibliography make this a great report source. The black-and-white reproductions and eight-page color section augment the text and add browsing appeal. The maps increase the informational power of the text, and the narrative flow is involving enough to provide booktalk or read-aloud material.

Collins, James L. *Exploring the American West.* New York: Watts, 1989. $11.90. 64p. index. ISBN 0-631-10684-5.

Today we think of reading specifically in terms of the ability to decode words in written language. We do refer to "reading faces" or reading "the writing on the wall," but these expressions are not taken with great seriousness. Daniel Boone made a living and built a legend out of his ability to "read sign," his cultivation of this art of being "able to spot and track quarry in the wilderness." It was this kind of literacy, a sort of wilderness literacy, that enabled Boone, and others like him, to open new lands to white habitation. They could read their way through unfamiliar terrain with an uncanny surety.

Covering several of the better known explorers—Boone, Lewis and Clark, Robert Stuart and Jed Smith, Joseph Reddeford Walker, and John C. Fremont—this book presents their adventures and explorations in clear, succinct language. The typeface is large and inviting, with a bit of extra leading, and the inclusion of period reproductions and maps extends the text beautifully. Especially useful is the chapter on Walker, who was hired in 1832 by Benjamin Bonneville as field commander of a well-equipped party of 110 men who went west to trap and trade in the Mexican Southwest. Walker, however, went on to explore California. He contrasts markedly with John C. Fremont, a rabid self-promoter, who, though he talked more than he acted, made those actions count.

The contents and index increase the accessibility of information in this ideal report book. Too dry for reading aloud, the book may be perused for pictures and factual material.

Conrad, Pam. *Prairie Visions: The Life and Times of Solomon Butcher.* New York: HarperCollins, 1991. $16.95. 83p. ISBN 0-06-021373-6.

He was a handsome man with a steady eye and hand and an iron will. These traits went into promoting and following his dream—recording the lives of the pioneers in turn-of-the-century Custer County, Nebraska. Solomon Butcher wanted to capture the pioneers' images in photographs and set down their tales on paper.

This combination of photobiography and pioneer narrative tells the story of Solomon Butcher's life through the stories that were told to him, the photographs he took, and the story of his own life which, like the pioneers', was full of hard work, disappointments, and small triumphs.

Conrad's admiration for Butcher and her love of the prairie infuse this tribute to a dreamer and his subjects. The prose is light, speculative, and easy to read, packed with stories of pioneer life. Butcher's photographs are lovingly reproduced, and Conrad's musings on their subjects make this a great inspiration for the type of creative writing that would encourage empathy and understanding of the pioneers' visions. A browser's delight, this book could be left in a classroom or library where it would soon find eager readers. Use this book to tie in with Conrad's *Prairie Songs* (see below) in which Butcher appears as a character.

Coulter, Tony. *La Salle and the Explorers of the Mississippi.* New York: Chelsea House, 1991. $18.95. 112p. index. bibliography. ISBN 0-7910-1304-7.

Following the same format as other books in the World Explorers series, Coulter's entry charts the travails of Robert Cavelier, Sieur de La Salle. Also giving background on Marquette, Joliet, and De Soto, the lucid text is extended by maps, period photographs, and a color insert composed of paintings done by nineteenth-century artist George Catlin (see Sufrin entry, below) in which La Salle is the subject.

La Salle's great ambitions and flawed personality are covered in readable, lucid prose. The detail is painstaking. The columnar text is dense looking, but there is enough interesting insight into characters and enough adventure to promote the book by reading bits of it aloud. A good table of contents lists the six chapters and gives a basic idea of content, while the index provides more detailed access. Fine as supplemental material, this book is also a creditable report source.

Fisher, Leonard Everett. *The Oregon Trail.* New York: Holiday House, 1990. $14.95. 64p. ISBN 0-8234-0833-7.

Using a sumptuous progression of clear, large text and half- to full-page black-and-white period photos and drawings, Fisher charts the journey of those who followed the Oregon Trail in the first half of the nineteenth century. Vivid descriptions of the obstacles and dangers the pioneers encountered are followed by a discussion of the Trail's eventual decline, prompted by the advent of the cross-country railroad.

There are no chapter divisions, but from the first page ("June 1 [1853]: It has been raining all day long, the men and boys are soaking wet . . . and comfortless . . . ") readers will be engrossed by the excellent, judicious use of primary source material, both visual and textual. The well-selected and composed black-and-white illustrations are large enough, generally, for group sharing, and the text is suitable for reading aloud, an unusual occurrence in nonfiction treatments. A brief but serviceable index increases access for those writing reports. This book works equally well for browsing, reading, reporting, or sharing.

Fitz-Gerald, Christine A. *Meriwether Lewis and William Clark.* Chicago: Childrens Press, 1990. $23.93. 128p. index. bibliography. ISBN 0-516-03061-2.

Sinnott, Susan. *Zebulon Pike.* Chicago: Childrens Press, 1990. $23.93. 128p. index. bibliography. ISBN 0-516-03058-2.

Both of these books are entries in The World's Great Explorers series and have the same format. Nine chapters in Sinnott and 10 in Fitz-Gerald are followed by appendices, a timeline of events during the subjects' lives, glossary, bibliography, and index. Lower in reading level than the Chelsea House World Explorers series (see Coulter entry, above), the physical layout of the Childrens Press series also features more visual material, contemporary photos of areas covered in the text, and period photos and drawings.

Zebulon Pike describes the adventures of the young army officer who, prior to the War of 1812, explored the upper Mississippi, Great Plains, and Colorado area, where he gave his name to Pike's Peak. Nine chapters cover his life from birth in 1779 to death in 1813 at the age of 34. In this age of extended life spans and deferred careers it is easy to forget just how young many of these explorers were. Three chapters are devoted to background and the remaining six to young Pike's explorations, just on the heels of Lewis and Clark's expedition.

Fitz-Gerald's coverage of the 1803 Corps of Discovery's journey is simply written and much enhanced by present-day photos of the areas they explored. The prose is readable, the documentation sound, and the follow-up on the main players in the expedition satisfying. Both books have appendices, glossaries, sound indices, and bibliographies composed generally of adult books. These titles will prove to be of limited use as browsing books since the covers have a textbook look to them despite the pictorial aspects of the internal layout. They will see most concentrated use as report sources.

Fleming, Alice. *The King of Prussia and a Peanut Butter Sandwich.* Illustrated by Ronald Himler. New York: Charles Scribner's Sons, 1988. $12.95. 42p. index. ISBN 0-684-18880-5. **ER.**

Fleming's readable historical text is ably extended by Ronald Himler's scratchy, impressionistic ink drawings. The story of the Mennonites, who emigrated first to

Russia and then to Kansas in order to escape conscription into military service, is simply and accessibly told.

As there are no chapter divisions and the index, though serviceable, is brief, the book is not a suitable report source. However, it can certainly be used as a broadening, organizing element in introducing units on the westward exploration. Alice Fleming describes discoveries the Mennonites made about their homes in both Russia and the United States as a result of agricultural exploration. Linking the Mennonite development of Turkey red wheat to the homely peanut butter sandwich, and thus to each child's experience is canny and inspired.

Best used by the librarian or teacher as an advance organizer, this intriguing story introduces units on history, exploration, science, or social issues with equal facility.

Franck, Irene M. and David M. Brownstone. *The American Way West.* New York: Facts on File, 1991. $17.95. 120p. index. ISBN 0-8160-1880-4.

When we think of the westward expansion, we often picture wagon trains moving over open, exposed scrub between high cliffs where Indians wait to rush down like waves from the ocean. Most of us do not think in terms of established trails or trade routes, used reliably year after year. This is not to say that the way west was safer or more predictable than we imagine—only that the open scrub may have contained clearly marked trails.

Five chapters each take a look at different portions of our continent and the trails that crossed them. The Mohawk Trail ran from Albany to the eastern end of Lake Erie, and was one of the earliest westward routes. Trans-Appalachian Routes to the Mississippi Basin are considered next, followed by the Mississippi itself, which carried settlers more than 2000 miles into the heartland of the United States. The text then turns west to consider the Santa Fe and Chihuahua Trails, and the Oregon and California Trails.

Enhanced throughout by the inclusion of 50 maps and illustrations, containing thorough chapter bibliographies and an adequate index, this book provides solid report material on the exploration of our continent.

The prose is unfortunately plodding and of textbook quality. A snappy dust jacket showing an antique world map will help move this title, but it simply cannot be pushed as interest reading. Students looking for solid information on the roads west will find it here.

Frontier America: Arts and Treasures of the Old West from the Buffalo Bill Historical Center. Text by Paul Fees and Sarah E. Boehm. New York: Abrams, 1988. $40.00. 128p. index. bibliography. ISBN 0-8109-0948-0. **Ad.**

Oversize and printed on stiff, heavy paper, this pictorial volume introduces artists who explored, visited, lived in, or painted the West. The influences of landscape, the people, and the artifacts on what became a uniquely American art form are examined in a chapter entitled "Frontier America: The Artists' Environment." A second chapter, "The West and American Unity," explores what life in the West was like and how it developed into a symbol of the American spirit.

There is a great deal more picture than text—124 illustrations, 54 in color. This is fortunate because the prose varies in quality depending upon which of the two authors is writing. Sarah Boehm adopts an academic, distanced style that will not engage young readers simply wanting to know what the painting or piece of sculpture is about. Paul Fees's prose is much livelier and more direct. He has a more involved and readable style altogether. Both have in common use of complex vocabulary and an adult approach to their material.

The index and bibliography make this book useful for reports, but it will move on its own as a browsing work. Certainly it is important that students have access to the pictures. Many of these artists were explorers and, in a number of cases, their pictures provide the only remaining record of indigenous cultures that have ceased to exist. This is an excellent vehicle for introducing students to visual primary source material, and a natural link between the social sciences and fine arts.

Hargrove, Jim. *Daniel Boone: Pioneer Trailblazer.* Chicago: Childrens Press, 1985. $11.95. 124p. index. ISBN 0-516-03215-1.

Hargrove, Jim. *Rene-Robert Cavelier, Sieur de La Salle.* Chicago: Childrens Press, 1990. $23.93. 128p. glossary. index. ISBN 0-516-03054-X.

As a young man, Daniel Boone was so woods-wise that he was ". . . almost like an Indian boy." This uncanny talent for woodcraft won Boone his reputation, still current today, as a woodsman, trailblazer, and Indian fighter.

This eight-chapter biography traces the life of Boone from his youth in the Pennsylvania wilderness to his adventures in sparsely settled portions of Virginia, the Carolinas, Kentucky, and Missouri. Proceeding in a chronological manner, the text, written in simple, blocky sentences, is easy to read. The language is basic, though place names like Fort Duquesne may trouble some students. The style is not quite dry, but neither is it inspired. Black-and-white reproductions, approximately one for every two chapters, plus an added eight-page section of illustrations, flesh the text out.

An excellent index increases access to a sound report source on one of America's early pioneers. A detailed chronology sets Boone into the international scheme of events.

Similar in format to *Daniel Boone*, Hargrove's work on La Salle is simply written in readable, if not exciting prose. Amply illustrated, it presents the life of La Salle from his birth in Rouen, France, in 1643 to his tragic murder along the Trinity River in what is now East Texas some 44 years later. Mentioning numerous earlier explorers, among them De Soto, Cartier, and Champlain, Hargrove gives background and context to the exploring ventures of the man who followed the Mississippi, staking the vast territory of the Louisiana Purchase for France. Three of the book's eight chapters give background information, while five detail La Salle's explorations. The book concludes with a set of pictorial appendices, a timeline of events in La Salle's lifetime, an adequate index, and a brief glossary and bibliography.

The layout is attractive, providing nearly as much illustrative material as text. Photographs, period paintings, drawings, and maps, all in color, are used to good advantage, rendering the book appealing to browsers. The typeface is large and easy to read. With enough information for a report, this book has special applicability for use with students in need of high interest, low vocabulary reading.

Harris, Edward D. *John Charles Fremont and the Great Western Reconnaissance.* New York: Chelsea House, 1990. $18.95. 111p. index. bibliography. ISBN 0-7910-1312-X.

". . . cities have risen on the ashes of his lonely campfires." This assertion made by Jessie Benton Fremont about her husband's explorations of the western United States rings as true today as it ever has. Both supremely handsome and compellingly charismatic, John Charles Fremont was also impulsive, reckless, and selfish. Beyond that he was intrepid, daring, and capable of leading men into the unknown with such success that he earned the title "Pathfinder." He lead five exploratory surveys of the American West, helping to open the region to later settlement.

Six chapters discuss Fremont's childhood and early years, his rise as an explorer and surveyor, and his journey to the Oregon Territory (which reveals his more Quixotic side—he attempted to cross the Sierra Nevada during the winter). Explorations in California and the so-called "Bear Flag Rebellion," his court marshall, light sentencing, disastrous winter expedition of 1848, and final journey of 1854 are covered subsequently. Throughout this soundly written and reasoned narrative, the sociopolitical tenor of the times and the complex interplay of personality and circumstance that moved Fremont to prominence act as a backdrop. Black-and-white photographs, lithographs, reproductions, and maps are sprinkled liberally throughout, extending the text and amplifying it. A color center section adds an extra bit of information. A brief but serviceable index and bibliography further this volume's use as a report source. This attractive entry in the World Explorers series combines the factual with the browsable most felicitously.

Jacobs, W. J. *Robert Cavelier de La Salle.* New York: Watts, 1975. $11.95. 57p. index. source notes. ISBN 0-531-02843-7.

On April 9, 1682, Rene-Robert Cavelier, Sieur de La Salle, planted the flag of France alongside a wooden cross at the mouth of the Mississippi River. With that simple ceremony he had, at the age of 38, laid claim to the vast territories that comprise what Lewis and Clark would explore 121 years later as the Louisiana Purchase.

La Salle is intriguing because, almost alone among the earlier explorers of the New World, he was not interested in financial gain. He explored in order to quench his thirst for great enterprises, as a test of his will, and for the glory of France. That he failed to realize his dreams, dying tragically five years after laying claim to the Louisiana Territory, in no way diminishes his accomplishments. Divided into seven short chapters, this account of L Salle's life is readably presented in accessible, engaging prose. La Salle is described in all his complexity, a man who ". . . carried within his own personality the seeds of his triumph and also of his destruction." The book covers La Salle's emigration to Canada, early explorations, support from the

Count de Frontenac, and final expeditions. Liberally illustrated with period drawings and maps, the book includes contemporary maps as well. This use of primary source material adds depth and immediacy. The lack of a table of contents poses a problem, but the solid index compensates to some extent.

Good interest reading, Jacobs's book will need promotion because of a lackluster cover. It is an excellent and penetrating report source, and a superior example of use of primary source illustrations. The "Note on Sources" on page 54 references primary source narrative. This book can be either booktalked or excerpted for use with groups.

Journeys in New Worlds: Early American Women's Narratives. Edited by William L. Andrews, et. al. Madison, WI: University of Wisconsin Press, 1990. 232p. $14.94. ISBN 0-299-12584-X. **Ad.**

Rarely do we find the viewpoints of colonial women expressed, yet women made up half the population of the colonies. In a small way, this book sets out to rectify the predominantly white male voice of colonial history. The text includes Mary Rowlandson's history of her captivity among the Narragansetts (1676), the journal of Sarah Kemble Knight (1704), the autobiographical account of the early life of Elizabeth Ashbridge (1755), and the travel diary of Elizabeth House Trist (1783-84). These women were of differing backgrounds, from independent teacher to minister's wife.

The essays preceding each of these primary source accounts are informative but scholarly, and may prove prohibitive reading for most middle schoolers. However, the female voices and first person nature of the documents presented make this book an invaluable source for balance. It is best used by a teacher or librarian who can give background information on the women, then excerpt their journals. Excellent bibliographies and black-and-white period reproductions increase access to information and enhance the text.

Lavender, David. *The Way to the Western Sea: Lewis and Clark Across the Continent.* New York: Harper & Row, 1988. 444p. $22.95. appendices. notes. bibliography. index. maps. ISBN 0-06-015982-0. **Ad.**

In twenty chapters, Meriweather Lewis and William Clark's historic journey to map the Louisiana Purchase is given a detailed, scholarly treatment. Beginning with biographical information on the explorers and historical background on the time period, Lavender moves on to preparations for the trek, then details the actual journey in the bulk of the text. He finishes with the histories of both Lewis and Clark after their great adventure was over.

This is excellent historical writing, detailed, readable, and consistently engaging. The maps are invaluable in showing where the explorers were at any time. The narrative explores their psychological states with equal exactitude. More than a chronicle of an historic expedition, this book also marks out the American mind set at a point of tremendous national expansion. Appendices contain Jefferson's commission to Lewis and a listing of the permanent party. The bibliography (all adult works) and the index are superb.

This is an adult book, but it can be used to introduce students to serious historical literature and research aspects. It is wonderful background for the interested educator, offering insights into both historical and cultural contexts of the early colonial years. It is equally well suited for the gifted or high ability reader.

Lawrence, Bill. *The Early American Wilderness as the Explorers Saw It.* New York: Paragon House, 1991. $23.95. 295p. index. bibliography. ISBN 1-55778-145-1. **Ad.**

We all have our ideas about the United States, that vast land that stretches "from sea to shining sea," each region having its own distinct flavor though blended these days by the ubiquity of Sears stores, the Golden Arches, and our television culture. What was it like before all this? What was it like when the human hand upon the land was that of the Native Americans who "...did not live in the wilderness—they were as much a part of it as the animals, plants, and trees." The first explorers on the continent saw it pristine, untainted.

Ten chapters cover in turn the earliest explorations (the Vikings, Cabot, Cartier), the exploration of Florida, the South (De Soto), the Southwest (Cabeza de Vaca, Coronado), the early English settlements in Virginia, the settlement of New England, the early exploration of the West Coast, the exploration of New York and the Great Lakes (Hudson, Champlain), the North American interior (Joliet, Marquette, and La Salle), and, finally, the Lewis and Clark expedition. Inspired by the author's desire to make history interesting for his junior high students, the narrative is characterized by vigorous prose and wry humor. The historical detail is complete and accurate, and the sense of freshness palpable.

Nonetheless, it is not a book students will sit down and read, despite the use of numerous black-and-white period maps and pictures which break up the text, and despite the inviting prose. The appearance is simply too intimidatingly adult. It is, however, a superb teacher's resource and does read aloud beautifully, providing a good classroom reading source. So introduced to the work and encouraged to read it, some students may pick it up on their own, while many will use it as a report source, for which role it is admirably suited. The index is sound and the bibliography, though composed mostly of adult titles, is little short of breathtaking.

Marrin, Albert. *Inca and Spaniard: Pizarro and the Conquest of Peru.* New York: Atheneum, 1989. $13.95. 211p. bibliography. index. ISBN 0-689-31481-7.

The Incas had created a sophisticated civilization with an intricate bureaucracy supporting an absolute monarch. The road and communications systems were impressive, efficiently linking vast areas. The Inca Empire covered all of Peru and parts of Chile, where messengers covered tremendous tracts on foot over the seemingly endless sands of northern Chile. This rich, diverse civilization was brought down by a small band of men lead by a single-minded opportunist named Francisco Pizarro.

The conquest of Peru is an inherently dramatic story, given the ruthless nature of both the Inca and the Spanish conquistadores. Francisco Pizarro was typical of the type of man who became a conquistador—crafty, self-interested, and single minded in the pursuit of opportunity. The conquest is yet another chronicle of the triumph of technology over a less technologically advanced civilization; Marrin describes how Pizarro reduced the powerful Inca Empire of Atahuallpa to rubble within a few short years. Marrin's prose is lucid and readable, conveying the complex machinations that went on within the Inca nation and among the squabbling Spaniards. Given the amount of information presented in 211 pages, students could report on several different aspects, from the Spanish conquest to the Inca Empire itself, from social issues dealing with servitude to governmental power and the influence of politics. The text is extended by black-and-white illustrations, many of which came from the contemporary accounts of Guaman Popo, an Inca who served the Spanish as a minor official. These line drawings have a piercing immediacy that communicates the suffering of the native population. Not a source for quick information, this book is good enrichment material for students who want to explore the topic in depth. It reads aloud well, and also serves, with grace and ease, as a discussion starter. Index and contents offer access, and the bibliography points out other sources for those who want to continue to explore the Inca Empire.

Pelz, Ruth. *Black Heroes of the Wild West.* Illustrated by Leandro Della Piana. Seattle: Open Hand Publishing, 1990. $9.95. 55p. bibliography. ISBN 0-940880-25-3.

This book comprises tales of nine black heroes and heroines who helped settle the American West. The chronicle begins in 1539 with Estevan, a black man who marched through North America in search of the Seven Cities of Cibola. A powerful and extremely intelligent person, he is remembered in Zuni legends. Other black explorers are Mountain Man James Beckworth, coureur du bois Jean Baptiste Point Du Sable, cowboy Bill Pickett, and five pioneers, three of them women, who possessed significant mettle and merit.

The prose style is straightforward and easy to read either silently or aloud. Chapters are short enough for classroom reading, and the racial issues raised are excellent discussion starters. This book shows the black contribution to westward exploration and settlement with great clarity and conciseness. The bibliography is divided into juvenile and adult lists. Most of the books listed are, unfortunately, rather old and may be out of print. One could not write a report from this brief text, so the bibliography is necessary for interested students, making the out-of-print issue of even greater concern. The illustrations are black, white, and grey acrylic, rather amateurishly executed. Though strong of line, shapes often have an ill-defined, out-of-proportion look. Use this book to fill in an under-examined portion of the history of westward exploration.

Peterson, David and Mark Coburn. *Meriwether Lewis and William Clark: Soldiers, Explorers, and Partners in History.* Chicago: Childrens Press, 1988. $23.93. 152p. index. ISBN 0-516-03264-X.

The 1803 Louisiana Purchase so increased the size of the United States that Thomas Jefferson justifiably wondered what he'd gotten for his $5 million dollars. The result was the commissioning of Meriwether Lewis and William Clark to explore and map the area west of the confluence of the Missouri and Mississippi Rivers.

This book presents a biography of the leaders of the two-year expedition which explored both the Louisiana Purchase and the Pacific Northwest. While the emphasis is on the dangers faced and the scientific contributions the expedition made, concerns about politics, social issues, and personality inevitably intrude.

The book is divided into 17 chapters; the first 11 set the scene and then follow the expedition to the West Coast and back. The remaining six chapters (one-fourth of the book) discuss the remainder of the lives of Lewis and Clark. (Peterson and Coburn indicate that Lewis may have been murdered, when in fact it is certain that he died a suicide in the throes of alcoholism and depression.) In conclusion, the effects of the opening of the West and related scientific discoveries are considered.

Though some of the illustrations (all black-and-white and all from period sources) are sprinkled throughout, most of them are gathered into a central section. This is less effective than placing them with the corresponding text. The prose is readable, but dull. However, the thorough index, detailed timeline, and clear route maps make this book a recommended report source.

Schlessel, Lillian, Byrd Gibbens, and Elizabeth Hampston. *Far from Home: Families of the Westward Journey.* New York: Schocken Books, 1989. $19.95. 264p. index. ISBN 0-8052-4052-7. **Ad.**

Using letters and diaries to tell the stories of three separate families who moved west between 1848 and 1911, the authors bring a variety of pioneering experiences to life.

Written in three separate accounts dealing with the Malick family, the Brown family, and the Neher/Martin menage, Schlessel concludes in the fourth essay the ". . . the Western ideals of mobility and individualism are still stronger forces than the notion of keeping families together, and this, too, is part of our frontier legacy." A clearly set up and visually accessible index aids the researcher, as does the first person nature of the narratives. The inclusion of photographs of the subject families extends the text well.

This book brings the exploration and opening of the West to the reader in a particularly immediate and approachable manner. It will appeal on the basis of interest, and as reference or research material.

Scott, John Anthony. *Settlers of the Eastern Shore: The British Colonies in North America 1607-1750.* New York: Facts on File, 1991. $16.95. 133p. bibliography. index. ISBN 0-8160-2327-1. **Ad.**

The early settlers to the shores of New England found life bleak and hard, yet by 1750 they had changed the face of the Northern American continent beyond recognition. In 10 brief but involving chapters, John Anthony Scott offers a detailed look at our first European and African settlers. Along the way, he discusses the plight of the Native Americans, the trial of Peter Zenger, the outburst of religious revival ("The Great Awakening" of the mid eighteenth century), the European view of the colonies, and the songs of these early settlers. These stories paint a clear picture of the growth of the character of the nation that would one day become the United States. The writing style is lucid, but lends itself well to reading aloud. A section from "The Captivity of Mary Rowlandson," which details the ordeal of a white woman captured by Narragansett Indians during King Philip's War in 1676, or a snippet of song from "The Sycamore Tree" will arouse student interest.

The type font is clear and attractively leaded, giving the text a nonthreatening appearance. Judicious use of primary sources adds life to the narrative as well as setting a fine example of historical research techniques. Each chapter contains at least one black-and-white map or period reproduction, all of which are faithfully and clearly reprinted. The index is good and the bibliography is detailed and specific, with applicable works listed for each chapter.

An excellent report source, this book could be used in short excerpts to introduce units on Colonial America or the early phases of westward expansion. If used for library programming, this book would be perfect for discussing what types of things can by found in the Dewey 970s, and to pique student interest in historical nonfiction.

Sufrin, Mark. *George Catlin: Painter of the Indian West.* New York: Atheneum, 1991. $14.95. 153p. index. bibliography. ISBN 0-689-31608-9.

George Catlin was born in 1796 in Wilkes Barre, Pennsylvania, a town which was, at that time, on the edge of the western frontier. Earmarked by his father to be a lawyer and sent through an esteemed law school in Lichfield, Connecticut, Catlin practiced for only a short time before turning to his hobby, painting, as a full-time occupation. A talented miniaturist and portrait painter, he found this too tame and conceived of a grand project: to record the life of the wild, free American Indian before that life disappeared. Between 1831 and 1836 he travelled west and did just that, painting 500 or so portraits, group pictures, and landscapes at lightning speed, and acting as the first ethnographer of the Native American people.

This biography of a simultaneously heroic and tragic life captures the West as the white settlers began to invade it. The writing style has life and color which just about compensates for its lack of elegance and the occasional poorly constructed sentence. Illustrated with numerous black-and-white plates of Catlin's paintings , this book provides primary source information on a little-known explorer, on Native Americans as they were first encountered, and on the American West itself. With a good index and fair bibliography, this fine report source is good for interest reading and would even make intriguing read-aloud nonfiction.

Tolan, Sally. *John Muir.* Milwaukee: Gareth Stevens, 1989. $14.95. bibliography. glossary. chronology. index. 68p. ISBN 0-8368-0099-0.

John Muir was eccentric, inspired, and crusading. Many of our national parks would not exist today if it were not for this odd, nature-loving, solitary man. He holds a chapter in the westward expansion precisely because it was his mission to halt it, leaving some of the natural beauty of our land untouched by the advance of civilization. Born in 1838 in Dunbar, Scotland, he emigrated to the United States when he was 11. His hiking and exploring began in 1864 after he was temporarily disabled in a factory accident.

The book is divided into sections from a few paragraphs to several pages long, and it gives a detailed account of Muir's life. The prose is factual; it never sparkles and sounds similar in life and verve to the encyclopedia. Numerous black-and-white and color photos, maps, and sidebars are sprinkled throughout. Wide margins facilitate the captioning and sidebar material, but do run the rather small type into the gutter. A good bibliography, serviceable glossary, detailed chronology, and basic index round out this entry in the "People Who Have Helped the World" series.

Wexler, Sanford. *Westward Expansion: An Eyewitness History.* New York: Facts on File, 1991. $40.00. 418p. index. bibliography. ISBN 0-8160-2407-3. **Ad.**

When the westward expansion is mentioned, we often think of the Gold Rush of 1849, or of Conestogas moving across the plains, or perhaps of the Donner party. However, the westward expansion actually began 86 years earlier, on February 10, 1763, when the historic Treaty of Paris was signed, surrendering most of France's American territories to Great Britain.

In this heavy tome, literally hundreds of first person accounts are provided from numerous sources—diaries, letters, speeches, newspaper articles, memoirs. The well-known as well as the common citizen are represented here, and the immediacy of testimony is generally as fresh now as it was when written.

Ten chapters cover the the Colonial Frontier (1754-1794), the Trans-Mississippi Frontier (1795-1810), the West in the War of 1812 and Economic Depression (1811-1820), Early Traders and Explorers (1821-1830), Across the Plains (1831-1840), the Gold Rush and the Debate over Slavery in the West (1840-1860), Overland Transportation and the Civil War in the West (1860-1869), Opening the Plains (1870-1879), and the Closing Frontier (1880-1897). Each chapter begins with a detailed essay on the time period under examination, gives a chronology, and finishes with a section of primary source material.

The book has a large, thick, and dense type font that is unlikely to appeal to students despite frequent black-and-white photos. However, this book is an excellent teacher resource and reference tool. The primary source material is fascinating, well accessed through a good index, and backed up by a huge bibliography.

Whitman, Sylvia. *Hernando de Soto and the Explorers of the American South.* New York: Chelsea House, 1991. $18.95. 111p. index. bibliography. ISBN 0-7910-1301-4.

Born in about 1500 in Jerez de los Caballeros in central Spain, Fernando de Soto died 42 years later along the banks of the Mississippi River in what is now the American South. A man of his time, with a conquest mentality that allowed for incredible abuse of the native population in order to achieve his goals, de Soto wasn't mourned by his men who had tired of ". . . his merciless, endless journey of destruction."

The first two of six densely written chapters cover the first contacts between the American Indians in the southern United States and the abusive relationship that developed. The remaining four detail de Soto's life and his fateful journey from Florida, across the Appalachians, to the Mississippi River. The text, clearly and concisely written, if a bit lacking in flair, raises moral issues surrounding the treatment of the native population. Thus the book, while definitely set up more as a report source, also has potential as a discussion starter, especially if read in excerpt form.

Numerous black-and-white illustrations and a central color insert extend the text skillfully. Use this title for unit support, excerpt reading, report sources, and discussion.

Fiction

Conrad, Pam. *Prairie Songs.* Illustrated by Darryl S. Zudek. New York: Harper & Row, 1985. $11.95. 167p. ISBN 0-06-021336-1.

Louisa's home is the Nebraska prairie. She loves the wild beauty of the huge landscape. She is thrilled, too, by the contrasting cultured beauty of young Emmeline Berryman, the new doctor's wife, who just arrived from New York City. At first open and warm, Emmeline gives reading lessons to both Louisa and her shy younger brother, Lester. Yet as time passes and she find herself expecting a child, Emmeline becomes despondent, dependent on her husband, and despairing when he leaves on his rounds. Gradually, her condition worsens; when her son dies at birth, Emmeline gives in to madness and death. Yet, though the reader senses the hardness of life, Louisa's love of the prairie is also evident.

Written with a stark, simplistic beauty and extended by five full-page soft pencil drawings, Conrad's book introduces young readers to a woman's view of life in pioneer society—loneliness, grinding work, heartbreak, loss, and the sudden surprise of joy, love, and continued life. Too personal for reading aloud, the large, clear type font and open spacing make the book attractive independent reading for moderately good to very capable readers. The subject may attract mostly girls, but boys could benefit from it as well. A quick classroom or library booktalk could move this book out into students' hands.

DeFelice, Cynthia. *Weasel.* New York: Macmillan, 1990. $12.95. 119p. ISBN 0-02-726457-2.

Many of the dangers to be braved when settling new lands wore human faces. In Ohio in 1839 an 11-year-old boy named Nathan Fowler runs up against such a man. Nathan's mother is dead, and his father has been gone hunting for six days, when a strange, speechless man appears with a sign from Pa. Nathan and his sister follow the man, Ezra, who leads them to their father, a victim, like Ezra himself, of a savage former Indian soldier whom the Shawnee call Weasel.

Touching on issues of good and evil, revenge and impotence, and the inhumanity of people, Nathan's story encompasses a range of emotions. It is a powerful tale of one child's effort to understand the nature of evil and to avoid being infected by it. Prose and characterization have a depth and penetration belied by the simple, almost stark language. The settlement of the West began nearly 200 years ago, but human emotion and intellect are still the same. An excellent read aloud and discussion starter, *Weasel* brings frontier America to life.

Fleishman, Paul. *Saturnalia.* New York: Harper & Row, 1990. $12.95. 113p. ISBN 0-06-021912-2.

Set in Boston, in December 1681, Fleishman's stylistically complex novel examines the lives of several of the town's inhabitants as they prepare for Saturnalia, the ancient Roman holiday in which masters and slaves exchange places. The sober tapestry of colonial life is presented through the various peregrinations of several people: The sour Mr. Baggot, a tithingman who teaches scripture to 10 of the town's families; William, his brightest pupil, a Narraganset Indian raised by a printer as the equal of his own children; Mr. Hogwood, a pompous wigmaker; and Malcolm, Hogwood's Cassanova of a servant. Various others come and go, mysterious grieving figures that give the book its air of mystery and contemplation.

Fleishman's elegant prose has energy and impact, and presents his complex story with deceptive simplicity. The typeface is large and clear. Seven chapters tell this story and expose many elements of colonial life, raising questions about the value of assimilation. The pivotal character is William, who feels the pull of his Native American past and yet has become an educated and accepted member of the white culture. Taut and exciting at times, and dreamy and thoughtful at others, this is, based on content not vocabulary, recommended reading for advanced independent readers. This could be read aloud in class as an opening to the idea that westward expansion and exploration had human costs and effects that we do not always consider.

Gregory, Kristiana. *The Legend of Jimmy Spoon.* New York: HBJ, 1990. $15.95. 165p. bibliography. glossary. ISBN 0-15-200506-4.

Adventurous 12-year-old Jimmy Spoon is always ready for a challenge. When two Shoshone boys offer him a horse on condition that he ride it to their camp, he sneaks away from his family to do so. The journey, however, is much longer and more arduous than Jimmy anticipated. When he arrives at the camp, he discovers the truth: he has been kidnapped to become the son of the chief's mother. The remainder of the book covers Jimmy's three years among the Shoshone as he adjusts to his new culture. Inspired by the memoirs of Elijah Nicholas Wilson who lived with Chief Washakie's tribe in the mid-1800s, this book is a high interest approach to cross-cultural experiences during the period of white westward expansion.

Gregory's style is not inspired, but she does show a nice alternation between high excitement plotting and periods of relative calm in which Native American tribal life is explored. The large typeface and short chapters make this book attractive for interest reading, especially for boys. It reads aloud or booktalks with equal ease. A glossary of Shoshoni words and a bibliography that cites several primary sources give natural lead-ins to nonfiction treatments of similar issues.

Hotze, Sollace. *A Circle Unbroken.* New York: Clarion, 1988. $13.95. 202p. ISBN 0-89919-733-7.

Captured by a roving band of Sioux Indians and brought up as the chief's daughter, Rachel is adjusted to her life and, at 17, thinks of herself as Kata Wi, Burning Sun. One day in early October 1845, white men show up in the Sioux camp when the men of the tribe are absent. The men have been paid to find Rachel Porter and bring her "home" to her white family.

Based on historical incidents in which white children, seized by Indians, were later returned and failed to re-assimilate into white culture, this novel is divided into 20 reasonably brief chapters. The type font is large and clear, appears approachable, and is appropriate for younger middle school readers. Characterization and prose style are both adequate. The story line is contemplative and will be most useful as recommended independent reading for students interested in considering some less examined aspects of acculturation and exchange between white and indigenous populations on the western frontier. While not as powerful a treatment of this issue as Douglas Lee's *The Season of Yellow Leaf*, the happy ending to this story may make this book more palatable to the young.

Kellogg, Steven. *Johnny Appleseed.* New York : Morrow Junior Books, 1988. $13.95. unpaged. ISBN 0-688-06417-5. **P.**

This colorful, kinetic picture book purveys the tale of John Chapman, a.k.a. Johnny Appleseed, in an interesting, tellable manner. Based on solid research, Kellogg not only gives background on John, but chronicles the way tall tales grow and spread.

His brightly colored watercolor and ink illustrations are large enough for group sharing. Indeed, this is the only recommended use for this book with middle schoolers, most of whom would rather die than be seen with anything like a picture book. Shown and read, or told and then shared, this can provide a stimulating introduction to both the westward expansion and the process of myth-making that is so much a part of our frontier culture. As a humorous, artistically sophisticated opener to units on frontier exploration, Kellogg's offering is hard to beat.

Lasky, Kathryn. *Beyond the Divide.* New York: Macmillan, 1983. $11.95. 253p. ISBN 0-02-751670-9.

When Meribah Simon is 14, her Amish father, Will, shunned by his community, leaves Pennsylvania for California. Unable to let him go alone, Meribah joins him. At first Meribah and Will find the journey encouraging, if difficult. The group of emigrants they sign on with at St. Joseph, Missouri, are of divergent backgrounds but all are willing to labor and share together. However, as the company travels through the brutal terrain toward the Great Divide of the Rocky Mountains, and the struggle for survival grows desperate, the other travellers display increasing cruelty and violence. As the first signs of winter approach, Will, now dangerously ill, and Meribah are abandoned in the foothills of the Sierra Nevada.

This is a story of survival grippingly told in literate, complex, comprehensible language. There is great brutality here—a rape, a murder, abandonment—and great humanity. Most important, it is the story of a young woman who maps not only the road she travels west, but herself. This is recommended for mature middle school readers who want a personal but historically based view of the westward expansion. Divided into 29 relatively short chapters, it could be excerpted for in-class reading, but the sustained narrative of the story is such that individual reading and contemplation seem the best modes of employment. An afterword and author's note add historical background. A map gives a clear graphic expression to the route Meribah followed on her westward journey.

Lawlor, Laurie. *Addie's Dakota Winter.* Illustrated by Toby Gowing. Niles, IL: Albert Whitman, 1989. $10.50. 160p. ISBN 0-8075-0171-9.

Ten year-old Addie is the oldest of five children in the Mills family which has just finished a year homesteading in Hutchinson County, Dakota Territory. In this 15-chapter episodic book, Addie survives a harsh winter. Whether it's apologizing to a friend, getting her brother to school in good shape, or trying to find her way through a blizzard, Addie is a spunky heroine who embodies the pioneer spirit.

This book gives an unstinting view of the harshness of prairie life—the deaths, the madness the lonely space engendered—without either the lyricism or starkness of Pam Conrad's *Prairie Songs* (see entry, above). This altogether homier piece of work is extended by Gowing's pencil drawings. Girls will find it reminiscent of Laura Ingalls Wilder's Little House books, and teacher and librarians will find numerous passages that read aloud beautifully. It would make a good classroom book or group reading, and is fine for independent readers as well.

Luhrmann, Winifred Bruce. *Only Brave Tomorrows.* Boston: Houghton Mifflin, 1989. $13.95. 190p. ISBN 0-395-47983-5.

When her father, exiled for his religious preferences, returns to Sussex to reclaim 15-year-old Faith Ralston from the aunt who has raised her, Faith is not pleased. She is even less happy when, a scant few weeks later, she finds herself aboard the "Venture," seeking a new life in the Massachusetts colony. It is 1675, and the colonies are engaged in King Philip's War, a war in which both the Native American and colonial populations suffered tremendous losses. By 1676, Faith has lived through a massacre in which her father died and is happily married to Zachary Steadman, a guide she had formerly distrusted. This is standard historical fiction. The scene setting and delineation of the period are adequate, though character development is sketchy. After a slow start, continuity is maintained by the plotting and the nice little romance between Faith and Zachary.

This is light reading that is nonetheless historically accurate and gives some life to a period of American history that is rarely examined. For a more sophisticated treatment of the same time period, see the annotation for Paul Fleischman's *Saturnalia* (above).

McClung, Robert M. *Hugh Glass, Mountain Man.* New York: Morrow, 1990. 166p. $12.95. bibliography. ISBN 0-688-08092-8.

Few of us have heard of Hugh Glass, and yet he was one of the Old West's legendary heroes. This well-researched, compellingly told historical novel will serve to spread Hugh's name around. In August 1823, Hugh Glass was on a hunting expedition for the Rocky Mountain Fur Company when he surprised a she-grizzly. He was attacked and horribly mauled. Left behind with two companions, John Fitzgerald and the youthful Jim Bridger, Hugh hung onto life with incredible tenacity. At last, fearful of an Indian attack and certain that Hugh would die, the two abandoned Hugh without food, supplies, or weapons.

Hugh did not die. He revived and sustained by an incredible will to live and the burning desire for revenge against the two who abandoned him, he began a 200-mile crawl through the South Dakota wilderness to Fort Kiowa on the Missouri River.

This book is literally impossible to put down. Along the way that readers travel with Hugh, they receive a wealth of information on the exploration of the West and the considerable role of the fur companies in the trapping and mapping aspects. The use of period paintings by artists who actually helped explore the West and maps of Hugh's crawl add to the book—as does a good annotated bibliography. This is one book, however, that does not need the help. Terrific read-aloud material, this is also superb pleasure reading.

Moore, Robin. *The Bread Sister of Sinking Creek.* New York: HarperCollins, 1984. $14.95. 154p. ISBN 0-397-32418-9.

There were many ways to make a living on the western frontier. Not all of them were obvious, and a number of professions were arrived at out of necessity. Such is the case of young Maggie Callahan. Leaving Philadelphia in the hot summer of 1776, she crosses into the Pennsylvania wilderness, intending to live with her loving Aunt Franny. But Franny has gone further west, leaving her niece only an empty cabin and the "spook yeast" Maggie wears in a pouch at her breast. Forced to become a bound-out girl, Maggie finally figures a way out when she uses her sourdough starter to begin a business.

Moore's story is engrossing and well written, his characterization solid, and the plotting swift. The story gives a clear window into the early days of the westward expansion at the close of the colonial era. The book reads aloud well and includes recipes for sourdough bread. Making bread from the recipes could become a creditable class project and a first-hand experience with a bit of culinary Americana.

Turner, Ann. *Grasshopper Summer.* New York: Macmillan, 1989. $13.95. 166p. ISBN 0-02-789511-4.

The White family has always lived in Kentucky and young Sam is happy there, even though he is confused by some of the changes wrought by the Civil War. His father is more than confused. Restless and haunted by the bloody legacy of the war, he vows to "find the future" and decides to begin a new life for himself and his family in the Dakota Territory. Leaving Kentucky is hard, and the journey west is harder. Sam struggles to adjust to the grave-like soddy the family must live in and to the endless, empty prairie sky. Just as the family begins to feel at home, a plague of grasshoppers strikes, eating everything in their paths and destroying the crops. It is then the Whites show their grit, ingenuity, and determination.

Turner's prose is precise and involving, her plotting quiet but sure. The contrast between Kentucky and the Dakotas is vivid, as are the descriptions of the hardships faced by the settlers. All told, this book has a ring of realism that makes the time and place palpable. Fine read-aloud fare, this book is also good independent reading. The young male protagonist guarantees strong appeal to boys.

CHAPTER 6
Dark Continent or Land of Light: The European View of Africa

In 1913, passage to Africa from Europe took 13 days. It may have seemed even longer to young Tanne Dinesen as she journeyed to her "Vita Nuova" with a new husband in a new land: Kenya.

> ... I had a farm in Africa, at the foot of the Ngong Hills. The Equator runs across these highlands, a hundred miles to the North, and the farm lay at an altitude of over six thousand feet ...

> The geographical position, and the height of the land combined to create a landscape that had not its like in all the world. There was no fat on it and no luxuriance anywhere; it was Africa distilled up through six thousand feet, like the strong and refined essence of a continent (Dinesen, 1985).

Dinesen came to Africa at the end of an era of white exploration that had fired the world's imagination. The "opening" of the "Dark Continent" found the location of the source of the Nile River, and explored the Congo and Kenya. Though it seemed a story of a strange and foreign place to Europeans, Dinesen's memoir, *Out of Africa*, is serene, lyrical, and at home in its love of the Kenyan highlands.

The land has a primordial essence, a sense of timelessness that is found only where the bones of the earth are old. Dinesen did not leave until 1931, years after the marriage begun with her coming to a new land had ended, and shortly after her lover and best friend, Denys Finch Hatton, had died in an airplane accident. Even then she left only because she had become financially unable to run the farm any longer and had been forced to sell it.

Truly, Africa was in her own bones, and her return "home" to Europe marked the beginning of an entirely new, and in some senses less free, life for her.

Not too far from Dinesen's Ngong Hills lies the Olduvai Gorge. It is here, in the washed African light, that the Leaky family has excavated the remains of some of the oldest human ancestors. Contemporary paleoanthropologists are almost unanimous in their agreement upon Africa as the birth place of humanity. Perhaps this alone is enough to account for its continuing reputation for mystery and darkness. The womb, too, is dark, and it was, after all, slightly after the beginning that God created light.

The coming of Europeans to the African mainland has a long history. Over 500 years ago, the Portuguese began their push down the western coast of the continent in search of a way around it to Asia. Most of the commerce between Africa and Europe over the next several hundred years, and later between Africa and the New World, had to do with the slave trade. Early European explorers also bought gold and ivory. Most of these commercial dealings were carried on at the coastal harbors where ships could dock, slaves could be detained, and goods gathered and loaded. The African interior remained largely unexplored. The golden age of African exploration waited until the nineteenth century and the British Empire. During that era, for reasons similar to those that earlier generated the Lewis and Clark expedition in the United States, it became not only intriguing but important to find out just what the nature of this vast continent was.

Tanne Dinesen left Europe in 1913. Later that year, shortly after her arrival in Nairobi, she married Bror Blixen, and began to go by her given name, Karen, rather than her childhood nickname, Tanne. By the time she left Africa, almost 20 years later, Karen Blixen was going by yet another name, Tania. Whether or not the woman who was best known to the world as Isak Dinesen would have gone through a series of name and personality changes wherever she was is not ascertainable. However, Africa did seem for her, and for many others, to be an ideal place to change one's identity or to build a new one.

Another person who found this to be true of Africa was Eduard Schnitzer.

> [Schnitzer was] the son of well-to-do Jewish parents . . . . He had studied in Breslau and Berlin and practiced medicine in Albania, then part of the Ottoman empire, where he adopted the name Emin Effendi Hakim. Later he went to Egypt as a medical officer until, working his way up through the ranks of the administration, he became a provincial governor under [British General Charles] Gordon. He followed the customs and outward forms of Islam, although there was some doubt whether he had formally converted to that religion (Bierman, 1990, p. 267).

Emin Pasha, as he was known in the late 1880s, became the focus of a concerted British rescue attempt. After General Gordon's murder at Khartoum by "... followers of the Ayatollah Khomeini of the day, the Mahdi Mohammed Ahmend ..." (Bierman, 1990, p. 260) it seemed that Emin, the governor of the Sudan's Equatoria Province, along with 4,000 loyal Sudanese troops, was single-handedly holding off the further advances of the Mahdi's forces. There was a popular outcry from the British people to send someone to his aid. In October 1886 a man who had been tailoring both his past and his persona for years was approached and asked to head an expedition for Emin's relief. The man was Henry Morton Stanley, as great a forger of identity as existed, and one who had found Africa instrumental in creating the myth of himself.

His birth name was not Henry Morton Stanley. He was born on January 28, 1841, and listed as "John Rowlands, Bastard" in the records of St. Hilary's Church, Denbigh, in North Wales. His mother was a 19-year-old housemaid named Betsy Parry who abandoned the child "... to the care of her father and returned to London and whatever it was she did there" (Bierman, 1990, p. 5). When his grandfather died, the boy was sent to a workhouse, where, though life was harsh and unpleasant, he received a fairly decent education. He learned to read and write, was exposed to geography and arithmetic, and was taught to write a neat, clear hand. He left the workhouse in 1856 to go to his uncle who employed him as a teacher. Eventually, as the job with his uncle palled and other relatives proved unable to give him support, the boy, now 16, signed on as a seaman on a vessel bound for New Orleans. It was the beginning of his fabrication of a past, and the creation of a legend. He was, though he did not yet realize it, on the road to Africa.

"David Livingstone was fifty-seven when Stanley set out to find him, a former Scottish mill hand turned medical missionary whose epic travels in the uncharted interior of Africa had made him a British celebrity" (Bierman, 1990, p. 90). In 1871, Stanley was 30 years old, a veteran (if not a particularly glorious one) of the American Civil War and now a newspaperman. His publisher, James Gordon Bennett, Jr., of the *New York Herald*, had given him the injunction to "Find Livingstone" (Bierman, 1990, p. 75). Livingstone had set off on his second expedition to the African interior in 1866. His goal had been to ascertain the source of the Nile and, incidentally, to try to save Africans from slavery and convert them to Christianity. He had last been heard from two years before, according to John Kirk, the British consul in Zanzibar, and the world wondered where the good doctor was. Stanley was to cash in on this, and, in the process, to elevate himself to a status rivaling Livingstone's own.

Stanley's first impressions of Zanzibar, the island off the eastern coast of Africa where his journey began were lyric. He compared Zanzibar with Baghdad, and was entranced by all he saw there. The interior of the continent was a different story. "I do not think I was made for an African explorer, for I detest the land most heartily" (Bierman, 1990, p. 77). He proved to be wrong about his destiny, and the pugnacious spirit that had enabled him to survive workhouses and wars helped him pull together his expedition.

The first roadblock was funding. Bennett, the publisher, had made no financial provision for the expedition. Stanley arrived in Zanzibar with $80, all the cash he had available. He was fortunate enough to meet Francis Webb, the American consul, who took a liking to him and vouched for Stanley's credit with local merchants. It cost Stanley a huge amount of money for those times—about $20,000—to outfit his motley group of travellers, but at last, on February 4, 1871, he left Zanzibar for the mainland. Six to eight to weeks later (the dates are conflicting in various sources), sometime between March 21st and April 1st, he left the coastal town of Bagamoyo, heading for the interior and Livingstone.

Livingstone had been on the move. On the day that Stanley left Zanzibar, the doctor had received a supply train sent by Kirk. Though the store of supplies was small, it was enough to send Livingstone out again a week later, not proceeding east, toward civilization and Stanley, but, with typical stubbornness, west toward the Lualaba River to investigate the source of the Nile. Though he had made a remarkable recovery from the illness that had plagued him earlier in his sojourns, Livingstone's attempt to move farther west was not successful. At the end of March 1871, he reached Nyangwe, on the Lualaba River, and there his progress was halted. His porters were fearful of going further, and he himself was "...broken in spirit and again failing in health after witnessing an apparently purposeless massacre of the innocents at Nyangwe by Arab slavers" (Bierman, 1990, p. 101). He turned eastward to the village of Ujiji and thus traveled slowly toward Stanley. He had traversed half the African continent, but had not achieved his goal.

Stanley was setting land speed records for covering the increasingly difficult terrain of the African interior. The first two weeks went well, although it rained and two of Stanley's three riding horses died on the third day out. "But then they came to 'the terrible Makata swamp,' a five-day slog through knee-deep water and black mire, and 'from here commenced the list of calamities which afterwards overtook [us]'" (Bierman, 1990, p. 97). These calamities were the diseases to which the African wilderness subjects the unwary or uninoculated. Fevers, smallpox, and dysentery assaulted the party, the latter illness removing 40 pounds from Stanley's usually sturdy frame. This, however, did not slow him down. "Stanley drove his men through the swamp with demonic determination and a liberal application of the lash. He had no sympathy at all for those he termed malingerers" (Bierman, 1990, p. 97). His zeal pushed two of the men working for him to attempt to kill him. The attempt failed and Stanley continued to work with one of the men. The other died of a malady which may have been either dropsy or elephantiasis. During this miserable portion of his journey, Stanley turned to the Bible, reading it with what he believed to be deep understanding. He felt that Africa was causing him to change, and indeed it would change the course of his life.

On June 23rd, Stanley's caravan, much the worse for wear, reached a village called Kwihara. "He had made the march in record time, covering 525 miles in 84 days, a trek that had taken Burton and Speke 134 days and Speke and Grant 115 days" (Bierman, 1990, p. 100). A legend was a-making, and was furthered by news Stanley received. Several informants had seen Livingstone, and one told Stanley that the man he sought was on his way back to Ujiji.

A war between an African chief and the Arab traders blocked Stanley's route to Ujiji and Livingstone, and he was savage in his treatment of his men once he got back on the road. Though weak and suffering from one of the endless African fevers (probably the result of malaria) that plagued him the entire trip, Stanley was still perfectly capable of applying his dog whip with relish to those who did not move fast enough to suit him. He forged onward, putting down the mutinies his treatment of his men engendered, and burning to find the man he sought.

Livingstone arrived in Ujiji, a creature of literal skin and bones. He had hoped to take possession of supplies there, but arrived to find that the goods had been sold off. The supplies had arrived a year earlier and the Arab in charge disposed of them, assuming Livingstone to be dead. Livingstone stayed in Ujiji, living on charity, and hoping for rescue.

Stanley was coming. A week's march west of Lake Tanganyika, the news of Livingstone's arrival reached Stanley. On November 10, 1871, he greeted the doctor with the words that were to be associated with him for the rest of his life: "Dr. Livingstone, I presume." Stanley's reputation as an explorer was made, and his addiction to the African interior began. He started out as a newspaper man; he returned an explorer.

Africa seems to exert a strong hold. Be it explorers, farmers, hunters, or tourists, those who go are drawn back. It is more than the chance of making a fortune. It is the draw, the distillation of something finer.

> Looking back on a sojourn in the African highlands, you are struck by your feeling of having lived for a time up in the air. The sky was rarely more than pale blue or violet, with a profusion of mighty, weightless, ever-changing clouds towering up and sailing on it, but it has a blue vigor in it, and at a short distance it painted the ranges of hills and the woods a fresh deep blue . . . Up in this high air you breathed easily, drawing in a vital assurance and lightness of heart. In the highlands you woke up in the morning and thought: Here I am, where I ought to be. (Dinesen, 1985)

References

Bierman, John. (1990). *Dark Safari: The Life Behind the Legend of Henry Morton Stanley*. New York: Knopf.
Dinesen, Isak. (1985). *Out of Africa*. New York: Vintage Books.

ANNOTATED BIBLIOGRAPHY

Nonfiction

Asher, Michael. *Two Against the Sahara: On Camelback from Nouakchott to the Nile.* Photographs by Mariantonietta Peru. New York: Morrow, 1988. $19.95. 301p. index. ISBN 0-688-08926-7. **Ad.**

"In Chinguelti Sid'Ahmed advised us to hand the camels over to the keeping of a man called Mohammed. He was a Hartani built like a wrestler with the biggest calf muscles I had ever seen."

Many of us would balk at a 4,500 mile journey in a car, even though there were frequent rest stops and four-star accommodations. Few of us would even dare to envision a camel journey of that length across the harsh sands of the Sahara Desert Yet this is exactly what Michael Asher and his wife of but a few days, Mariantonietta Peru, decided to do. Taking three camels, one for each of them and one for their guide, relying on their fluency in Arabic and knowledge of desert travel, they set out on a trip that sent them into themselves as much as across northern Africa from Nouakchott on the west coast to Aswan in Egypt.

The book carries readers through Mauritania, Mali, Niger, Chad, the Sudan, and into Egypt, in the process giving these places a setting and life that renders them more than just names on the map. Asher writes in informed, easy prose, but his style and word sense do justice both to the external terrain of the Sahara and to the internal terrain of a marriage being forged by physical and emotional demands far beyond the usual.

The reading level is adult and the book lengthy. Two sections of photos, one black and white and one color, extend the narrative. Nonetheless, few middle school readers will attempt this cover to cover. In a teacher's or librarian's hand, however, this is a potent tool, packed with anecdotes and incidents that help to flesh out, in a pithy, visual way, the land and people, and the political climate of northern Africa. Have it in the classroom or library to read from, or leave it about for students to dip into. They will.

Bierman, John. *Dark Safari: The Life Behind the Legend of Henry Morton Stanley.* New York: Knopf, 1990. $24.95. 401p. index. bibliography. source notes. ISBN 0-394-58342-6. **Ad.**

The man who would become famous as Henry Morton Stanley, explorer of darkest Africa, was born on January 28, 1841, in the village of Denbigh, Wales. The child was registered in the records of St. Hilary's Church as "John Rowlands, bastard." His mother was 19-year-old Betsy Parry, a housemaid. The identity of his father was murky, though a village drunk, the original John Rowlands, claimed paternity. Young Rowlands had a harsh childhood, and at an early age he fled to the United States, fought in the Civil War, and took up journalism, eventually becoming a foreign correspondent. It was in this capacity that Stanley, sent to Africa to find David Livingstone, the British explorer, found both international acclaim and notoriety.

He subsequently led two further African expeditions, enduring perilous circumstances, but succeeding in completing Livingstone's work by finding the source of the Nile. He also charted the Congo River and created the so-called Congo Free State (now Zaire) for his patron, King Leopold II of Belgium.

Bierman presents readers with a definitive biography of a man almost as enigmatic as the continent he explored. In accomplished prose, Bierman paints a detailed picture of the early years of African exploration by Victorian whites—the dangers, the discoveries, the atrocities, and the effects on colonization. Advanced, mature readers with a taste for biography and travel lore will find themselves hooked into this involving story. Generally, however, it will be most effectively used in excerpted, read-aloud form. Excellent maps, frequent black-and-white photographs and drawings, and a thorough index and source notes make this an excellent source of information on both the opening of the African continent to whites and the life of one exceptional man.

Clinton, Susan. *Henry Stanley and David Livingstone.* Chicago: Childrens Press, 1990. $23.93. 128p. index. bibliography. glossary. ISBN 0-516-03055-8.

If Bierman's book (see entry, above) is a definitive biography, Clinton's treatment of the lives of both Henry Stanley and David Livingstone is the definitive report source. In slightly over 100 pages, it traces the lives of these two men from birth to death, giving coverage not only to their professional lives but to personal aspects as well. If the psychological depth of Bierman's book is missing, much is gained in succinctness.

Beginning with Stanley's meeting with Livingstone at Ujiji on the shores of Lake Tanganyika in November 1871, Clinton backtracks to devote a chapter each to the men's childhoods, then covers each man's African exploits in the remaining seven chapters. She paints a clear picture of the times, the political exigencies, and the intertwined lives of these two very different explorers. Both had the urge to find out what was there, but one was a missionary and the other a journalist.

The page layout and type font are both attractive, and the copious use of period drawings and photos as well has present day photographs of the regions discussed in the narrative extend the text well. An excellent period map of Africa takes an entire double-page spread and is most helpful in tracing Stanley's and Livingstone's routes across this large continent. The bibliography is mostly composed of adult works, but does give access to primary source material. The index is sound and the timeline and glossary both helpful. This is an excellent and highly readable report source that can be used to augment or introduce oral reading from Bierman's more comprehensive work.

Daniels, Anthony. *Zanzibar to Timbukto.* London: John Murray, 1988. $24.95. 232p. ISBN 0-7195-4533-1. **Ad.**

Similar in approach to Asher's *Two Against the Sahara* (see entry, above), Anthony Daniels's recounting of his travels across Africa is personal and as much internal as external. Avoiding the Saharan sands, he travelled through Central Africa, tracing some of the same roads covered by Stanley and the elusive object of his search, David Livingstone. Daniels, however, was not testing his endurance, nor was he searching for anything so concrete as another person. The object of his search was hope. His two years as a doctor in Tanzania and earlier periods in Zimbabwe and South Africa had left him with grim impressions of the continent.

From the arresting cover photo of a sculpted-looking Niger boatman to the witty, conversational prose, this book provides excellent travel writing and an outsider's inside view on an unfamiliar continent. Each of the 12 chapters treats Daniels's experience in a different area. Beginning with Zanzibar, he chronicles travels through Tanzania, Burundi and Rwanda, Zaire, Gabon, and Mali. One comes to know not only the landscape but the highly diverse cultural make-up of the area. And Daniels finds what he is looking for in "...the ordinary African's ability to find happiness long after we would have given up looking."

The prose is adult, but the anecdotal nature and quick pace lend the book to reading aloud. This could well be used to introduce any number of African nations. Given Daniels's recapitulation of Stanley's route, the book also facilitates study of the Africa of a century ago.

Houston, Dick. *Safari Adventure.* New York: Cobblehill Books, 1991. $15.95. 160 p. index. ISBN 0-525-605051-2.

Dick Houston had been fascinated with Africa since his childhood in Ohio. Any movie about African safaris absorbed him, but the documentary film of Martin and Osa Johnson grabbed his imagination and would not let go. The final necessary push to go to Africa came from one of his junior high students, who suggested that

Houston ". . . stop talking about [Africa] and start doing something about getting there . . ." Houston did.

This is the story of Houston's safari through Kenya. From his opening sentence ("I got everyone lost on my first safari."), the narrative catches attention and holds it. Houston writes directly to his middle school audience in an experienced way that combines the informative with the wryly humorous.

Fourteen chapters cover differing aspects of Houston's sojourn in Kenya, from climbing Mt. Kilimanjaro to releasing a mired land rover from mud (a process shown in the arresting cover photo). A good map, two sections of color photos, and a fine index all extend the text well. This is good read aloud or independent reading material, excitingly and enticingly written.

Lasky, Kathryn. *Traces of Life: The Origins of Humankind.* Illustrated by Whitney Powell. New York: Morrow Junior Books, 1989. $16.95. 144p. index. bibliography. notes. ISBN 0-688-07237-2.

Beginning with a clock analogy to point out how recent is man's advent on the terrestrial scene, Lasky provides a wealth of both historical and current information on the evolution of Homo sapiens. Lucidly written, attractively formatted in a central columnar style with very large print, and copiously illustrated in soft pencil, this book is great browsing material. Interested students will also find it a superior report source. The index and source notes are serviceable, but the bibliography lists mainly adult works. The illustrations show female hominids from A. Afarenesis to H. sapiens sapiens with bared breasts, so a preview of the book is recommended.

As a background for works on the exploration of Africa, this has some distinct merits. Africa may well have been the birthplace of humanity, and this book puts the idea of the white "opening" of Africa into a proper perspective. Lasky's millenial approach gives a feel for the ecology of the region. She opens discussion, too, on another sort of physical exploration, as archaeologists go down through layers of rock and years instead of out across land, sea, or space.

Brief chapters are perfect for reading aloud and can also be used to start discussions. This book is natural browsing material and may awaken some students to an interest in paleoarchaeology and the study of the evolution of humankind.

Paton, Jonathan. *The Land and People of South Africa.* New York: Lippincott, 1990. $14.89. 288p. index. bibliography. ISBN 0-397-32362-X.

That South Africa is a land of intense conflict, both in the physical and ideological senses, is something that is apparent from the daily news. However, in many books dealing with the country, these issues tend to be glossed over. The emphasis is placed on the spectacular scenery and natural resources while the political upheaval is downplayed. Yet this political unrest, this intense internal division, is as old as the white settlement of South Africa.

Jonathan Paton, son of writer Alan Paton and professor of literature at the University of the Witwatersrand in Johannesburg, has given a measured, honest treatment to his native land, portraying both the natural beauty and the tragedy of a people at war with each other. His explanations and descriptions are clear, and his use of the poetry and prose literature of native South Africans, both black and white, adds dimension to the text and increases readers' understanding of the tortured situation in a land that pits the need for change against a firm societal resistance.

Covering geography, history, economics, and the contemporary situation to within two years (thus missing some of De Klerk's later reforms and much of the black-on-black violence of 1991 and 1992), this is an indispensable book for any young adult who wants to understand South Africa and its diverse peoples.

Clear black-and-white photographs and maps are carefully placed to both augment and clarify the text. A wonderful report source, segments of this book might also be read aloud in class to arouse interest or promote discussion. The book includes a fine bibliography and index, but its most important feature is the provision of a psychological portrait of this strife-torn land.

Pavitt, Nigel. *Kenya: The First Explorers.* New York: St. Martin's Press, 1989. $25.00. 208p. index. bibliography. ISBN 0-312-03186-6. **Ad.**

The Reverend Dr. John Ludwig Krapf, Johann Rebmann, Joseph Thomson, Count Samuel Teleki von Szek, and Lieutenant Ludwig von Hohnel. How many of us have heard of these men? What have they in common?

Until the 1840s, the interior of the country we now call Kenya was unknown to the outside world. The tribes were hostile and fought continually between themselves, and the scrub land was inhospitable. Yet from 1844 to 1888 the five men listed above faced considerable danger and hardship to travel to the Kenyan interior. Between 1844 and 1853, John Ludwig Krapf and Johann Rebmann, fired with missionary zeal, became the first white men to set eyes on the snows of Kilimanjaro. Thirty-five years later, a Scot named Joseph Thomson penetrated Masai lands to reach Lake Victoria. He came back with reports of an unknown lake in northern Kenya which in turn fired the Hungarian Count Samuel Teleki von Szek and his companion Ludwig von Hohnel to undertake a 13-month journey to reach Lake Turkana and Lake Chew Baher, formerly Lakes Rudolf and Stephanie.

This beautifully crafted volume contains clear maps and numerous black-and-white line engravings and sketches. Three sections of color photos ensure browsing appeal and open the Kenyan land to students. The prose is densely written, the primary appeal of the book being in the pictorial elements and the frequent use of primary source material. The sheer volume of information makes this book a prime teacher resource. Additionally, the division of the book into three sections—one covering Krapf and Rebmann's exploration, one covering Thomson's, and one covering Teleki von Szek and von Hohnel's—makes it easy to focus in on one explorational experience. This book has utility as a report source (though students will need to be encouraged to wade into it), a browsing book, and a read aloud-booktalking tool. There are African explorers beyond Stanley and Livingstone. This is a resounding, in-depth introduction to five of them.

Sandak, Cass R. *Remote Places.* New York: Watts, 1989. $10.50. 32p. index. glossary. chronology. ISBN 0-531-10458-3.

Surtsey, named after a figure of Icelandic folklore, is an island off the coast of Iceland that came into existence in 1963 as a result of an undersea explosion. We look to the stars as our frontier now, forgetting that our earth still holds potential for exploration, just as it did for nineteenth-century explorers.

Sandak uses two-page spreads to discuss 11 areas on our earth that are still being explored. Rain forests, the Amazon, Africa, grasslands, deserts in general, and Asian deserts specifically, Old and New World mountains, islands, and caves are all covered. The text is brief and awkwardly phrased at times, and the information sketchy. Generally, each area receives a definition, e.g., "Grasslands...are areas where grasses and grains are the predominant types of vegetation." A brief history of the exploration, ecology, and population of each is also put forward. The one-page index is good, and the "dateline" section provides 25 brief entries noting explorational trips between 1906 and 1988. The glossary uses curt little definitions and could have been omitted.

A significant number of the areas discussed are in Africa, thus the book's inclusion in this chapter. The illustrations of African tribespeople and their environs range from interesting to fascinating. Since the information is scanty, students may well be tempted to look for answers elsewhere. For example, a 1913 photo of "...a Congo rain forest native in a headdress made from snail shells..." displays a young man whose chest and shoulders are impressively scarred in a Braille-like pattern. No explanation for this is given, but readers will wonder and can be pointed to books with more depth. Useful for introducing units on African exploration, this volume in the *New Frontiers: Exploration in the Twentieth Century* series may also be used as a supporting book for Viking exploration, mountaineering, or the journey of Marco Polo.

Excellent pictorially, the book is good for browsing, but is too brief and narrow in scope for report writing.

Simon, Charnan. *Richard Burton*. Chicago: Children's Press, 1991. $23.93. 128p. index. bibliography. timeline. glossary. ISBN 0-516-03062-0.

Most of today's middle schoolers will think of the actor, if they think of anyone, when the name "Richard Burton" is mentioned. Yet the nineteenth-century Richard Burton was one of the foremost explorers of the African continent, as well as being the translator of the classic "Arabian Nights."

Burton was born in Torquay, Devonshire, England in 1821. Before he was a year old, the family moved to France, and the Burtons never again lived permanently in England. It was a fitting early life for a man who was to travel widely, who seemed happier moving through new lands and cultures.

Simon's able biography covers Burton's youthful years and the explorations of his adult life, including his African travels with fellow explorer John Hanning Speke. She employs a fluent, accomplished prose that captures the time and place (or places) competently. There is ample information for a report, and the generously illustrated format encourages browsing. A section on early mapping of the Nile, shown in the appendices, gives visual context to the physical difficulty of Burton's search for the elusive source of the great river. Sections could easily be read aloud, for example, the story of Speke's estrangement from Burton, and the effect that had on Burton's fortunes.

The glossary, timeline, index, and bibliography are all helpful in elucidating not only a life, but the urge to explore the unknown. This book is a worthy addition to the The World's Great Explorer series.

Smith, Anthony. *The Great Rift: Africa's Changing Valley.* New York: Sterling, 1988. $24.95. 224p. index. ISBN 0-8069-6907-5. **Ad.**

Running southward from the Lebanon to Mozambique, the Great Rift Valley cuts a 4,000-mile swath through eastern Africa. It is, in total, the greatest rupture in the land surface of the earth. The geological phenomena which resulted in the formation of the Great Rift have given birth to an incredible diversity of terrain and plant and animal life. In a competent (if not compelling) text, Anthony Smith discusses the fecundity of life forms in this fascinating valley.

For units on exploration, Chapter III, "'Pockets' Gregory," is of special interest. John Walter Gregory was a Scotsman born in 1864. Though he was a geologist by profession, he was also an explorer and scientific polymath. His passion was for in situ geography. In pursuit of this, he brought the Great Rift Valley to the attention of the European community. This account of Gregory's expedition into the African interior along the Great Rift provides riveting reading and, for purposes of discussion, can also be contrasted with Henry Stanley's experiences on the African continent. Questions that might be raised include the purposes of their respective expeditions, what the explorers were trying to find, their attitudes toward their guides and other African natives, and how the different orientations of their explorations may have affected the results of their expeditions.

Six lavish color sections feature the flora, fauna, and landscape of the Great Rift. These are great browsing pictures and offset the adult level of the prose, perhaps pulling in younger readers. The index adds accessibility. Though this is certainly a good report source, it is unlikely that students will go beyond the pictures without encouragement. However, used as a teaching resource, and made available for browsing, this has real potential for classroom use.

Tessendorf, K.C. *Along the Road to Soweto: A Racial History of South Africa.* $14.95. 194p. index. bibliography. ISBN 0-689-31401-9.

Why a racial history? If one looks at South Africa, the answer is clear—the entire history of the nation is infused with a racial aura, conflicts between blacks, blacks and whites, white English and white Boers. From the days of the earliest incursions and explorations of the white settlers, racial issues have been the country's major social issues.

Twelve chapters cover South African history from around 1 A.D. to the present. The focus, despite a chapter devoted to Shaka and the Bantu Holocaust, is on the white settlers. Criticisms have been leveled at Tessendorf for an approach that is ethnocentrically white. Whether or not this is true, he does a superb job of giving insight into the Boer point of view. Boers are whites who have lived in South Africa for hundreds of years. They have fought for, bled for, and died for "their" land. If one hopes to understand the current turmoil in the rich and lovely southernmost land of Africa, there is no better way than to read this involved history.

An excellent report source, this book also provides insight into the social context, making it a good discussion starter. For example, it could be paired with Fisher's *Prince Henry the Navigator* (see Chapter 3, above) to look at a history of African slavery. Likewise, a contrast to the American westward expansion yields surprising parallels. The text is augmented by black-and-white photographs and reproductions as well as clearly drawn maps. A good bibliography and sound index add both extension and access to the 12 information-packed chapters.

Thompson, Leonard. *A History of South Africa.* New Haven, CT: Yale University Press, 1990. $29.95. 288p. index. notes. ISBN 0-300-04815-7. **Ad.**

From the hunting-gathering ancestors of the Khoisan tribes to the slow breakdown of apartheid in today's world, this book covers the history of South Africa with depth and penetration.

The book is divided into seven chapters: the original African inhabitants, the Cape Colony, the African Wars of 1770-1870, the age of British imperialism, the segregation and apartheid years, and apartheid in crisis. There is a detailed chronology, excellent source notes and index, and a center section of black-and-white photographs beginning with aboriginal paintings and ending with the racial havoc on the Cape Peninsula in 1988.

Thompson's precise prose is scholarly in the extreme, and the density of the typeface will not attract young readers. However, advanced middle schoolers will find a tremendous amount of meticulously researched historical information to help flesh out Jonathan Paton's *The Land and People of South Africa*, or stand in contrast to K.C. Tessendorf's *The Road to Soweto* (see entries for both, above). Thompson's term for the Caucasian explorers, "The White Invaders," is thought-provoking and potentially opinion altering. A good reference and report source for both teachers and more capable students, this book has a supportive place in units on Africa.

CHAPTER 7

Fire in the Ice: The Northern and Southern Polar Regions

It sounds almost like a riddle. There are two of them. We think of them as white. They are both cold. They are amazingly different. What are they? They are, of course, the poles, north and south. A contemporary person's most likely point of departure for contemplation of these frozen regions will be ecological. We all hear about the ozone hole over Antarctica and the smaller one over the North Pole. We are aware of the damage human ingress is doing to the beautifully balanced but fragile ecosystems of the northern tundra and the southern ice-bound continent. We may applaud the initiatives taken to save them.

In the late twentieth century, exploration of the polar regions is a thing of the past. Not that we know everything there is to know, but the times of dogsleds racing across the frozen southern waste or the northern pack ice, of hotly disputed "first" arrivals at the poles, seems antique, quaint. Now we look to the skies, confer anxiously over meteorological information coming from polar lab installations, gaze with concern as the whales begin to die due to human alterations in their environment. And yet there is still debate and interest in those fur clad explorers of an earlier time, a time when their clothing betokened only a need for warmth and not a political stance. These driven men and women still speak to us of the need to find out, to achieve a goal simply because one must.

The recurring motif for early twentieth century polar exploration is embodied in the dogsled. Humans are linked to the dogs by lines, ropes, tied to their tools for safety, somehow held to the earth. This image of binding recurs through many sorts of exploration in our century. The rope links the underwater explorer to air and thus to survival; it links one mountaineer to another, to the solid earth. Lines link astronauts or cosmonauts to their craft, thus holding them in some way close to the blue planet floating far below. These fragile lines link us to our mother, the Earth, link us to human support; or, in the case of the polar explorer, to animals that may be crucial in maintaining life. The reins link the driver to the rest of creation. The sign of a fundamental interrelatedness is clear.

Although both are white and cold, the North Pole and the South Pole are vastly different. How? The impression the northern lands give is bleak, but recognizable. The tundra appears from under the snow at certain times of the year. There is a rich animal life, with predators largely dependent on the incredibly prolific lemmings, which multiply until they outgrow their territory, then rush to fling themselves off cliffs in a population reduction measure of astounding brutality and effectiveness. The Arctic is bleak, but not barren, for the tundra supports not only animal but human life. The Inuit and Aleut cultures have found homes here, created civilizations and social structures. In the early years of the current millennium the Norse colonized Iceland and Greenland, farming the land as best they could. The climate and terrain do not forbid life. However, to the farthest north, the territory surrounding the North Pole, there is no land, only floating, shifting pack ice. Animal life survives here, harp seals and polar bears, though few humans venture so far toward the top of the planet. Yet even in this extreme, there is the knowledge that not too far away is terrain resembling that to which humans are accustomed.

Antarctica gives a quite different impression. Looking at the wind-swept mountains of the south, one has the sense of looking at an alien world, a place where men and women do not fit in. The silence, broken only by the noise of calving glaciers, the sigh of the sea, and the sounds of penguins and seals, does not seem fitted for the echo of the human voice, the crack of the rifle, or the mechanized whop of the helicopter. Antarctica is foreign turf in the most elemental sense, a place of silence and cold that is not hostile to humankind so much as simply and hugely indifferent. It's exploration came later than that of the Arctic, and this ice-bound continent has seen more attempts toward limitation of human encroachment than its northern counterpart. It's wildness and overwhelming stillness, even in the face of technology, makes it seem deserving of protection. "Antarctica . . . retains much of the mystery that it has always had and remains one of the most . . . in hospitable parts on the face of the globe" (Flegg et al., 1990).

What images are conjured up when we think of polar exploration? Dogsleds are certainly part of the popular conception, as are disputes, those between Peary and Cook (contenders for the honor of reaching the North

Pole first) and Scott and Amundsen (competitors for the South Pole). The time period seems frozen in the late nineteenth and early twentieth centuries. While the exploits of these men may be the most clearly remembered, they were merely the culmination of a long line of polar explorers, reaching back over hundreds of years to the south and over 2,000 years to the north.

"The written record of man's exploration of the Arctic opens, amazingly, as early as 325 B.C., when a Greek explorer, Pytheas, sailed north from Britain in search of a land already known as 'Thule.' Most of his contemporaries adhered to the strict Roman view that voyaging north was impossible because of an unbroken sheet of ice, but Pytheas certainly penetrated far enough north to encounter and record the nightless mid-summer Arctic days" (Flegg et al., 1990, p. 29). The intrepid Greek mariner (perhaps following in the tradition of Odysseus, as he certainly could not have gotten home any too fast) was followed by various European explorers who, during the years of the first century A.D., pushed northward. Others came later, such as Irish monks, "who seeking solitude for religious contemplation, found it in Iceland in about A.D. 770" (Flegg et al., 1990, p. 29). Later Viking voyages north have been mentioned in Chapter 1, above.

The first relatively modern surge in Arctic exploration began not as a strict urge to find out what was to the north, but, as was typical of the Age of Exploration, for commercial reasons. As the Spanish and Portuguese began to tie up the sea lanes to the Orient and the New World, the northern countries, finding overland routes blocked by hostile Moslem nations, began to consider the possibility of a Northwest Passage, a northerly sea route to the Far East that, cutting through or passing above the North American continent, would allow swift sailing to the Orient.

The first attempt to find the Northwest Passage was made by John Cabot in 1497. His London-based backers must have been disappointed in the outcome of the expedition, for it failed to find any trace of a sea lane through the northern land mass. A later attempt, commissioned by the Company of Merchant Adventurers, sent Sir Hugh Willoughby, with two ships, off to the north in May 1553. Willoughby landed on the coast of what is now Lapland in northern Scandinavia, but died of scurvy, as did most of his crew. His navigator, Richard Chancellor, survived, as did the crew of the second ship. They made landfall near what is today Archangel. Chancellor managed to make profitable contact with the Russian Tsar, Ivan the Terrible, and establish trade between England and Russia, but he did not come one whit closer to finding a northern passage to Asia.

Perhaps the best known and most persistent explorer in the search for the Northwest Passage was Henry Hudson. Hudson is intriguingly reminiscent of Columbus in his insistence on the existence of such a passage, eventually giving his life to the search. Like Columbus, he seems to have been at once charismatic and difficult, imprudent in his choice of officers, and blinded by his own determination and preferences.

Born in the late 1500s, Hudson was a third generation sailor. He made four northward voyages in 1607, 1608, 1609, and 1610. In the course of the third expedition, he sailed up the St. Lawrence Seaway, alienated the native population, set the scene for the settlement of New Amsterdam, and made his way, along with his ship, the *Half Moon*, into American literature by way of Washington Irving's "Rip Van Winkle." His final voyage took him far to the north. The circumstances quickly grew dire and and the crew, living on a ship trapped in the pack ice, grew more and more discontented. Hudson faced a mutiny. He was finally left to die by a treacherous young man who had been a trusted officer and friend of Hudson's family. The Northwest Passage remained undiscovered.

Even though expeditionary motivations changed over the centuries from commercial pressure to an interest in mapping and exploring for its own sake, the search for a way through the northern latitudes to the Pacific Ocean continued to be peppered with lost lives. In 1845, Sir John Franklin departed from Great Britain in two tested ships seeking the Northwest Passage. By 1847, when nothing had been heard from him, a series of rescue missions were launched. Though they contributed to the mapping of the puzzle of islands and channels between the Beaufort Sea and Baffin Bay, the area separating Greenland from the North American mainland, no trace of Franklin's expedition turned up. Except for a few personal possessions found in Eskimo hands, he and all his men seemed to have vanished off the face of the earth. Franklin had married an extraordinarily devoted and strong-minded young woman. Where others might have given up, Lady Jane Franklin, outwardly unprepossessing and shy, proved to be a ferocious fund raiser. In 1857 Leopold McClintock, financed by Lady Jane, left from Aberdeen, Scotland, in a steam-assisted vessel to determine the fate of the Franklin party.

> During the summer of 1859, sledge parties led by McClintock . . . found substantial traces of the Franklin expedition in various places on King William Island [a small island northeast of Hudson Bay, just north of the North American mainland] . . . Beside a cairn nearby were medical apparatus and...a sealed cannister containing [a] record [stating that Franklin's boats] had been abandoned on 28 May 1847 . . . . Another note had been added . . . almost a year later—registering the deaths of twenty-four of the men, including Sir John Franklin, during the intervening year (Flegg, 1990, p. 33).

This tragedy did not mark the end of the ill-fated expedition. Crozier, one of the surviving officers, had recorded his intention of attempting to move southward to the Back River. Some years later, Charles Hall, an American, set out by himself on foot to find out more about the fate of Franklin's men by living with the local people. He did not find much, except to report that the Prince William Island Inuit admitted to abandoning Crozier and his men to die of starvation.

The Northwest Passage was eventually formally negotiated. In 1862 an impetuous 26-year-old American named Robert McClure, part of one of the Franklin rescue missions, sailed his 400-ton ship, *The Investigator*, on an uncharted course through the Aleutian Islands, around the northwest coast of Alaska, and on eastward. The navigation of this circuitous course marked the culmination of 365 years of searching.

The later purely explorational expeditions of the far north of Cook, Peary, and Henson had many warnings from these earlier voyages about the great difficulty of travel and the need to befriend the Inuits and Aleuts.

What of southern exploration?

> The Greek geographer and astronomer Ptolemy, writing in Egypt, then one of the centers of the civilized world, described a vast land mass far to the south. How he was aware of this land mass about 150 years after the birth of Christ is a complete mystery, but he described it as 'Terra Australis Incognita' and depicted it as a place of evil, occupied by various legendary beasts and malign influences (Flegg et al., 1990, p. 43).

Formal exploration of this "Terra Incognita" was to wait many centuries. It was not until the fifteenth and sixteenth centuries that Portuguese and Spanish sailors navigated around the tip of the Cape of Good Hope and that Magellan rounded Cape Horn, the southern tip of South America. Mistaking Tierra del Fuego for the northern extremity of Antarctica, Magellan thought that this land, apparently having a reasonable climate and fertile soil, might be hospitable enough to colonize. His inaccurate information spurred some eighteenth-century explorations, notably that of Captain James Cook, who set sail from England in 1772 with two small ships. He spent the next three summers circling the southern continent, kept offshore by the pack ice; he reported that the area was extremely cold and murderous to navigate. Further navigations were made in the early nineteenth century by sealers and whalers, and the first landing on the continent itself was made by John Davis, a sealer from New Haven, Connecticut. As the extremes of climate decreased sealing and whaling activity in the Antarctic Circle, exploratory geographers, inspired by the location of the North Pole, began to launch expeditions to locate the southerly equivalent. As was the case with the North Pole, the location of the South Pole was followed by the desire to "discover," and set foot upon it. Two explorers, spurred on by Peary's attainment of the North Pole in 1909, set out to be the first to reach the South Pole.

That year Robert Falcon Scott announced that he would mount an expedition to "conquer" the South Pole. Having travelled to within 600 miles of the pole on a previous expedition and already famous for his exploits, Scott intended to field a relatively large expeditionary force. It also turned out to be cumbersome, slow-moving, and inadequately equipped.

Norwegian explorer Roald Amundsen was also inspired by Peary's attainment of the North Pole. Cancelling other plans, he and a team of four hastened to Antarctica. In contrast to Scott's large force, Amundsen's small team was well equipped and experienced. He was also unimpeded by the interest in scientific discovery which seriously slowed the Scott expedition. The fact was that the expeditions to the South Pole had become a race, which ended tragically in early 1912.

> The "winner," if the term can be applied in such a situation, was Amundsen. Superior experience and planning paid off as he and his team reached the most southerly point previously explored early in December. A week later they reached the South Pole, leaving a tent with a Norwegian flag to mark their success. They returned to their base camp late in January 1912, having covered almost 2,000 miles of the worst terrain in the world in just under 100 days. Such progress is a tribute to planning skills, to equipment, and to Amundsen's expertise in coping with the logistic problems of varying progress and the location of supply dumps, plus an element of that good fortune that so often accompanies success (Flegg et al., 1990, p. 52).

Scott's luck was not nearly so good. Bedeviled by blizzards and heavy loads of supplies, the expedition's morale dropped at the sight, on January 18, 1912, of the Norwegian tent at the South Pole. The attempt at a homeward journey, begun in mid-January, was tragic. The men were completely fatigued and the weather was horrible. Frostbite was a besetting problem, and with winter closing in the weather became worse and worse. By early February food was growing short and the members of the expedition were increasingly ill. On March 21 they set up their last camp. By then two members of the expedition had died, and the rest followed shortly. Eight months later a relief expedition found the bodies and Scott's diary, which closes with the plea: "For God's sake look after our people."

Tragedy, indeed, and such must be anticipated in these extremes of climate and terrain. As technology has increased in sophistication and expanded our ability to reach into formerly inaccessible areas, we are well advised to rephrase Scott's anguished words: "For God's sake look after our fellow creatures." People will continue to investigate the northern and southern extremes of our planet, but perhaps with a different slant. It may be that we will explore with the intent of preservation of the cold and alien landscapes that are home to animals that can live nowhere else, home to seals named for an Englishman and penguins named for a Frenchwoman, home to microorganisms that support the life of the largest mammals on earth, home to a richness of life belied by its barren appearance.

Reference

Flegg, Jim, et al. (1990). *Poles Apart: The Natural Worlds of the Arctic and Antarctic.* New York: Pelham Books/Stephen Green Press; distributed by Viking.

ANNOTATED BIBLIOGRAPHY

Nonfiction

Abramson, Howard S. *Hero in Disgrace: The Life of Arctic Explorer Frederick A. Cook.* New York: Paragon House, 1991. $21.95. 250p. index. bibliography. ISBN 1-55778-322-5. **Ad.**

Robert Peary is generally credited with being the first man to reach the North Pole. Frederick Cook comes into the story only as a sort of afterthought, the stumbling block to Peary's immediate, rightful recognition. In most accounts Cook is a footnote, an unfair, would-be usurper of Peary's hard-won distinction.

This adult biography of Frederick A. Cook paints a different picture entirely. Rather than highlighting the unlikely aspects of Cook's polar claims, Peary is subjected to the same sort of cynical scrutiny that Cook usually receives. The author not only discusses the validity of Cook's claim, but gives enough background on him to support the contention that Cook indeed reached the North Pole before Peary. Cook was not a neophyte to exploration. He weathered a winter with Amundsen in Antarctica and climbed Alaska's Mount McKinley. He was certainly no stranger to the exigencies of the Arctic and Antarctic climates. Abramson's arguments in Cook's defense are persuasive.

The book is divided into three parts covering Cook's explorations prior to his bid to reach the North Pole, his conquest of the Pole, and his subsequent smearing by Peary's advocates. The writing style is easy and conversational but clearly adult. It could, however, be excerpted and read aloud. Given its alternative viewpoint to an almost 100-year-old controversy, it is an excellent discussion starter. For ambitious older middle schoolers, this book is a fine report source, with ample detail and a thorough index. The bibliography lists adult titles only. Nonetheless, this book is a good supplemental and balance title for units on polar exploration.

Brown, Warren. *The Search for the Northwest Passage.* New York: Chelsea House, 1991. $16.95. 111p. index. bibliography. ISBN 0-7910-1297-2.

The search for the Northwest Passage, a route to Asia through or above the northern regions of North America, is for most of us inextricably tied to Henry Hudson. But along with this intrepid and obsessed seventeenth-century Englishman, many others attempted to discover the way to the Orient from the north. The Passage was actually negotiated as a result of Sir John Franklin's tragic 1845 expedition. Departing in May of that year, Franklin's expedition disappeared without a trace. Loved ones in England endured three years of silence before a rescue expedition was sent. When the 1848 rescue expedition failed to answer anxious questions, Lady Jane Franklin, John Franklin's tenacious wife, enlisted American aid. It was in the course of this expedition that a hot-headed and impetuous 26-year-old named Robert McClure sailed his 400-ton ship, *The Investigator*, on an uncharted, unauthorized course through the Aleutian Islands, around the northwest coast of Alaska, and on eastward. This marked the first official navigation of the Northwest Passage.

Brown's prose style is rhythmic and readable. Though clearly a work of strict nonfiction, this volume in the World Explorers series could certainly be read aloud in segments; the picture of the harsh Arctic climate and the driven explorers is enthralling. Covering explorers from Cabot to McClure, this good report source may keep students reading out of interest. Numerous black-and-white reproductions and maps help explicate the text. A good index and bibliography increase this volume's potential as a report source.

Dolan, Edward F. *Matthew Henson: Black Explorer*. New York: Dodd, Mead, 1979. $7.95. 193p. index. bibliography. ISBN 0-396-07728-5.

Matthew Henson, born just after the Civil War in August 1866, seems to have been destined for adventure. In his teens he set to sea and sailed to Asia and Europe. In 1887, the 20-year-old black American met Robert E. Peary, and became his personal servant for the duration of a surveying trip to Nicaragua. Henson's resourcefulness in the swamps and jungles of Central America led Peary to invite Henson along on his explorations to the far north. Between 1891 and 1909, Peary took several expeditions north to explore, map, catalog flora and fauna, and, eventually, reach the North Pole. Matt Henson was with him the entire time. In six words, Peary succinctly summed up a relationship based on mutual esteem and devotion: "I can't get along without him." Henson stands, along with Peary and Cook, as one of the foremost early explorers of the Arctic reaches.

Beginning with a flashback, Dolan moves forward in a strictly chronological manner, covering the nearly two decades in Greenland in great detail. His use of the active voice and consistent sense of involvement with his narrative give the text a lively and immediate air that holds readers. His coverage of the polar expeditions is detailed as is his unflinching examination of Peary's shabby treatment of Henson at the end of their association—a rift only barely mended at the end of Peary's life.

The index is useful for those interested in writing a report based on specific incidents or Arctic phenomena. The table of contents provides access by year. Black-and-white photographs and clear maps augment the text. The maps are especially helpful in giving a feel for the push across the floating ice fields that mark the way to the North Pole. This is a fine example of biography and might be excerpted for reading aloud. Henson certainly deserves more credit than he has received, and this lively true adventure story will help bring him recognition.

Ferris, Jeri. *Arctic Explorer: The Story of Matthew Henson.* Minneapolis: Carolrhoda Books, 1989. $9.95. 80p. bibliography. index. ISBN 0-87614-370-2.

This straightforward, accessibly written biography covers Henson's life from birth to death, but concentrates on his years with Peary from 1887 to 1909. Beginning with the debate over whether Peary in fact reached the North Pole at all in 1909, author Ferris goes on to discuss Matthew Henson's "indispensability" to Peary. The chronicle of Henson's usually harmonious but ultimately acrimonious relationship with the determined Arctic explorer is chronicled in six brief chapters. Though not as detailed a treatment of Henson as Edward Dolan's (see entry, above), this book gives the basic story in brisk, crisp prose.

The index and bibliography add to the accessibility of this solid report source. Black-and-white photographs enhance the text. The formatting employs a large, readable type font and gives the book a nonthreatening look that should appeal to reluctant readers.

Flegg, Jim, et al. *Poles Apart: The Natural Worlds of the Arctic and Antarctic.* New York: Pelham Books/Stephen Green Press; distributed by Viking, 1990. $29.95. 192p. index. bibliography. ISBN 0-7207-1838-4.

This lush pictorial treatment of the ecology of the Arctic and Antarctic regions is divided into nine chapters. The first chapter discusses the prehistories of both polar regions, their similarities and differences. The next two chapters concern exploration of the Poles, and consider the following life forms of the two areas: plant, insect, mammal, and avian. The final chapter discusses contrasts in terms of the flora and fauna of each polar region. The typeface is clear but small, and is tightly packed in columns between numerous striking color plates. These color photographs are the book's most notable feature, being uniformly clear and graphic in demonstrating the differences between the two Poles.

The prose style is straightforward and scholarly without being pedantic. It remains approachable and accessible to those with no background on polar ecology, though the vocabulary is adult in level. The historic accounts of polar exploration are low-key and reportorial, but manage to give a picture of the high risk and human stakes involved in exploration carried out in harsh, frigid climates. The prose is enhanced by the aforementioned photos and by lovely color maps of the Arctic and Antarctic. The endpapers feature Landsat photos of both areas. A good index and brief ecology-based reading list round out the book.

The most obvious use for this title is as browsing fare. The pictures will entrance students, and some will go on to read further about these majestic areas of our planet. A decent report source, both for exploratory and ecological themes, this book will need relatively little promotion.

Halsey, David, with Diane Landau. *Magnetic North: A Trek across Canada from the Pacific to the Atlantic by Foot, Dogsled, and Canoe.* San Francisco: Sierra Club Books, 1991. $12.00. 252p. index of place names. bibliography. ISBN 0-87156-566-8.

In early May 1977, four young men set out from Fort Langley, British Columbia. Though they looked to the casual glance like any group of weekend backpackers, they were, in fact, attempting something much more ambitious than a two-day hike. Calling themselves the "1977-78 Trans-Canada Expedition," the four had a final destination of Tadoussac, a village on the St. Lawrence River in Quebec Province, 4,700 miles from Vancouver. Their intent was to use only essentially primitive means of transport—snowshoes, cargo toboggan, canoe, and foot—to complete their journey. Four days later, with his three companions having opted out of the arduous trek, Dave Halsey undertook the journey on his own.

He completed his journey, picking up two partners: his dog, Ki, and photographer Peter Souchuk. The book, written in diary fashion, has the engaging and immediate quality of first-hand observation. The hardships and satisfactions of pitting oneself against the untamed and harsh, yet beautiful, Arctic terrain are newly felt. A one-page bibliography and index of place names give the reader pointers to other works and add reference aid, but this is largely an account to be read for sheer interest. A center section of color photos satisfies curiosity, and the excellent maps sprinkled throughout allow readers to follow the Trans-Canada Expedition's route with ease.

This book will read aloud or booktalk beautifully, with cliff-hanging passages throughout the story. Dave and Pete's triumphant arrival in Tadoussac on August 17, 1979, invites readers to share their jubilation, as well as their bittersweet sense that with this goal attained, there was nowhere left to go. Halsey never saw the publication of his book, dying a probable suicide at the age of 26. Much of the text has been ably completed from Halsey's notes by Diane Landau. She makes us understand quite clearly that this is a recounting of the high point in a young man's life.

Huntington, Lee Pennock. *The Arctic and the Antarctic.* Illustrated by Murray Tinkelman. New York: Coward, McCann, & Geoghegan, 1975. $5.95. unpaged. ISBN 0-698-20322-4. **P.**

This picture book introduction to life in the polar regions will serve best as a teaching tool. Each page of information is faced by a full-page illustration of the landscape or life form addressed. The illustrations, employing a scratchboard technique, are quite impressionistic. Best seen from a distance, they are possessed of a startling sense of arrested energy. However, their character necessitates a group approach to presentation.

The brief text, too, is impressionistic, but taken as a whole gives a fairly clear picture of Arctic and Antarctic ecology. This book offers excellent background material for units on polar exploration, giving students a landscape and set of environmental conditions into which to place the men and women who explored the southern and northern extremes of our planet.

Kent, Zachary. *The Story of Admiral Peary at the North Pole.* Chicago: Childrens Press, 1988. $8.95. 31p. ISBN 0-516-04738-8.

On the morning of March 1, 1909, despite unfavorable weather conditions, Commander Robert Edwin Peary and his expeditionary party set out from Cape

Columbia, the northernmost point of Ellesmere Island, Canada, to travel to the North Pole, 413 miles away. The weather was terrible—clear but driven by high winds that blew flaying ice particles into the men's faces. However, Peary felt that he could wait no longer. He was 52 years old and obsessed with being the first person to reach the North Pole. It was, he said, ". . . my dream, my destiny . . ."

This large print, heavily illustrated book tells Peary's story in an engaging, easily understood manner. Kent is not a particularly elegant stylist, but he knows how to make a yarn hold together coherently, and Peary certainly supplies the necessary dramatic tension. The book is neither divided into chapters nor possessed of an index, which somewhat limits its use for reports. The information on Peary is generous, but difficult to access. Despite this drawback, the book is useful in a number of ways. Kent covers Peary's life from his 20s on in enough detail for readers to gain insight into the man. The 1909 journey to the North Pole is chronicled succinctly but with enough interesting detail to make this good read-aloud or booktalking material. Kent gives full credit to Matthew Henson and the four Eskimo guides of the expedition, and also covers the controversy over whether Peary or Frederick Cook reached the Pole first.

The period photographs and use of Peary's and Henson's own words give a compelling immediacy to the whole, which could be used as a lesson in the use of primary source material.

Lyttle, Richard B. *Polar Frontiers: A Background Book on the Arctic, the Antarctic, and Mankind.* New York: Parents' Magazine Press, 1972. o.p. 264p. index. bibliography. notes. ISBN 0-8193-0601-0. **Ad.**

Before there was polar exploration, there were the Arctic and the Antarctic. If history seems to us to begin with the time when humans first recorded setting foot on virgin terrain, it behooves us to remember that the ecosystems existed before, creating a way of life and a challenging environment to overcome.

Opening with a discussion of the differences between the Arctic and the Antarctic, this book is subsequently divided into two sections. The chapters of Part I, "The Arctic," present archaeological work in the Arctic followed by a brief history of exploration and discovery. The text then considers polar flight and Arctic life to the year of publication. Along the way, information is given on the flora and fauna, as well as environmental issues.

Part II, "The Antarctic," follows much the same pattern, though it allows for the vast differences in the two regions. The book's dated character shows most in this section; many of the environmental issues challenging the southern-most continent were only incipient 20 years ago.

Written for adults, this book provides a valuable background resource for teachers, putting polar exploration firmly in environmental and temporal contexts. Lyttle's prose is readable, if not exceptional in quality, and the information imparted is sound. Older advanced middle school readers could certainly use this as a supplemental report source. The index is thorough and gives guidance where the table of contents does not. The lengthy bibliography is composed mostly of out-of-print works, but does cite a number of primary source documents which might conceivably be obtained from libraries.

May, John. *The Greenpeace Book of Antarctica: A New View of the Seventh Continent.* New York: Doubleday, 1989. $24.95. 192p. index. bibliography. ISBN 0-385-26280-9. **Ad.**

Exploration, that human impulse, is a mixed blessing for our earth. The Antarctic environment is a particularly fragile one, a trait it shares with the rain forests. As we have found more and more out about this fascinating netherworld, the inevitable problem of exploitation has arisen. Greenpeace is in the business of preventing this, and in aid of that has produced this impressive, information-packed pictorial examination of the seventh continent.

The range of subjects covered is impressive. Antarctica's continuing evolution, six sections on ice formations, oases, weather, optical phenomena, three sections on atmospheric phenomena, land and sea flora and fauna, 48 pages on the human presence, and 20 pages on Greenpeace's perspectives are included. The format is columnar, inset with color photos and drawings, and reminiscent of *Time* magazine, though the reading level is a bit higher. There are numerous excellent maps and isometric views of the continent. The index and bibliography are both excellent.

This superb report source gives information on almost any aspect of Antarctic life or exploration that comes to mind. An excellent complement to Jim Flegg's *Poles Apart* (see entry, above), this book will extend that title. It's a natural for browsing and for discussion starting, sparking debate on how exploration and exploitation of resources are related.

Miller, Luree and Scott Miller. *Alaska: Pioneer Stories of a Twentieth-Century Frontier.* New York: Cobblehill/Dutton, 1991. $14.95. 116p. index. bibliography. glossary. ISBN 0-525-65050-4. **Ad.**

If there is still a frontier in the United States, it exists in Alaska. Despite cosmopolitan cities like Anchorage and Fairbanks, the extremes of climate are incontrovertible. Children journey to and from school in darkness all winter, fight off mosquitos in the summer, when the daylight is endless, and deal with earthquakes, heavy snowfalls, and man-made disasters like the Valdez oil spill. The pioneering spirit is alive and well in the northern extreme of our country.

Conversationally written, *Alaska* traces the lives of early pioneers like Frank and Mary Miller, as well as modern-day pioneering Alaskans. From native leader Willie Hensley, to Marty Rutherford (a state official), to teen-aged fisher Faith Van De Putte, these people celebrate the rugged but breathtaking country where they live, and give primary source testimony to the challenges they face daily.

A clear, open typeface and attractive page arrangement give this book an accessible appearance. Inset black-and-white photos add a pictorial dimension to the stories, and the map of Alaska at the beginning of the book is helpful in locating the scenes of the action in the following chapters. This unusual report source could be creatively used for informational studies of the Alaskan frontier, and Arctic ecosystems generally. The narratives read aloud well and might be effectively excerpted for classroom reading or library booktalking. The index is good, and the bibliography though brief and eclectic, is fairly recent.

Murphy, Joseph E. *South to the Pole by Ski: Nine Men and Two Women Pioneer a New Route to the South Pole.* Saint Paul, MN: Marlor Press, 1990. $19.95. 202p. index. ISBN 0-943400-49-X.

There are a number of ways to get to the South Pole, the most frequently employed of which is dogsled or its modern equivalent, the snowmobile. Skiing is not an option usually considered, but in the winter of 1988-89, nine men and two women pioneered the first route from the Ronne Ice Shelf to the South Pole, and they did it on cross country skis.

This first-person account is divided into three sections. The first, "The Expedition Begins," consists of three chapters and covers pre-expedition training. The next two chapters recount the ski journey to the South Pole. The South Pole Overland Expedition, as the 11-person team called itself, battled extreme cold and winds of up to 50 miles an hour, at times moving in whiteout conditions. Yet they persevered to achieve several polar firsts: a new route pioneered, the first Americans to reach the Pole overland by ski, and the first women to reach the South Pole overland.

Murphy's style tends toward the purple and exclamatory, but he weaves a good yarn. This book lends itself to reading aloud or to booktalking, but is probably best suited for individual interest reading. A section of black-and-white photographs satisfies curiosity but, due to their home snapshot quality, does little else. Rather amateurish pen and ink drawings pepper the text, which would have done just as well without them. Nonetheless, this book is an exciting adventure, engagingly, if idiosyncratically, told.

Osborn, Kevin. *The Peoples of Arctic.* New York: Chelsea House, 1990. $18.95. 111p. index. bibliography. ISBN 0-87754-876-5.

An essay by Daniel Patrick Moynihan concerning the wide range of ethnic groups that comprise our population as well as our heritage of white intolerance of native cultures opens a detailed consideration of indigenous Northerners. The peoples of the north, the first Americans, Arctic ecology, spiritual and social structures, cultures, and contact with other cultures each have a chapter devoted to them. A picture essay entitled "Between Two Worlds," consisting of eight pages of captioned color photographs, comes at the midpoint of this volume in the Chelsea House The Peoples of the Americas series.

The prose, though informative, is a bit dry. The text is arranged in columns down the center of each page, leaving wide margins for pictorial materials and sidebars. This has the effect of driving the main text into the gutter, but the black-and-white illustrations, mostly photographs but including some period drawings, serve to break up the narrative and add information. The table of contents and index are both acceptable, but the bibliography contains mostly adult titles, some of them standard reference works, but all a bit difficult for the middle school age range.

This book has applications. The sixth chapter, "Contact with Outsiders," gives a capsule look at Arctic exploration. The book also gives insight into the cultural and ecological milieu into which explorational parties have found themselves injected.

Pictorial enough to be suitable for browsing, this book is also an accessible report source.

Perkins, Robert. *Into the Great Solitude: An Arctic Journey.* New York: Holt, 1991. $19.95. 219p. ISBN 0-8050-0727-X. **Ad.**

The Back River in the northern Canadian wilderness empties into the waters of the Arctic Circle. Rapids, rocks, unpredictable weather, and blustering winds were all challenges battled by George Back, its original explorer, who made a voyage down it in 1834. In 1987, Robert Perkins decided for a number of reasons, most of them personal, to recapitulate Back's trip. He, too, faced the same hazards, and he, too, survived to tell about his journey down the river by canoe.

Perkins's prose is descriptive, poetic, and intensely personal. Following the river, he also follows himself within, finding in extreme hardship, in "solitude and suffering," a way to look into himself and discover what matters. While students may not read this themselves, and the prose is a bit orotund for younger middle school readers, this book is a rare thing: read-aloud nonfiction for grades eight and nine. The prose bogs down now and again, and the teacher or librarian, in order to keep the story flowing, may have to read ahead and be selective as to which parts are presented. Nonetheless, the book provides a nearly unique introduction to the rigors of traveling in the polar reaches, as well as presenting the terrain, for all its bleakness, with a kind of lyricism. Illustrated with monoprints and line drawings by the author, this volume also has a PBS companion film of the same name.

Rodgers, Eugene. *Beyond the Barrier: The Story of Byrd's First Expedition to Antarctica.* Annapolis, MD: Naval Institute Press, 1990. $24.95. 354p. index. bibliography. source notes. ISBN 0-87021-022-X. **Ad.**

My mother was born in 1928, so that is a year of considerable significance for me. However, that was also the year that Admiral Richard E. Byrd made his celebrated expedition to Antarctica, building his settlement at Little America. Encountering extreme dangers, Byrd and his men claimed a series of impressive achievements. They made the first flight over the South Pole, discovered vast new territories, conducted significant scientific studies, and made pioneering use of technological advances such as the airplane, snowmobile, and long-range radio communication.

Detailed and adult in scope and prose level, this exhaustive narrative is divided into 18 chapters and an epilogue. The entire scope of the expedition is explained and examined. Using interviews, diaries, letters, unpublished manuscripts, and Admiral Byrd's private papers, Rodgers gives us a realistic view of a thoroughly human expedition. Problems with clashing egos, personality differences, drinking, and the stresses of working in an extreme environment all took their toll.

A 14-page center section of black-and-white photos adds faces to the names and a sense of reality to the white-out environment. A thorough index and detailed bibliography are added pluses for report writers. This adult book will be read only by capable readers. It's best use may be as a teacher resource for background on a fascinating, all-too-human mission.

Rosen, Mike. *The Journey to the North Pole.* Illustrated by Doug Post. New York: Bookwright, 1990. $11.40. 32p. index. bibliography. glossary. ISBN 0-531-18344-0.

Between 1886 and 1909, Robert Edwin Peary made six attempts to reach the North Pole. The success of the final 1909 expedition was firmly grounded in experience gained during the previous five.

This short, pictorial treatment gives background on Peary's expeditions; but it also gives readers a look at earlier attempts to reach the Pole. Including information on Arctic ecology and native lifestyles, this book is remarkably comprehensive for a 32-page text. Nothing is dealt with in detail, but the background information is valuable. Thirteen two-page chapters discuss Peary, the peoples of the Arctic, early European explorers and the results of their voyages, and Peary's attempts at reaching the North Pole. The writing style is succinct if uninspired, though the vocabulary is fairly complex. Those students unable to read the text fluidly will be able to piece together the stories by virtue of the copious illustrations. Maps, photographs, period reproductions, and artist's representations are used to recreate history and extend the narrative.

This book would not be useful as a source for in-depth reports, but all the basic information and solid background are here. The index, table of contents, and glossary are adequate. The bibliography, listing only books by the publisher, is self-serving, but gives an idea of other topics related to Arctic exploration. A browser's delight, this book provides good classroom support for units on the northern reaches.

Sipiera, Paul P. *Roald Amundsen and Robert Scott.* Chicago: Childrens Press, 1990. $23.93. 128p. index. bibliography. glossary. ISBN 0-516-03056-6.

On the verso opposite the table of contents of this volume in The World's Great Explorers Series, there is a photograph of a husky tethered at Scott Base, Antarctica. The dog is yawning hugely, a reaction that the outwardly textbookish look of this title might engender. A quick dip into its pages will dispel this illusion. The writing style is neither inventive nor inspired, but the subjects of the work are fascinating and virtually impossible to render lifeless and dull.

The introduction covers the prior history of polar exploration, and the clearly written text gives background and then looks at the ultimately deadly competition for the honor of reaching the South Pole first that fired both Amundsen and Scott. The emphasis is on their respective personalities, giving an effective psychological bent to the narrative. The layout is attractive, with a great many photographs and drawings breaking up and extending the text. The account of the race to the South Pole is lucid and precise without being distanced. The hardships of polar exploration are made clear by example rather than by list.

This book reads aloud well, and the more action-filled portions might be used effectively as classroom oral reading or booktalking material. The extension of the text provided by the index, glossary, and bibliography makes this an excellent report source.

Weiner, Eric. *The Story of Henry Hudson, Master Explorer.* Illustrated by Maria DeJohn. New York: Dell, 1991. $2.99. 105p. chronology. ISBN 0-44-40513-0.

Henry Hudson has for centuries been a shadowy figure despite the myriad places in the Northeast named for him, and despite the Hudson's Bay Company. Perhaps Washington Irving can be credited with this, for his nine-pins playing Heinrich Hudson in "Rip Van Winkle" and his shadowy *Half Moon* have become etched into both the historical and the popular psyche.

Hudson, the historical person, was born in the late 1500s. A third generation sailor, Hudson was infused by the certainty that he could discover the elusive Northwest Passage, a water route through the Arctic to the spice rich East. Remarkably similar to Columbus in the obsessional nature of his explorations, Hudson made four northward voyages, one in 1607, two others in 1608 and 1609, and the final voyage, in the course of which he died a victim of mutiny, in 1610.

Hudson appears to have been a complex and compulsive man, but Weiner's informational book is too brief to examine that in any detail. The prose, while easy to read, is more than a little wooden, and contains occasional non-sequiturs. The 12 chapters and introduction are short and fairly interesting. The full-page ink and pencil illustrations are not terribly accomplished, but do break up the text. Good for reports at the lower middle school level, this book will also pique interest in a recklessly single-minded explorer.

Fiction

Houston, James. *Frozen Fire: A Tale of Courage.* New York: Atheneum, 1977. $6.95. 147p. ISBN 0-689-50083-1.

Matt Morgan's prospector father is a geologist who is always sure that his next expedition will yield a lucrative copper strike. With his mother recently dead, Matt is sent to school at Forbisher Bay in the Canadian Arctic to wait out his father's latest prospecting trip. But things do not go as planned, and when Matthew's father and his helicopter pilot are lost in an Arctic storm, Matt and his Eskimo friend, Kayak, set off by snowmobile to search for them.

This survival story is based in part on a journey undertaken by an Eskimo boy in the 1960s. The narrative is gripping, the plotting brisk. Giving a window on the traditional Eskimo way of life, this book also serves to introduce readers to the searing cold of the Arctic regions, and the hazards of travel in this inhospitable northern climate. A natural lead-in to works on Peary's and Cook's expeditions to the North Pole, this novel is classic classroom or interest reading that gives as much information as nonfiction in an easily assimilable form.

Newth, Mette. *The Abduction.* Translated from the Norwegian by Tina Nunnally and Steve Murray. New York: Farrar, Straus & Giroux, 1989. $13.95. 248p. ISBN 0-374-30008-9.

Along with settlements, the Vikings who sailed into cold northern waters also brought disruption to the lives of the native Inuit people. This piercing narrative tells the story of Osuqo and Poq, two Inuit adolescents who are abducted from their people and brought back to Norway as curiosities.

Told alternately in the voices of Osquo and Christine, a Norwegian girl who is ordered to guard the two Inuits, the story brings to the fore the collision of two cultures, mutually incomprehensible to each other. Dealing with the violence inflicted in the name of civilization, it also speaks to the attunement to nature which is part of the traditional Eskimo way of life, and, perhaps most significantly, to the growth of understanding across cultures as Christine slowly comes to regard Poq and Osuqo as her peers.

Vivid prose and unstinting vision mark this eye-opening, discussion-provoking book. Characterization is entirely three dimensional and the narrative flow is smooth and believable. This book is sure to change readers' visions of the lives of seventeenth-century Norsemen and their Eskimo contemporaries. The subject matter is raw, including the rape of Osuqo, but for those with a strong moral sense, this is reading that will produce questions and induce pondering.

CHAPTER 8
The High Places

Two hours later I stepped down onto the snow at the foot of the wall. Waves of relief swept over me. The vise that had been squeezing my temples and gut was suddenly gone. By God, I had survived. I sat down in the snow and began to laugh.—Jon Krakauer, *Eiger Dreams**

I am afraid of heights. I'm fine on airplanes because the space is small and enclosed and I don't feel like I am going to fall out. But those little glass elevators that tony shopping centers use to run up their insides give me the shakes, and being up on a ladder causes me to sweat and tremble. It's called vertigo, and I am not as afflicted as some people; but it has kept me off mountains for all of my adult life.

I live south of Seattle, Washington. About 60 miles still further south stands Mount Rainier, solid as a fortress. When we first moved here, just looking at it frightened me. It was too big, too looming, too unreal. Now, 12 years later, I think it's beautiful, though you couldn't pay me to climb it. However, the exhilaration one gets just looking at that graceful pile of rock must have some sort of contagion in it, for from the time we moved here I've read books about mountaineering. Though I carry my car keys attached to a carabiner that I'll never use for anything more than a key chain, I know all about tough climbs and physical effects of altitude and which of the

---

*Krakauer, Jon. (1990). *Eiger Dreams: Ventures Among Men and Mountains*. New York: Lyons & Burford.

Himalayan peaks are the most treacherous. I know the names of climbers (quite a number of them dead now), and I admire the less foolhardy of them. Still, you would not get me out on a high exposed flank of ice and rock for any reason. For all my reading, I haven't experienced that need to reach for the heights, the motivation that might push me to stand on top of some big mountain, having very likely risked my life to do it, having very likely caused someone I love a terrible lot of worry.

Why do people climb? Like all exploratory activities, there is an element of personal gain in scaling high peaks. It's just that in this case the gain is more ephemeral, less material than in other areas of endeavor. You might get a reputation out of it, maybe a job advertising climbing boots or rope, but hardly huge financial remuneration.

If we buy into the idea of evolution, we came out of the trees. Perhaps some of us are trying in some way to get back up there. Or perhaps, taking a more spiritual view, we are perpetually trying to reach God, who is usually perceived as inhabiting the upper air. Whatever the reasons may be, the peaks of the world continue to draw men and women from all walks of life, and continue to inspire acts of daring and total impetuosity that, under ordinary circumstances, would undoubtedly be eschewed. There seems to be something in the human psyche that reaches up, that wants to be on top looking back at the place from which it came. The closest one can come to "the roof of the world" is the top of a huge Tibetan peak.

The natives call it Chomolungma, The Mother Goddess of Heaven. To those of us raised in the West, it is Mount Everest, the highest mountain in the world, named after Sir George Everest, the Surveyor General of the Survey of India in the early 1800s. It is a mountain that, like many of the Himalayan peaks, exerts a strong fascination; and perhaps as a result of that has claimed a number of lives. The renowned British climber George Leigh-Mallory was last seen hiking into the mist along the west ridge in 1927. More recently, Joe Tasker and Peter Boardman lost their lives in an attempt to ascend the northeast ridge. Perhaps the indigenous people are right in considering the mountain holy and in leaving her undisturbed. However, the trend is for more and more people to attempt the climb, or to come to the mountain and ski around it; to challenge it some way, so that what Mallory began, and Edmund Hillary carried on, has become almost a mass phenomenon. Every serious mountaineer, it seems, comes sooner or later to Everest.

The first well-known Western expedition to Everest was the 1924 Mallory expedition. Ending in the disappearance of both George Leigh-Mallory and Andrew Irvine, it may have been the first expedition to set a man on the peak of "The Mother Goddess of Heaven"; or it may not have.

Years later debate still rages over just exactly how high Mallory got before he died. Mountaineers going up the Chinese side of Everest, through Tibet, still look for evidence, relics of his passage.

In his mid-30s in 1924, Mallory was exceptional in many ways. Long and lithe, distinctively graceful, he had a body toned by years of gymnastics and weekend climbs on the challenging Welch cliff faces. His first expedition to Everest had been the British expedition of 1921. At that time, Mallory "had become one of the greatest names in British climbing, more because of whom he knew and his future promise than for what he had done" (Rowell, 1983, p. 81). Ever the maverick, ready to face any challenge that should present itself, Mallory found himself in the Himalayas along with seven other men, bidding to scale the highest mountain in the world. The expedition was not a success. One of the party, Dr. A. M. Kellas, weakened by dysentery and dehydration, died before reaching sight of Chomolungma. The next check was the reluctance of the monks at the Rongbuk Monastery, set at 16,500 feet, to permit the party to pass through the area freely. This frustrating stalemate continued for some time before the monks agreed to allow the party to explore. Once allowed through, Mallory spent some days in reconnaissance with another climber. They found two cols that dropped directly into steep ice or rock, and scanned the South Col, rejecting that route to the summit, the very one that Edmund Hillary and Tenzing Norgay would use to make the first ascent 32 years later.

Despite passing time and growing frustration, Mallory persisted in his search for a potential route to the summit. Months more passed without finding a suitable route from the Tibetan side. Part of the problem lay in the fact that Mallory had wrongly judged the course of the glacier descending from the North Col. When the expedition surveyor, Major Oliver Wheeler, produced a map showing the correct course of the East Rongbuk Glacier, Mallory labeled Wheeler's map as "notably wrong in some respects" (Rowell, 1983, p. 83). This was untrue, but Mallory didn't want to look inexpert or uninformed. At any rate, it was by then far too late in the year to attempt to climb the mountain. Additionally, the climbing party had by that time been reduced by illness and Kellas' death to three. They were forced to retreat.

Though he vowed never to return, Mallory was back in April 1922 to make a second attempt at scaling Everest. This time he was with a team of 13 men equipped with a complex oxygen apparatus that used four tanks per climber. From the beginning there were problems among the members of the party. Though he had considerable charm and expertise, Mallory was not an easy person with whom to work, having about him more than a little of the prima donna. The expedition leader, General Charles Bruce, found Mallory's constant philosophizing on any and every subject highly aggravating. This acrimonious air plagued the expedition for its entire time on the mountain. With tempers worn thin by altitude and stress, this expedition, too, failed to gain the summit, though in proceeding up the East Rongbuk, the climbers attained greater heights than any mountaineers in history. In June, Mallory led 17 summiters toward the North Col for another attempt at reaching the peak. In the early afternoon, with a short, sharp sound like a rifle firing, an avalanche struck, partially burying the British but killing seven sherpas. The loss of life signalled the end of the 1922 expedition.

It would be another two years before Mallory would attempt Everest once more. In the meantime, he spent considerable time on the lecture circuit in the United States where he gained public recognition if no further climbing experience. It was in Philadelphia that he, when asked why he wanted to climb Everest, replied: "Because it is there" (Rowell, 1983, p. 86). Those who knew Mallory well believed this to be an off-the-cuff answer to an obvious question. In his more contemplative moments, and in his writings, Mallory offered much stronger explanations of the motivation to climb:

> Our case is not unlike that of one who has, for instance, a gift for music. There may be inconvenience, and even damage, to be sustained in devoting time to music; but the greatest danger is in not devoting enough, for music is this man's adventure . . . . To refuse the adventure is to run the risk of drying up like a pea in its shell. (Rowell, 1983, p. 86).

Mallory was certainly not one to refuse adventure. In 1924 he was back in the Himalayas.

On the morning of June 8, 1924, Mallory set off before dawn for the summit of The Mother Goddess of Heaven. He left from Camp IV at 26,800 feet, taking with him Andrew Irvine, a 22-year-old Cambridge undergraduate of strong constitution and good endurance, but little mountaineering experience. Mallory sent messages down with a sherpa: "Perfect weather for the job . . . . It won't be too early to start looking for us either crossing the rock band or going up the skyline at 8:00 a.m." (Rowell, 1983, p. 87). It was the last that was heard from him.

The only eyewitness to the remainder of Mallory and Irvine's summit bid was Noel Odell. A geologist who initially hadn't acclimatized quickly, Odell, by the beginning of June, moved about the mountain with an uncanny ease, alone and without oxygen. At 12:50 p.m., he looked up from a vantage point at 26,000 feet and "'noticed far away on a snow slope leading up to what seemed to me to be the last step but one from the base of the final pyramid, a tiny object moving . . . . A second object followed, and then the first climbed to the top of the step. As I stood intently watching this dramatic appearance, the scene became enveloped in cloud . . .'" (Rowell, 1983, p. 87). Not only was Odell the only eyewitness, he was also the only member of the expedition who staunchly maintained that Mallory and Irvine had a strong probability of success. "Viewed by later mountaineers and historians, the disappearance of the two men has become as much a mystery as a tragedy. Unquestionably they gave their lives on the summit bid—but did they make it to the top?" (Rowell, 1983, p. 87).

> I have climbed a steep section of mountain and now, breathless inside my tent, the realization hits me that I cannot get back down again. I lie rigid, unable to move, and am sweating profusely even though it is so cold. Hoar frost coats the drab fabric above my head. I mutter to myself, call out, yet cannot hear the sound of my own voice. Panic has me in its clutches and all I want to do is to scream (Messner, 1980).

This could be the voice of an inexperienced mountaineer just learning about the perils of climbing dangerous peaks in weather that is at best unpredictable, at worst, deadly. It could be, but it is not. The writer is Reinhold Messner, a man acknowledged to be the greatest mountain climber of all time, a man who has virtually dominated the world of mountaineering since his early twenties. Messner wrote the lines quoted above of his tiny solo attempt to climb Nanga Parbat, an 8,000-meter peak in the Indian Himalayas. He had tried to climb the mountain some years earlier as a member of an expedition. At that time, weather conditions had forced Messner and his brother, Gunther, over the far side of the mountain. Against tremendous odds, they nearly made it back to safety. As they came down the face of the mountain, the end in sight, Gunther was swept away in an avalanche. Reinhold returned two years later to climb the peak again, alone, unsure of whether he was laying ghosts or making a pilgrimage. This, his first solo attempt, failed. His second, in 1978, succeeded.

Messner is a legend. He has tremendous physical strength and stamina and an uncanny mountain sense that has kept him alive in situations in which others would have died. His accomplishments are legion, among them the distinction of being the first person to climb Everest without artificial oxygen. He has been an inspiration to countless climbers, but also a continuing, if inadvertent, source of mountaineering deaths. Jon Krakauer argues that Messner's example allows less experienced climbers to assume that the sort of climbing he does is easier than it looks, and that this assumption leads them to attempt climbs for which they are not prepared.

Not too far from Nanga Parbat, in the northernmost corner of Pakistan, is a peak that rises 28,250 feet. It is K2, 800 feet lower than Everest, but sharply and gracefully shaped. It is more striking than Everest and much more difficult to climb. Jon Krakauer observes that "of the fourteen mountains in the world higher than eight thousand meters, K2 has the highest failure rate" (Krakauer, 1990). Not only do expeditions fail to get to the top, but the loss of life on the mountain is catastrophic. Never was it worse than in the summer of 1986. At the end of that summer, 27 climbers had made it to the top, but for every two who stood on the summit, one died. Krakauer observes that "The toll would raise some thorny questions about the recent course of Himalayan climbing, a course some people believe has become unjustifiably reckless" (Krakauer, 1990). He lays the blame for this course directly in the lap of Reinhold Messner.

In the summer of 1975, Messner and his partner Peter Habeler tackled a slightly less lofty neighbor of K2 called Hidden Peak, climbing without support teams, fixed ropes, a set string of camps, bottled oxygen, or any of the other accepted accoutrements of high altitude climbing. They would climb Everest in just the same way three years later. Messner called this approach "climbing by fair means," seeming to imply that he considered it unfair to get to the top of a mountain by any other method.

Mountaineers play a sort of one-upsmanship that comes with the territory of any competitive sport. Once Messner had climbed an eight-thousander in the same manner that others climb the Tetons or the Alps, anyone hoping to keep up with him felt obligated to climb in the same way. The result was to make an already dangerous sport more dangerous. The death toll on K2 in the summer of 1986 is at least in part a result of this trend. John Krakauer states the concern succinctly.

> It is natural in any sport to seek ever-greater challenges; what is to be made of a sport in which to do so also means taking ever-greater risks? Should a civilized society continue to condone, much less celebrate, an activity in which there appears to be a growing acceptance of death as a likely outcome? . . . . Messner's brilliance has, perhaps, distorted the judgment of some of those who would compete with him . . . [and] . . . given unwarranted confidence to many climbers who lack the uncanny 'mountain sense' that's kept Messner alive all these years. (Krakauer, 1990).

Whatever the case, it is apparent that men and women will continue to climb the tall peaks, to pioneer new routes and new methods, to exercise that drive upward. The high places beckon, they draw, and there are those who draw from them strength and knowledge.

> Despite my tiredness . . . I am aware of a deep consciousness, all the enigmas of this baffling world are contained within me—the questions and the answers; I have in me the strength of life, the power to give life, death and the beginning and the end. (Messner, 1980).

References

Krakauer, Jon. (1990). *Eiger Dreams*. New York : Lyons & Burford.
Messner, Reinhold. (1980). *Solo: Nanga Parbat*. New York: Oxford University Press.
Rowell, Galen. (1983). *Mountains of the Middle Kingdom: Exploring the High Peaks of China and Tibet*. San Franciso: Sierra Club Books.

ANNOTATED BIBLIOGRAPHY

Nonfiction

Blum, Arlene. *Annapurna: A Woman's Place.* San Francisco: Sierra Club Books, 1980. $16.95. 256p. index. bibliography. ISBN 0-87156-236-7. **Ad.**

First ascended in 1950 by a French climbing team under the leadership of Maurice Herzog, Annapurna, "the harvest goddess," had an unsettling track record. One of the 14 peaks in the world to top 8,000 meters, it had been attempted only 12 times since its first ascent. Eight climbers of all those expeditions reached the summit, but nine others had died in the attempt. In August 1978, 13 women set out from Berkeley, California, for Kathmandu, Nepal. Their goal was to scale the 26,540 foot peak. In October, two of the company succeeded, becoming both the first women and the first Americans to climb the awe-inspiring mountain. Two days later the celebratory atmosphere was drastically changed when two other members of the team died in a second summit bid.

Blum's writing style is straightforward but, as the length of the book attests, perhaps overly detailed. The complex inter-relational web between all participants is given a close examination that does not add to narrative propulsion but does give added depth and fuller comprehension of just how the human element responds to the stresses of altitude and fierce exertion. Blum's descriptions of the impact of the deaths of Alison Chadwick-Onyszkiewicz and Vera Watson is slightly numbed, but infused with emotion.

Numerous black-and-white photographs of the terrain and the climbers extend the text. The color insert shows both the bleakness and beauty of "the harvest goddess." Route maps are especially detailed and helpful. This is a good book for browsing, picking up snippets of information about mountaineering and women on mountains, and increasing understanding of the urge to climb. The extensive bibliography can point interested readers to other titles of interest. Like many mountaineering books, this one contains numerous exciting sections suitable for reading aloud as classroom or library attention-getters.

Bonington, Chris. *Mountaineer: Thirty Years of Climbing on the World's Greatest Peaks.* San Francisco: Sierra Club Books, 1990. $29.95. 192p. ISBN 0-87156-618-4.

Chris Bonington is indeed a phenomenon. He has spent 30 years climbing the world's greatest peaks and is still alive—a remarkable achievement, given the attrition rate among climbers. He has managed to stay in the top rank of his sport for three decades despite injury and even tragedy, such as the loss of Joe Tasker and

Peter Boardman during the 1982 assault of Everest by the Northeast Ridge (see the Bonington and Clarke entry, below). This large format photographic autobiography supplies information about the impulse to climb paired with breathtaking photographic illustration.

Ten chapters cover Bonington's career, from the Alpine peaks and the big walls, to the major Himalayan peaks. The book concludes with a climbing record. Bonington is matter of fact and wry in reporting on his career; little psychological insight comes to the fore. Students who want adventure stories will find this appealing, and those sheer rock faces and blue peaks cause an inward gasp even in reproduction. This book shows why climbers go back for the sheer glory and challenge, despite tragedy and loss.

A beautiful browsing book, *Mountaineer* is also full of climbing lore and story. It may be enough to hook many a youngster into reading more books like it—and into taking to the mountains.

Bonington, Chris and Charles Clarke. *Everest: The Unclimbed Ridge.* New York: W. W. Norton, 1983. $24.95. 132p. index. ISBN 0-393-01875-X. **Ad.**

The dedication is "To Pete and Joe." The reason for this becomes clear as one reads this account of the attempt of a six-member British team to reach the summit of Everest by a previously unclimbed route without oxygen. On May 17, 1980, Joe Tasker and Peter Boardman, two exceedingly able and talented mountaineers, set off up the Northeast Ridge. It was the expedition's final assault, and one that ended tragically, with both climbers lost.

Twelve densely written chapters, with much material taken from journals, diaries, and letters, chronicle the expedition from April 1981 when the project was conceived, until June 1982, when the deaths of Tasker and Boardman occurred. The view given is compellingly personal and emotional in nature, making the psychological aspects of climbing clear. Bonington usually comes across as measured, objective, and chilly. This provides a rare glimpse into the man behind the cool-thinking expedition leader.

Though definitely an adult book, the many lovely color photographs give it browsing appeal. Read aloud, this book has force and power. It may well inspire interest and respect for those who risk their lives on the high peaks, and it may even create a climate of understanding.

Cobb, Sue. *The Edge of Everest: A Woman Challenges the Mountain.* Harrisburg, PA: Stackpole Books, 1989. $16.95. 214p. ISBN 0-8117-1681-3.

The perils of climbing the world's highest mountain, or of climbing any tall peak, may be as much in the psyche as in the physical realm of frostbite and altitude sickness. Certainly the physical realm affects the mental, and medical science can probably even chart the dynamic; but the fact remains that at times the flesh may be more willing than the spirit. More than one mountaineer has had the experience of turning back even though physically capable of going on because his or her mind had reacted against the stress, danger, and loneliness.

When Courtney Skinner put together the Wyoming Centennial Everest Expedition, he wanted to show that ordinary people could do extraordinary things. One of the people he invited along was Sue Cobb, a 50-year-old attorney. This book is Cobb's chronicle of what was called The Cowboy Expedition. Between August and October 1988 Cobb was immersed in the attempt to climb Everest as a member of the summit team. Written in journal format, Cobb's book charts the ups and downs, the stresses and small triumphs, of the Cowboys' ultimately unsuccessful Everest bid in a personal, at times wrenching, manner. Only the most advanced middle schoolers will read through this book, but it is an excellent teacher and librarian resource. The descriptions of the effects of altitude sickness, hypothermia, and cerebral edema are riveting, as is the examination of the mental state that accompanies these ills. For booktalking or discussion-starting, this book excerpts beautifully and is sure to hold students' attention.

Gaffney, Timothy R. *Edmund Hillary: First to Climb Mt. Everest.* New York: Children's Press, 1990. $23.93. 128p. index. bibliography. glossary. ISBN 0-516-03052-3.

Edmund Hillary, born in Aukland, New Zealand, on July 20, 1919, developed no interest at all in climbing until he was 20. It quickly became a passion and, over the next 12 years, he tackled increasingly challenging peaks until, in 1953, he and Tenzing Norgay, a Nepalese Sherpa, attained the top of the world's highest peak.

Factual but chatty, the brief biography details several of Hillary's most demanding expeditions, looks at his family life, and brings readers up to date on Hillary's current job as ambassador from New Zealand to India and Nepal. The profile is sunny and easy to read, presenting a picture of a man who is as much altruist as mountaineer.

This solid report source is accurate and factual and enhanced by a good index and a bibliography consisting mostly of Hillary's works. The glossary is brief and its definitions uneven in quality. Copious use of black-and-white and color photographs portray both the beauty and the danger of mountaineering. Hillary's debonair public image is denied by a picture taken shortly after his 1953 descent from Everest. He looks haggard and worn, living evidence that climbing at altitude is death defying. Even if the text doesn't ask it, the visual evidence raises a question about the human cost of such endeavor.

Gardner, Steve. *Why I Climb: Personal Insights of Top Climbers.* Harrisburg, PA: Stackpole Books, 1990. $12.95. 130p. bibliography. glossary. ISBN 0-8117-2321-6.

In this slim paperback, 29 top-notch climbers talk about why they feel the urge to scale the heights of our planet. Their insights vary in intensity. "Maybe I can express myself through climbing. I am different from any other person" (Naoe Sakshita). "There's no way I'm going to stop taking risks. Whatever confidence I have comes from striving . . . " (Yvon Chouinard). "I . . . happen to be a visual thinker, good with three dimensional space, which enables me to plan moves in advance. But the most important factor is desire. I love to climb" (Lynn Hall).

Beginning with a brief introductory essay on the motivation for climbing, the book follows with interviews that range from two to eight pages. The typeface, though clear, is very small, but the brevity of the essays compensates to some extent. An insert following page 68 provides the reader with black-and-white photos of 27 of the climbers. The bibliography is excellent, and the lack of index is partially compensated for by a decent table of contents.

Reading one of the shorter essays would provide a good booktalk strategy. Interested young mountaineers will pick the book up for pleasure reading and might even be encouraged to contemplate the psychological motivation for tasks about which they are passionate.

Fraser, Mary Ann. *On Top of the World: The Conquest of Mount Everest.* New York: Henry Holt, 1991. $14.95. unpaged. ISBN 0-8050-1578-7. **P.**

One may object to the word "conquest." The mountain, after all, is as it has always been, and doesn't, one presumes, give a fig for the miniscule humans crawling about on its face. Apart from this quibble, Fraser's book has some unique strengths.

In a picture book format with a brief, trenchant text that gives credit equally to Edmund Hillary and Tenzing Norgay, Fraser traces the last 1128 feet of climbing the pair did from Camp Nine at 27,900 feet to the 29,028 foot summit. With emphasis on teamwork and mutual respect, this book speaks not only to human tenacity but to the positive effects of group orchestration. Fraser's afterword reinforces this by discussing input from expeditions that had gone before.

Fraser's acrylic paintings vary in quality, from the very effective to the amateurish. In one of her pictures of Norgay and Hillary on the summit, the figures are so oddly foreshortened as to appear dwarfish. One thing these acrylics do is to set the stage for some of the really breathtaking photographic treatments, like Bonington's *Mountaineer* (see entry, above).

One can hardly imagine a better introduction to a unit on mountaineering than reading this aloud to students. It will raise questions, spark curiosity, and most definitely send students on to more in-depth works.

Herzog, Maurice. *Annapurna: First Conquest of an 8000 Meter Peak.* Translated by Nea Morin and Janet Adam Smith. New York: Dutton, 1967. $6.50. 314p. glossary. LC 52-12154. **Ad.**

Herzog's account of the first scaling of an 8,000-meter peak is by now a classic. Though successful in attaining the summit, a number of mishaps during the descent left the two summiters permanently maimed. Herzog was, as he noted toward the end of the march out from Annapurna, "to be spared nothing." Climbing technologies in 1950 were much less sophisticated than they are at present, and this book shows the ghastly shape of Herzog's hands and feet after the descent.

The translation from the French is lively and immediate, and although the book is quite long, the chapters are fairly short. Over all, the book has read-aloud potential and could perhaps be read to a class over a period of eight weeks if read on a daily basis. The narrative is gripping enough to sustain interest and will serve to raise questions. Certainly Herzog reached the summit, but in so doing lost fingers, toes, and health. One must ask whether it was worth it.

Numerous black-and-white diagrams, photos, and maps extend the text and give depth to the explanations. Dictated in large part by Herzog as he lay, nearly a year later, in the American Hospital at Neuilly, France, attempting to recover from having challenged "nature at her most pitiless," this book is an enduring testimonial to human suffering. Interest reading both for individual and group situations, *Annapurna* should spark both discussion and debate.

Krakauer, Jon. *Eiger Dreams: Ventures Among Men and Mountains.* New York: Lyons & Burford, 1990. $17.95. 186p. ISBN 1-55821-057-1.

> When I lay down to sleep I was overcome by a soul-wrenching loneliness. I'd never felt so alone, ever.
>
> That night I had troubled dreams, of cops and vampires and a gangland-style execution. I heard someone whisper, 'He's in there. As soon as he comes out, waste him.' I sat bolt upright and opened by eyes. The sun was about to rise. The entire sky was scarlet. It was still clear, but . . .a dark line was visible just above the horizon. I pulled on my boots and hurriedly strapped on my crampons. Five minutes after waking up, I was front-pointing away from the bivouac" (p. 182-83).

When he was 23, Jon Krakauer decided to climb The Devil's Thumb, a peak that rises out of the Stikine Icecap near the Alaska-British Columbia border. He was young enough to believe in his own immortality, and surprised when he nearly lost his life in this quixotic solo gesture—one which was ultimately successful. Each of the 12 essays in this book is equally riveting, whether it be a look at Chamonix, the climbers' Alpine Mecca, the horrors of being tentbound, canyoneering, or the tragic 1986 climbs of K2.

Krakauer's style is spare, wry, and humorous by turns. He is one of the more introspective and psychologically revealing mountaineering writers, rivaling (if not topping) Reinhold Messner (see entry, below). His examination of mountaineering as a sport penetrates to the moral/ethical levels: "It is natural in any sport to seek ever-greater challenges; what is to be made of a sport in which to do so means taking ever-greater risks? Should a civilized society continue to condone, much less celebrate, an activity in which there appears to be a growing acceptance of death as a likely outcome?" Thought-provoking and gripping, this book is ideal for interest reading, starting class discussions, or booktalking.

Long, John. *How to Rock Climb!* Evergreen, CO: Chockstone Press, 1989. $9.95. 160p. glossary. ISBN 0-934641-20-X.

Probably no one has just hauled off and climbed Mt. Everest without some kind of background in arduous climbing. A young person reading stirring first-person accounts of climbing endeavors like Herzog's *Annapurna* (see above) or Messner's *Solo: Nanga Parbat* (see below) may well be inspired to pack his or her bags and head for the nearest big mountain. A measured look at the situation should, however, point out a few problems with skills (or the lack thereof) in scaling sheer rock faces and hazardous trails. And what if you can't climb a rope? Where do you go for information?

John Long, an experienced climber, has provided a detailed primer on the sport of rock climbing. Background on the sport is the subject of the first chapter. Following chapters deal with climbing skills, protection systems, leading, getting down, training, and climbing and staying alive. Equipment and injury protection are discussed in detail. Long makes no bones about the perils of the sport, but gives sound advice for minimizing risks while enjoying the challenge and exhilaration of clawing up a sheer rock face.

The book contains numerous photographs, drawings, and diagrams illustrating everything from movement patterns to handholds, equipment to taping for injury protection, rope techniques to belaying. The prose is clear and concise without being dry, though a bit more anecdotal material would have been an enhancement. The lack of an index is a real problem. The chapter titles are general and most chapters contain a great deal more information than their labelling indicates. These findings reduce accessibility and make quick answers virtually impossible without a thorough knowledge of the text. Nonetheless, this book is a good reference for young would-be climbers as long as they realize that you can't just read this and hit the slopes. A good teacher remains a necessity.

Messner, Reinhold. *Everest: Expedition to the Ultimate.* New York: Oxford, 1979. $16.95. 253p. ISBN 0-19-520135-3. **Ad.**

"Sometimes I am able to keep from my mind the possible consequences of this Everest expedition. Death is a subject one doesn't dwell upon." That's one form of intensity. "The banality of Base Camp conversation and the overall greyness of the surroundings combine to force me into my own thoughts . . . " That's another. Climbing in high places produces physical effects that produce emotional effects that may in turn produce spiritual effects. No one assesses himself as he moves through these changes more thoroughly than Reinhold Messner. This highly subjective book is about the first ascent of Everest "by fair means," i.e., without the use of oxygen tanks.

Messner's first-person account is riveting and personal, if at times a bit self-conscious. He is occasionally raw and always revealing, and he shows to perfection the deterioration of self-confident cockiness under extreme conditions. His style is unique and easily identifiable, for he has a singular and authoritative voice. Strong in his opinions and set in his viewpoint, Messner's strength as an observer is impeccable and his affection for the Himalayan area and people is a shining source of warmth.

Beginning with accounts of previous attempts to climb Everest oxygen-free, Messner then gives his account of his ascent of Everest with Peter Habeler. The book concludes with a history of Everest climbs. Black-and-white and glorious color photos, as well as detailed route maps, add immediacy to the text.

While this book could certainly be used as a report source given the amount of information and excellent indexing, it can be used to much better effect as interest reading or excerpted for reading aloud to spark interest or introduce a unit.

Messner, Reinhold. *Solo: Nanga Parbat.* New York: Oxford University Press, 1980. $19.95. 276p. ISBN 0-19-520916-5. **Ad.**

A climber's experience depends not only upon physical condition but upon mental state. When Reinhold Messner set out in 1978 to solo climb Nanga Parbat, a particularly nasty Himalayan peak, he was suffering from considerable emotional stress. He and his wife had decided to separate, and he was still mourning the death of his brother, Gunther, who had died eight years earlier on a previous expedition to Nanga. The mountain, a high ice desert, finally yielded to Messner.

The most startling thing about this account of a solo climb is the depth of psychic intensity that it reaches. Messner's self-examination is penetrating, and his descriptions of his mental and psychological state at altitude are extremely revealing. Few readers who have not climbed, and climbed high, know the torsions the mind goes through. Messner, a prodigious climber with incredible mountaineering sense, knows well, and tells about it well. An additional positive aspect of the books is its infusion with Messner's love of the Karakhorum and its people.

This complicated book with adult vocabulary and sense of abstraction will probably appeal only to advanced readers. Teachers should have it on hand, however, for what it says about the impulse to climb and about the obsessive nature of the urge to forge upward. Including color and black-and-white photos and excellent maps—one of them hand drawn with felt-tipped pens—this book is an excellent tool for both reference and enrichment. The last 30 pages give a history of exploration and ascent of Nanga's icy flanks.

Miller, Luree. *On Top of the World: Five Women Explorers in Tibet.* Seattle: The Mountaineers, 1984. $9.95. 222p. index. bibliography. ISBN 0-89886-097-0. **Ad.**

"What had I dared to dream . . . Into what mad adventure was I about to throw myself?" These questions, posed by Madame Alexandra David-Neal, refer to a more than 2,000-mile walk she intended to take from China to Lhasa in Tibet. In the West, we attribute risk-taking and high adventure to men. However, as this book so amply illustrates, women also engage in these kinds of pursuits. We just don't hear about them; and if we don't hear much about adventurous women now, how much less were they heard of or from at the turn of the century?

The five women profiled in this book—three British, one American, and one French—were all drawn to the roof of the earth, to Tibet. Fanny Bullock Workman, for example, was a staunch New England feminist who believed that women could equal and even excel men in arduous pursuits. Unlike her circumspect, corseted peers, Mrs. Workman accompanied her husband on journeys that were characterized by an intensely vigorous schedule of hikes and walks. Beginning her climbing in New Hampshire's White Mountains, she next tackled the Alps and finally trekked, drawn by the Himalayas and the mountains of the Karakhorum, to Tibet.

The book is divided into three sections, the first devoted to the three British adventurers, the second to Fanny Bullock Workman, and the third to Alexandra David-Neal, a Frenchwoman. The prose is direct and lively, proceeding in a conversational manner. As a result the portraits of these women are as natural and casual as unposed snapshots. The reading level is adult, but the subject matter is well suited to units that take into account women's contributions to history. Any of the five biographical portraits could be used as report sources, especially given the access provided by the table of contents and index. The book could also be used as read-aloud material to aid in starting discussions about women's roles and expectations and how these have changed over the last 100 years. The book's use as an historical source is enhanced by the frequent inclusion of primary source material. Maps and black-and-white photographs of the subjects clarify and extend the text.

Osius, Alison. *Second Ascent: The Story of Hugh Herr.* Harrisburg, PA: Stackpole Books, 1991. $19.95. 240 p. ISBN 0-8117-1794-1.

Hugh Herr started climbing during childhood, and by his mid-teens had a reputation as a fearless, obsessive rock climber, one of the world's best. Then, in his seventeenth year, he and a friend were lost for four days on New Hampshire's Mount Washington during an unrelenting winter storm. By the time they were rescued the damage from frostbite was severe and irreversible. Both of Hugh's legs were amputated four inches below the knees. In addition to this blow, the death of a young, talented, poplar rescue volunteer during the course of the search for the boys left Hugh feeling guilt ridden.

Fighting incredible pain, depression, and the guilt created by Albert Dow's death, Hugh nonetheless resolved to climb again. Using the same determination that had driven him up sheer rock faces in defiance of both gravity and human limitations, Hugh trained himself to climb wearing artificial legs, and came to surpass his prior climbing feats. Additionally, Herr's interests and energies have been invested in the design of prosthetic devices that enable the disabled to climb. His abilities in this area are so pronounced that he has been accepted into a doctoral program at MIT in advanced prosthetic engineering.

Herr's story is both fascinating and inspiring, but Osious' telling bogs down occasionally. A climber herself, she spends an inordinate amount of time on definitions of climbing terms and the technical grades of various climbs. Detailed route descriptions pepper the text, and this slows the narrative. However, many portions of the book are readable and involving, and would be excellent as oral reading material. The black-and-white photos are almost artistic, and satisfy curiosity. One of the real strengths of the book is its power as a discussion starter. A double amputation should close some doors, but for Herr it opened some. Why is this? How do you turn a dead end into a new road? This book is good mountaineering writing, but is even better for philosophical and psychological issues.

Ridgeway, Rick. *The Last Step: The American Ascent of K2.* Seattle: The Mountaineers, c1980. $25.00. 301p. ISBN 0-89886-007-5.

K2, Pakistan's magnificent contribution to the rolls of the world's highest mountains, is not as high as Chomolungma, Mt. Everest, but is much harder to climb. Endowed with the worst weather in the Himalayas, it had defeated five expeditions and cost five American lives, when in 1978 a 14-person team succeeded in putting four American men on the summit. The given wisdom is that if one has not reached the summit of K2 in 45 days, he or she will not reach it at all. The 1978 American team belied this by spending 67 days above 18,000 feet, suffering the exigencies of high altitude living, among them the frustration and monotony of living in tiny, confining tents.

Targeted for advanced middle school readers, this book, containing journal entries from several of the men and women who attempted or reached the summit, gives a subjective, multi-faceted view of the climb. The focus is largely on the interpersonal experiences of the group, though the technical angles receive considerable space. A section of color pictures gives life to the grandeur of K2 and faces to the personalities of the team members. Route maps show the way the expedition members assaulted the summit. Despite an abrupt ending, this book is good interest reading. Various of the journal entries could be read aloud to point up the effects of altitude on climbers' minds and perceptions.

Roskelley, John. *Nanda Devi: The Tragic Expedition.* New York: Avon Books, 1987. $4.50. 213p. ISBN 0-380-70568-0.

Nanda Devi Unsoeld was the daughter of Willi Unsoeld, a world class climber. In 1976, an expedition involving 11 climbers was planned—an expedition to ascend Nanda Devi, "Goddess of Joy." At 25,645 feet, it was the third highest mountain in the Indian Himalayas. The expedition was organized by Devi Unsoeld who was driven to climb the mountain after which her father had named her. The Indo-American Nanda Devi Expedition was difficult from the start, a complex and not always harmonious mixture of personalities and methods. The dominating personality was, however, Devi Unsoeld's. Ill from the outset of the expedition, she continued to climb until, finally, she died of sudden complications of a hernia and bowel obstruction. She was 22.

In an involving, emotional first-person account of a divisive climb, John Roskelley presents his viewpoint on what happened. It is patently an attempt to make sense of the terrible sense of loss and the futility of death experienced on the soaring Himalayan peak. The chapters are short, vocabulary is simple, and the style engrossing. Excellent independent reading, this book will also booktalk well. It can serve as a discussion starter for such varied topics as the moral issues of climbing, health concerns, and safety precautions.

Roth, Arthur. *Eiger: Wall of Death.* New York: W.W. Norton, 1982. $15.95. 350p. index. ISBN 0-393-01496-7. **Ad.**

Everest may be the highest mountain in the world, but the north wall of the Eiger, towering over the Swiss village of Grindelwald, is arguably the most challenging climb. It was not climbed until 1938, and in the ensuing 54 years this difficult and dangerous face defeated hundreds and killed 44 of those who attempted to scale it. Yet mountaineers have continued to assault the face, to try to explore its unforgiving walls, despite the threats of sudden, ferocious storms and rock showers.

The 32 chapters of this book are packed with riveting narratives of climbers who have braved the north wall of the "Ogre," as it translates into English.

Consummate interest reading, Roth's prose is novelistic in its ability to hold the reader rapt. For those who enjoy mountaineering literature, the small typeface will prove no impediment. This book is also a solid report source, both for exploratory and general mountaineering topics and for a specific look at the Alpine peaks. A serviceable index gives accessibility and approximately 50 black-and-white photographs add to the usefulness and interest of the book. This book will read aloud well or booktalk beautifully because there are exciting and involving incidents to be found anywhere the book falls open.

Rowell, Galen. *Mountains of the Middle Kingdom: Exploring the High Peaks of China and Tibet.* San Francisco: Sierra Club Books, 1983. $40.00. 208p. index. chronology of exploration. bibliography. ISBN 0-87156-339-8.

In 1980, after 30 years of closure, the People's Republic of China opened parts of their mountain provinces to outsiders. Galen Rowell, a photojournalist and mountaineer, travelled through eight provinces, producing the most extensive exploration of Chinese mountain territory by any American since World War II.

This gorgeous pictorial volume is a thorough documentation of this territory in China's remote and mountainous west. The people, landscape, flora, and fauna all appear in vital, engrossing color photographs. The text recapitulates the journeys of past explorers, giving detailed coverage to Marco Polo, George Leigh-Mallory, Eric Shipton, Heinrich Harrer, and Terris Moore. Looking at the changes that have taken place in each region since the explorers mentioned above were there, and providing detailed portraits of the fiercely independent mountain tribes, Rowell's text gives insight into present day China. The prose style and presentation are adult, and for middle schoolers the visual aspects must carry the reader along.

A good index aids in location of specifics, and the table of contents in locating geographic areas. A 12-page chronology of exploration gives excellent capsule histories. Despite the good text, *Mountains of the Middle Kingdom* is best used as a kindler of interest and a browsing book. Most students who pick it up will find it hard to put down, and when they do, they may well want to read something more about the 8,000-meter peaks of the Himalayas.

Sherwonit, Bull. *To the Top of Denali: Climbing Adventures on North America's Highest Peak.* Seattle: Alaska Northwest Books, 1990. $10.95. 347p. index. bibliography. glossary. ISBN 0-88240-402-4. **Ad.**

"Rising 20,320 feet above sea level, Mount McKinley is a perfect symbol of Alaska. In a land of superlatives and extremes, this monumental granite monolith is the state's most dominating feature." It is not just a physical landscape it dominates, but a mental one as well. Since the first ascent in 1913, numerous climbers have attempted the summit, and by the end of 1989, almost 6,000 had actually reached the peak.

Sheronwit recounts the history of Denali's ascents in a chronological fashion, beginning with pioneering attempts during the late nineteenth century. In the following nine chapters, he details expeditions in 1910, 1913, 1932, 1950, 1961, 1967, and several solo ascents made during the winter. The final four chapters examine facilities for rescues, the problem posed by huge amounts of trash left on Mt. McKinley, guides, and the opinions of five people with close ties to Denali regarding the future of the mountain given the current climbing boom. Use of primary source material is frequent and is well incorporated into the contemporary essays.

Chapters generally range between 20 and 40 pages and are engrossing and readable. Sheronwit's style is journalistic without being overly brief, giving a clear picture of both the dangers and satisfactions of climbing in the wild. Issues are raised implicitly and Sheronwit's chapter on the Wilson Expedition of 1967 could certainly be compared to Krakauer's "A Bad Summer on K2" (see *Eiger Dreams*, above) for detailing disasters. There is potential for discussion here, both ethical/ moral issues and environmental concerns. A detailed index will help readers find passages they want to re-read, and a lengthy bibliography points the way toward a wealth of books that can help readers to explore North American's highest peak from the safety of home.

Stokes, Brummie. *Soldiers and Sherpas: A Taste for Adventure.* London: Michael Joseph, 1988. $24.95. 250p. ISBN 0-7181-3119-3. **Ad.**

Brummie Stokes was born to a working class family living in a suburb of Birmingham, England. He always had a penchant for difficult endeavors. A member of the SAS, an elite regiment of the British Army, Stokes is much decorated and undeniably a success. His first love, however, is mountaineering.

This biography covers Stokes's early years in Hampstead, then goes on to discuss his military career and growing fascination with climbing. The second half of the book is devoted entirely to accounts of his assaults on Everest and other high peaks, notably Mt. McKinley in Alaska. A self-taught writer, Stokes claims that he is "no Will Shakespeare," and he's right. However, his prose is fresh, direct, informed by a lively enthusiasm, and has a merit of its own. Beautiful color photographs of the majestic peaks Stokes has climbed grace the latter half of the book, while black-and-white photos extend the first half. Maps of the routes up mountains are helpful and relatively frequent.

This book is excellent interest reading for advanced middle schoolers, and might well be considered for classroom reading in excerpt form. Neither contemplative nor psychological, this book is excellent action fare.

Stuck, Hudson. *The Ascent of Denali: First Complete Ascent of Mt. McKinley, Highest Peak in North America.* Seattle: The Mountaineers, c1977. $12.95. 188p. ISBN 0-916890-58-9.

Mt. McKinley, whose true name, Denali, has been severed from it as surely as Tahoma has been from Mt. Rainier, challenges climbers with a long cold climb in Arctic conditions but gives, as its reward, a spectacular view. Numerous experienced climbers have been defeated by its inhospitable slopes, yet the first expedition to attain the summit contained two Eskimo boys under 15 and only one person with any knowledge of hard trekking over long distances in perilous conditions.

Originally published in 1914, this unrevised reissue retains the Edwardian prose that was standard at the time. While the narrative is stirring, this old fashioned flavor to the text will limit appeal to middle schoolers. However, it has some definite merits as a teaching tool. The book includes a facsimile of Walter Harper's diary of the climb and is an excellent first-person account of an unassisted climb. Reading this book aloud will not only catch students' attention, but may encourage them to keep reading independently. It can also serve as a potent discussion starter. How was the ascent of Denali different from contemporary ascents of Everest? How have climbing conventions changed since 1914? How has equipment evolved? Frequent black-and-white photos and maps extend the text and add interest.

Fiction

Murphy, Claire Rudolf. *To the Summit.* New York: Dutton/Lodestar, 1992. $15.00. 160p. ISBN 0-525-67383-0.

Sarah Janson is an athletic teenager with a competitive edge. She also has problems at home. Her parents have recently divorced, and her father has been cold and critical of her. When the chance comes for her to be one of the youngest people ever to attain the summit of Denali, she jumps at the chance. Perhaps in this way she can win back her father's approval.

Murphy creates a realistic character in Sarah, but her real forte is in describing the climb—the hard work, fatigue, triumph, and disappointment. While offering middle school readers a gripping survival story with a protagonist they can care about, this book also gives insight into the climber's frame of mind. Good interest reading, this book will also booktalk easily, and could be excerpted for reading aloud.

Ullman, James Ramsey. *Banner in the Sky.* New York: Lippincott, c1988. $12.89. 150p. ISBN 0-397-32141-4.

This fictionalization of the first ascent of Switzerland's Matterhorn tells the story of young Rudi Matt, who in 1865 at the age of 16 climbed the Citadel. Rudi, a small, slim boy, had always felt a call to the mountains. On the day when he leaves his dishwashing job at the Beau Site hotel to try to climb the Citadel, " . . . he could not have said [why he had run off on that particular day]. He had had to—that was all." This is a sentiment that will surely resound in the hearts of all climbers: The irresistible impulse to push onward and upward toward the clouds.

Ullman catches to perfection the sense of challenge and impulse, the dangers that attend mountaineering. An excellent fictional treatment, with fully realized characters and setting, this book is excellent interest reading. Although too contemplative and slow moving in the more narrative portions, this book may still work as a read-aloud, especially in programs for the gifted. In a booktalk it will provide a riveting introduction to such nonfiction books as Arthur Roth's *Eiger: Wall of Death* (see entry, above).

CHAPTER 9
Full Fathom Five: Underwater Exploration

Full fathom five thy father lies;/ Of his bones are coral made;/ Those are pearls that were his eyes./ Nothing of him that doth fade/ But doth suffer a sea-change/ Into something rich and strange.—William Shakespeare, *The Tempest*

"Full fathom five" would put one under the waves about 30 feet, a not inconsiderable way below the level of air and light in Shakespeare's era. In our day, when submarines and camera sleds can plummet 12,640 feet to investigate the remains of ocean liners, or submersibles can descend the Marianas Trench in the Pacific to 35,800 feet this may not seem like much. It demonstrates how much our technology has advanced since Shakespeare's time.

Of course, we know a great deal more about the oceans and lakes of our planet now than we did at that time, almost 400 years ago. Many fearsome mythological monsters are no longer feared and some very real ones—the "bends" and carnivorous sea creatures like sharks—are better understood. We can predict tides and currents accurately. We have the benefit of years of observation and the experience of those who went before, intrepid men and women determined to discover the secrets hidden under the waters.

In the early twentieth century, a young man in a curious get-up stood at the edge of a still reservoir on the Yucatan Peninsula of Mexico. He must have been hot in his regalia, a version of the closed-dress diving suit, vented by a valve, designed by Englishman Augustus Siebe in 1837. The round helmet had a small viewing panel at the front, and heavy air tanks were strapped on the diver's back. His intention was to dive to the bottom of the reservoir at the historic Chichen Itza site, one of the monumental ruins of the ancient Mayan civilization. Similar to Robert Ballard's use of underwater technology to investigate sunken ships like the Titanic, this was an instance in which underwater exploration and archaeology walked hand in hand. Lowered slowly, the diver descended about 60 feet to the bottom of the reservoir. Green algae festooned the sides and the still dark water closed over his head leaving only outwardly pooling ripples. Who knew what he might find on the bottom? The first problem he encountered was the lack of light. At 60 feet below the surface it was extremely dark. Unable to see, the diver simply grabbed a handful of silt, felt something hard in it, and jerked on the line connecting him to the surface. As he rose, the water went from black to green to yellow. Then with a burst he was out into the open. Unclasping his gloved hand, he saw through the dark silt something shine gold, green, white. Carefully, he rinsed the muck away. There sitting in the light of the Central American afternoon were two small figures, one of jade and one of gold. The third item was a bone, a bone that proved to be one of the spinal links from a young girl. Unsettling as this was, the dive had provided the archaeologists with information that encouraged them to dredge the reservoir. At its bottom, they found literally hundreds of skeletons of teenaged girls. At last they were able to reconstruct the use of the pool. Each year, they deduced, the loveliest young girl in the area was taken, dressed in white, decked with jewelry, and, with great ceremony, thrown into the water to be the bride of the rain god, thus ensuring a bountiful harvest. From the courage of one young man, willing to drop to the depths of an ancient reservoir, part of the underpinning of the culture of a Precolumbian people's culture was resurrected.

The interests that send people diving are not always scholarly. Some underwater exploration is undertaken for commercial reasons by professional treasure hunters. Perhaps the best known contemporary member of that calling is Mel Fisher, the man who doggedly searched the area surrounding the Florida Keys until he located the wreck of *Nuestra Senora de Atocha*, a seventeenth-century Spanish warship.

On September 4, 1622, *Nuestra Senora de Atocha*, a handsome 550 ton three-masted galleon built only two years earlier set sail in a fleet of 28 ships from Havana, Cuba. It was a lively ship, bearing chickens and sea turtles, water, wine, and vegetables, as well as a cargo of gold and silver coins and ingots, tobacco, indigo, copper, and contraband rough-cut loose emeralds. There was human cargo, too. Forty-eight Spanish hidalgos (minor nobility) and their families crowded into the *Atocha's* cabins. There were also 82 soldiers, servants, slaves, and sailors. The manifest for the voyage lists 265 people.

These were all intrepid individuals, hoping and praying for the best. The weather in the Bahamas in September is unpredictable; it is the height of the hurricane season. Aside from the risks posed by the weather, there was the threat of pirates, who might well have chosen to attack such a treasure-laden ship despite its 60 cannon.

Two days out of Havana as the fleet neared the coast of Florida the sky darkened precipitously. The oily roll of the sea quickly became more and more violent. Sailors hurried to secure lines and hatches and reef sails against gale force winds. Within a short time, the fleet had been overtaken by a hurricane. As the decks of the *Atocha* were washed by waves, the wind drove it steadily toward a coral reef where it broke up and foundered. It's sister ship, the *Santa Margarita*, was also grounded on a shoal and sunk. A soldier sailing on the *Margarita*, Capitan De Lugo was later picked up by a Jamaican ship. Dazed and confused, he was distressed to learn that only 68 travelers from the *Margarita* were saved. Worse, only five had survived the sinking of the *Atocha*. In all, eight ships of the 28-ship fleet were lost with a grim human toll.

On his return to Havana, de Lugo found that the Cuban governor was anxious to salvage the wrecks. The Capitan therefore did his best to describe the positions of the *Margarita* and the *Atocha* when they broke up. Despite his first-hand testimony and the employment of numerous Indian and Mexican divers, very little was recovered. The divers, who could remain underwater only until their held breath gave out, were unable to bring any appreciable amount of the treasure to the surface. Then in 1626, an inventor named Francisco Melian approached the Spanish king, Felipe IV, with a plan for using a cast bronze diving bell to lower two divers to the floor of the ocean. The scheme succeeded, and the *Santa Margarita* was located. Numerous artifacts were pulled up from that ship, but the *Atocha* evaded any search efforts. Feeling that his job ended with the location of the *Margarita*, Melian wrote a detailed report on the recovery operation which he sent to Felipe IV, who apparently had lost interest in the salvage job. "For more than three hundred years, the scroll remained in the king's library in Spain, until Eugene Lyon [an historian working with treasure hunter Mel Fisher] eased the crumbling parchment out of its leather casing" (O'Bryne-Pelham and Balcer, 1989, p. 29).

In the late 1960s, Mel Fisher began exploring the waters near the Florida Keys in an attempt to find the wreck of the *Atocha*. Following a number of false leads, he spent some time exploring around the wrong Key when Eugene Lyon returned from Spain with a copy of Melian's letter. It pointed Fisher to a more southerly Key, and a later letter, forwarded by a librarian in Seville who remembered Lyon's interest, led them to the west side of the Key, one of the small islands in the Marquesas Keys. Nonetheless, the search continued fruitless for the next several years, and this despite the use of some instruments which were technologically superior to any previously used in treasure hunting.

The magnetometer was one. This instrument, towed behind a salvage vehicle, detects iron underwater and notifies the operator of any iron it passes over. Since old galleons contained considerable iron, the magnetometer is invaluable for locating the hulls of such vessels. In the way of all inanimate objects, the instrument is, however, completely indiscriminate. "Many times, the magnetometer fooled the divers. On one dive, two explorers descended to the sea bottom, only to find empty bombshells littering the barren seascape" (O'Bryne-Pelham and Balcer, 1989, p. 34). They had wandered into an old army test site.

Another tool that Fisher employed was called the "mailbox" and was used to deal with the problem of the shifting sands of the sea floor. One reason that the *Atocha* was so difficult to locate was that the sea currents and tides shifted the sands, covering the vessel. The mailbox is "a huge, elbow-shaped tube [that] fits over the propeller [of the salvage boat], forcing the water downward while the boat is anchored with engines running. The jets of water . . . swirl away tons of sand." (O'Bryne-Pelham and Balcer, 1989, p. 35). The boat carrying the mailbox, which is huge, has to be sturdy. Consequently, Fisher bought two tugboats to aid in the search.

The mailbox was responsible for the first find of any consequence. In the spring of 1973, the mailbox on one of the tugs uncovered hundreds of gold coins. A month later, the mailbox uncovered an astrolabe, a navigational tool used in the seventeenth century. That summer, Kane Fisher, one of Mel Fisher's sons, found the first certain evidence that they were close to the remains of the *Atocha*. Diving in the area where the gold coins were found, he noticed a dark colored loaf-like shape. He poked at it, then attempted to lift it, but it was too heavy. Returning to the surface, he commandeered a rope, and the ingot, for such it proved to be, was hauled to the surface. The ingot was not only pure silver, but was engraved. Upon its surface were both the symbol of the merchant who shipped it and the Roman numerals that translated to 4584, an identification number.

Eugene Lyon searched through all the documents he had pertaining to the voyage. These included a list of all the items shipped on the ill-fated vessel. After several days of wading through archaic lettering, he announced that the ingot had indeed been one loaded onto the *Atocha*. So the crew was close to the ship, but where was the vessel itself? Ghostlike, it persisted in evading them. It would take more than technology to help with the discovery. It would take an archaeologist.

With the opening of the diving season of 1975, Duncan Mathewson was on staff. Providing a calm, methodical influence, he helped the crew apply archaeological methods to their search by mapping the locations of the artifacts they had found. This systematic approach yielded up a clear trail which "stretched from a galleon anchor, to a pile of silver coins, to an astrolabe, and on to a small stack of silver ingots" (O'Bryne-Pelham and Balcer, 1989, p. 43). The picture it presented was puzzling, as was the fact that the 60 cannon the *Atocha* had carried were missing. Mathewson became convinced that the wreck lay in deeper water.

In July, Dirk Fisher, another of Fisher's sons, had moved one of the salvage tugs to the Hawk Channel, south of where they had been searching previously. Noticing that the ship had drifted in the night, he dived to check the anchor line. He swam in a smooth sweep down the line, but when he reached the bottom he stopped in astonishment. Resting on the rocky bottom were five cannons, the first indication of the true resting place of the vessel for which they had been searching for seven years. It was, however, an indication only, for again the vagaries of time and tide had hidden the true resting place of *Nuestra Senora de Atocha*.

The mapping continued until 1980. That spring a submerged vessel was located, but it was not the *Atocha*. Fisher's organization had found the *Santa Margarita*. The cash return from the salvage of the *Margarita* was impressive: $20 million dollars. It enabled Fisher's company to continue to search for the *Atocha*, even as it rekindled their enthusiasm for the project. Encouragement was a necessity. Five more years of meticulous mapping, inch-by-inch searching, and hoping passed before the *Atocha* was found at last.

A combination of the magnetometer and sonar confirmed an unusual formation on the floor of the ocean. It was July 20, 1985, and divers, heading to the bottom to investigate found strange hills of stones. What could they be? Ballast, it turned out, a five-foot wall of ballast. It marked the location of the *Atocha*, which would at last be excavated using the archaeological method of gridding it off. Plastic grids were laid over the sea floor and each small area was painstakingly searched. Artifacts were raised, preserved, and made ready for display. Much of the treasure is on display in museums, a bit of living history. As a result of Fisher's 17-year search, we understand a great deal more about life in the seventeenth century, the effects of undersea currents in shifting submerged items, and the degree of persever-ance it may take to make a discovery.

Treasure hunting and archaeological interests provide two motiva-tions for searching the seas, but there are others. Sylvia Earle, an underwater biologist whose interest in going far below the surface of the ocean has earned her the title "Her Royal Deepness," is motivated by the need to study and understand the animal life of the deep seas. Her concern is more than just that of an interested biologist. She is alarmed about the condition of the oceans and believes that there is an urgent need need for us to be aware of the life requirements of the creatures that live in them.

> The critters Sylvia met underwater had made her increasingly aware of the uniqueness of the planet Earth and its declining condition . . . She often warned of man's harm to the oceans—pollution, overfishing, overbuilding in coastal areas—reminding people of the need to take care of the planet. 'Each plant and animal, no matter how small, is somehow important to the Earth's whole system,' she would say (Conley, 1991).

Her quest is not to find out things about the human world hidden by the ocean, but to find out about how humans fit in with the context of life that breeds in the salty soup from which life first emerged.

Whether their reasons are biological, archaeological, military, or com-mercial, it is certain that men and women will move deeper into the ocean depths in search of answers to their questions. Enhanced technology improves our chances of performing difficult research—or plain searches—safely, and without disrupting the natural life of the oceans. It may well help us to see just how we fit into the interconnected web of life that comprises our world. Understanding our place in the larger environmental picture will help us investigate without despoiling, satisfying the need to find out without harming our fragile planet.

References

Conley, Andrea. (1991). *Window on the Deep: The Adventures of Underwater Explorer Sylvia Earle*. New York : Watts.

O'Bryne-Pelham, Fran and Bernadette Balcer. (1989). *The Search for the Atocha Treasure*. Minneapolis: Dillon.

ANNOTATED BIBLIOGRAPHY

Nonfiction

Ballard, Robert D. *Exploring the Titanic*. New York: Scholastic, 1988. $14.95. 64p. bibliography. timeline. glossary. ISBN 0-590-41953-6.

Ballard's nearly classic condensed edition of his adult work on the discovery of the wreck of the *Titanic* may need no introduction. It is sufficient to say that this beautifully formatted, absorbingly written book also maintains high illustrative and informational standards. It will give students an insight into both maritime tragedy and exploration.

Beginning with two attention-grabbing pictures of the *Titanic* as she sank and the hull as it looked when discovered 74 years later, the book then covers Ballard's background and his conception of the search for the sunken liner. Chapters 2 and 3 look at the ship's construction, its sinking, and the rescue of its survivors by the *Carpathia*. Chapters 4 and 5 move into present time, discussing the discovery and exploration of the sunken ship. Chapter 6 explains what caused the ship to sink. An epilogue, filling readers in on the fate of some of the survivors of the *Titanic* disaster, is followed by an adequate glossary, a timeline of the *Titanic* from planning state to its certification as an international memorial in 1987, and a brief bibliography. The information given, whether technical or personal, fully satiates curiosity. The paintings and photos are wonderful, full of flair and drama. The diagrams are worthy of note; they are exceptionally clear and make fine use of analogies to give the data relevance and accessibility to students.

This book is excellent introductory, report, browsing, or interest reading fare, and is likely to be available in most school libraries.

Ballard, Robert D. and Rick Archbold. *The Discovery of the Bismarck.* New York: Warner/Madison Press, 1990. $35.00. 231p. index. ISBN 0-446-51386-5.

This much expanded and prior version of *Exploring the Bismarck* (see entry, below), has many more pictures and a more complex, adult text. The information presented is much the same as that in the shorter version and, given the relative prices, the latter will be better suited for middle schoolers. However, for those seeking greater detail, this may be the preferred title.

Ballard, Robert D. and Rick Archbold. *Exploring the Bismarck.* New York: Scholastic/Madison Press, 1990. $15.95. 64p. glossary. bibliography. ISBN 0-590-44268-6.

Written and illustrated along the same lines as *Exploring the Titanic* (see entry, above), this book provides a riveting look at the exploration of the German battleship, *Bismarck*. Using eyewitness accounts of four young sailors who voyaged on the *Bismarck* and survived her sinking, the prose is immediate and enthralling.

Six brief chapters cover the search for the *Bismarck*, then flash back to the history of the boat and her final battle. The next two chapters cover the discovery and exploration of the wreck. Beautifully and intriguingly illustrated with period and contemporary photographs, charts, clear maps, and lovely oil paintings by a number of artists, this book not only presents state-of-the-art underwater exploratory techniques, but tells a riveting story. There is easily enough information for a report, though the fictionalization diminishes credibility a bit.

The lack of an index seriously hampers access. The table of contents gives insufficient guidance. The glossary is succinct and excellent; the bibliography is strictly incidental. However, this book will virtually sell itself, both through pictures and narrative.

Ballard, Robert D. and Rick Archbold. *The Lost Wreck of the Isis.* New York: Scholastic, 1990. $15.95. 64p. bibliography. glossary. ISBN 0-590-43852-2.

Using the same format that worked to such good advantage in his *Exploring the Titanic* (see entry, above), Ballard recounts the discovery of the fourth century A. D. wreck of a Roman ship, which sank in the Mediterranean. Chapters alternate between the story of Ballard's crew's discovery and exploration of the *Isis,* and a fictional account of her sinking. The similarity to the *Titanic* book may seem stultifying to adult readers, but the familiarity will be reassuring to younger readers.

The fictional approach lacks some of the immediacy of the eyewitness accounts of the Titanic's sinking, and though the photographic illustrations are good, only three of the paintings are by the very talented Ken Marschall. His oils exhibit his splendid ability with light and stormy seas, but Wesley Lowe's water-colors, which illustrate most of the fourth-century story, are washed out, uninspired, and look as if they came from a textbook.

Ballard's writing is engaging and the browsing aspects of the book make it an excellent supplemental or resource tool. There is enough information for reports, though there is no index. The mystery element can be a plus for teaching if the story is read in segments. The job of predicting the location of the ship may be left to the students. This book's best use is as an attractive reinforcing material for units on history, science, or social science.

Blos, Joan W. *The Heroine of the Titanic.* Illustrated by Tennessee Dixon. New York: Morrow, 1991. $14.95. unpaged. ISBN 0-688-07547-9. **P.**

The sinking of the *Titanic* was a disaster probably best captured in Ken Marschall's photographic oils (see Robert Ballard's, *Exploring the Titanic,* above) or in the bathos of celluloid treatments like "A Night to Remember." The visual media often serve when verbal expression proves inadequate. This book gives a visual treatment to one of the unforgettably and indelibly American characters to emerge from that night in the North Atlantic. Mrs. J.J. Brown of Leadville, Colorado, was a former frontier music hall girl who gamely entertained and comforted a lifeboat full of grief-stricken and panicky survivors during that long night before the *Carpathia* picked them up. Best known as "The Unsinkable Molly Brown," Mrs. Brown has come down to us in musical form, but with little known of her life before of after her starring role in one or the *Titanic* lifeboats.

Joan Blos's picture book fills in some of the gaps, but its real utility is in the zippy introductory function it has for units on underwater exploration. Picture books do work with middle schoolers, and Tennessee Dixon's large, loose water-color paintings, though occasionally off perspective, do invite viewing and give a clear image of feisty, red-headed Molly. The text in poetry and prose is direct and energetic, just the sort of thing to read aloud. This sprightly story is a natural lead-in to Ballard's books on the *Titanic,* or even to the *Atocha* salvage and environmental explorations.

Conley, Andrea. *Window on the Deep: The Adventures of Underwater Explorer Sylvia Earle.* New York: Watts, 1991. $13.95. 41p. index. bibliography. ISBN 0-531-11119-9.

Few people have heard of Sylvia Earle, but those who have have know her as "Her Royal Deepness." Earle is concerned with many things involving the ocean—its animal life, its ecology, its future as humans encroach upon it. However, her real interest is in exploring the deep sea. Using first a stiff-shelled diving suit called a Jim Suit and then a submersible called Deep Rover, Earle has plunged to record depths to look at the flora and fauna of the deep sea.

Four brief pictorial chapters, illustrated with beautiful deep-hued photographs, ably impart a wealth of information on underwater exploration, both its history and the current state of the art. This book would be a fine report source, excellent browsing material, or a good read-aloud introduction to deep sea exploration and research. With its index and fairly current bibliography, this New England Aquarium book is perfect supplemental material for units on the environment, marine biology, or investigation of life far beneath the waves.

Gennings, Sara. *The "Atocha" Treasure.* Photographs by Pat Clynet. Vero Beach, FL: Rourke, 1988. $11.89. 31p. glossary. index. ISBN 0-86592-874-6.

Rawlinson, Jonathan. *Discovering the "Titanic."* Vero Beach, FL: Rourke, 1988. $11.89. 31p. glossary. index. ISBN 0-86592-873-8.

————. *From Space to the Seabed.* Vero Beach, FL: Rourke, 1988. $11.89. 31p. glossary. index. ISBN 0-86592-872-X.

These three short books have the look of browsing material but pack enough information to act as report sources. Each volume is part of The Great Adventure Series, and each is identically formatted. The text, divided into six chapters of three to six pages, is set in a small, yet readable font and illustrated by photographs. The one-page glossaries and indices are rudimentary. Most glossary terms are sketchily defined and oddly selected. *The "Atocha" Treasure,* for example, defines "airlift," and "manifest" but not "artifact," or "galleon." Nonetheless, these books are approachable and informative.

The "Atocha" Treasure begins with the first discovery of artifacts and treasure from a Spanish galleon, *Nuestra Senora de Atocha,* in June 1971. The five chapters that follow cover the ship's final voyage and sinking in September 1622; the salvage operation, including the technology involved; the final location of the galleon's resting place in July 1973; the location of the *Atocha's* sister vessel, the *Santa Margarita,* in June 1980; and the final location of the *Atocha's* hull on July 20, 1985. The prose is concise, interesting, and informative, giving background on the technology and human persistence necessary to succeed in this undertaking.

If Rawlinson's *Discovering the "Titanic"* suffers in comparison to Ballard's *Exploring the Titanic* (see entry, above), it is still a valuable record of a remarkable discovery. Beginning with the search for the liner and a description of the techniques involved, the text then covers the building and appointments of the *Titanic,* its sinking, Ballard's dream of locating it, the discovery of the wreck 400 miles southeast of Newfoundland, and its exploration. It certainly poses no pictorial competition for Ballard's book, though the double-page spread of the "Alvin" being set into the water from the back of a research vessel is worth a second look. The prose, however, is lucidly and accessibly written in a lively style.

Scott Carpenter was the second astronaut to orbit the earth, shooting into orbit on May 24, 1962. In 1965, Carpenter set out to explore new environments in the other direction as an aquanaut on Sealab 2. A chapter of Carpenter's journey to space is followed by chapters on various types of vehicles used to explore the sea with a brief history of pre-Sealab exploration. The Sealab program, the journey of Sealab 1, Carpenter's experience of Sealab 2, life aboard Sealab 2, and the demise of the project are all covered. The inclusion of background material on diving and its attendant physical dangers is both informative and judicious.

All three books are excellent resources for student reports, interest reading, browsing, or unit support. They may also be used as introductory books for those who wish to go on to more detailed works.

Gibbons, Gail. *Sunken Treasure.* New York: Thomas Y. Crowell, 1988. $12.95. 32p. ISBN 0-690-04734-7. **P.**

Targeted for an elementary age range, Gibbon's pictorial treatment of the search for the Spanish galleon *Nuestra Senora de Atocha* has applications for middle school curricula. Simple text and large, clear pictures offer a schematic approach to the salvage operation. For example, a close-up map of the Florida Keys with the site of the ship's sinking and the direction of the hurricane that sank it clarify the location of and reasons for the galleon's demise.

The author covers Mel Fisher's 20-year search for the wreck in the same visual manner, with all equipment illustrated, labelled, and explained. Sections of the book record salvaging, restoration and preservation, cataloging, and distribution. A final five pages are devoted to other famous ship salvages—the raising of the *Mary Rose*, the *Vasa*, the *Shydah*, and the *Titanic*. A brief history of diving is also given. If used as a class introduction, students will not be put off by the picture book format and will find their understanding of how archaeological methods apply to undersea salvages deepened. The clear black-line watercolors lend themselves to reproduction and might well be used as information sheets.

Johnson, Rebecca L. *Diving into Darkness: A Submersible Explores the Sea.* New York: Lerner, 1989. $16.95. 72p. index. glossary. ISBN 0-8225-1587-3.

What is it really like deep below the surface of the sea, in inky blackness? What kinds of creatures life there? How do we know? In straightforward, if slightly dry, text, Rebecca Johnson fills readers in.

The book covers historical attempts to explore the sea bed, from the efforts of Alexander the Great to the diving bell and bathysphere. Consideration is then given to Edwin Link's considerable contributions to undersea technology. Further chapters discuss the Harbor Branch Oeanographic Institution and its prototype submersible, and a journey to the ocean floor in the Johnson-Sea Link II.

The prose answers many questions about ocean life and the workings of submersibles. With the text set in double columns, it bears an unfortunate resemblance to an encyclopedia article, though the clean typeface mitigates that impression. Frequent color photos give this rather small book considerable browsing appeal, but it cannot match Andrea Conley's *Window on the Deep* (see entry, above) for photographic excellence. The index and glossary are both serviceable. This excellent report source is small and slim and may have to be sold to middle schoolers.

McGovern, Ann. *Down Under, Down Under.* Photographs by Jim and Martin Scheiner and the author. New York: Macmillan, 1989. $14.95. 48p. index. ISBN 0-02-765770-1. **ER.**

Set in the waters around the Great Barrier Reef of Australia, this chronicle of a young girl's scuba dive is a lovely pictorial introduction to a magical world.

The narrator, a 12-year-old junior certified diver, is spending 10 days on a dive boat and making as many as three dives a day. Among the topics discussed are the ecology of the Great Barrier Reef, life on a dive boat, and the technology of scuba. The color photographs are clear and well composed, and certainly show some amazing sights: fish from the very small to the very large, flatworms, shell-less snails called nudibrachs, sea snakes, and even the wreck of a ghost ship.

The text is in present tense and at an easy reading level. The book will take some promotion, and perhaps booktalking or reading aloud, to prevent middle schoolers from being put off by the juvenile format

Though too brief for reports, this book is informative as to the protocols of diving, the work of marine biologists, and the teeming life of the Great Barrier Reef. It provides stage setting for more detailed looks at underwater exploration, and does so in an attractive and accessible way.

Munson, Richard. *Cousteau: The Captain and His World.* New York: Morrow, 1989. $19.95. 316p. index. ISBN 0-688-07450-2. **Ad.**

Jaques-Yves Cousteau's name is a household word. A charismatic, multi-talented man, Cousteau is known as an environmentalist, inventor, and consummate showman. His output has been prodigious: television documentaries, almost 100 films, 80 books, and inventions that have helped revolutionize undersea exploration.

This adult biography covers all these facets in straightforward, if occasionally turgid prose. However, this unauthorized biography contains a great deal about Cousteau's personal life that tarnishes his zesty public image. Munson gives time to other oceanographers' allegations that Cousteau "focuses more on showmanship than science" and to ecologists' laments that he does not use his political clout to further ecological protection. Munson also avers that Cousteau's filming techniques involve considerable cruelty to the sea creatures he claims to be protecting.

Few middle schoolers will plow through all 11 chapters of this detailed biography. It is best used as a teacher resource or reference work for dipping into when information is needed on underwater photography, whales, environmental issues, or a host of other controversial items. The index is comprehensive and renders information easily accessible. In the hands of an imaginative teacher, this book could be a potential discussion starter and source for debate.

O'Bryne-Pelham, Fran and Bernadette Balcer. *The Search for the Atocha Treasure.* Minneapolis: Dillon Press, 1989. $12.95. 108p. index. bibliography. glossary. ISBN 0-87518-399-9.

This small book can tell the reader everything he or she wants to know about the salvage of the Spanish galleon *Nuestra Senora de Atocha,* which sank off the coast of Florida in 1622. Students can learn about the indefatigable Mel Fisher who, using a subscription method to finance his search, persisted for 17 years until he discovered and salvaged the wreck of the ship.

Giving a history of both the galleon and Fisher's salvage enterprise in six chapters, the authors weave a readable tale, integrating information about salvage, underwater archaeology, library research, and underwater technology. The style is chatty and readable, the type font large and clear, and the whole book handsomely enhanced by photographs and diagrams. The pictures of the fabulous treasure taken from the wreck should move this book right into students' hands. Good for interest reading, browsing, and reports, this book will give students information while engaging their imaginations. A workable index, glossary, and bibliography round out the volume.

Rayner, Ralph. *Undersea Technology.* New York: Bookwright, 1990. $11.40. 47p. bibliography. glossary. index. ISBN 0-531-18347-5.

When we think of undersea vehicles, we often call up Disneyesque images of Captain Nemo's "Nautilus" battling giant octopi. However, in the daylight world of the twentieth century, submersible vehicles come in all shapes and sizes and serve all kinds of purposes, from exploration to mining.

Rayner's brief pictorial text contains 19 double-page sections covering the technology used in underwater exploration, mining, or oil production. He gives equal time to descriptions of submarines, bathyscaphes, and other vehicles, and finishes with a discussion of the protection of the undersea environment. Most spreads contain a diagram of the form of technology being focused on and at least one clear color photograph. Echo sounders, seismic surveys, a Jim Suit (for deep water diving), buoyancy control, and hydroplanes are all clearly diagrammed in full color, much enhancing the explanations given in the text. The prose, though generally clear and well composed, is rather dry. The illustrations carry the text, which lacks anecdotal material to liven it up.

Though there is not enough information on any one item for a report, there is enough for a general treatment of the technology used in underwater exploration. The book functions best as a reference source, giving quick, brief, and attractively packaged information on a wide range of equipment. The table of contents gives better access than the index, which is poorly cross-referenced. The bibliography, though brief, is fairly current, and the glossary serviceable. This information rich book is a good browsing or booktalking source with potential for use as reference material.

Swanson, June. *David Bushnell and His Turtle.* Illustrated by Mike Eagle. New York: Athenuem, 1991. $13.95. 40p. bibliography. ISBN 0-689-31628-3. **ER.**

We think of the submarine as a relatively modern development, first conceived of by Jules Verne in *Twenty-Thousand Leagues Under the Sea* with Captain Nemo and the *Nautilus.* The actual *Nautilus* was built in the late 1780s by Robert Fulton, who has generally been credited with the invention of the submarine. However, his *Nautilus* was in fact predated by the *Turtle,* a hand-grenade-shaped craft built in 1777 by David Bushnell, the eldest son of a Vermont farmer.

This brief biography of David Bushnell and the history of his *Turtle* raises almost as many questions as it answers. It answers questions about the construction and operation of Bushnell's craft; the explanations, nicely extended by Eagle's pen-and-ink and wash drawings, are clear and understandable. One could almost generate a set of plans for a homemade submarine using the information given. However, the most interesting aspect of the book is the figure of Bushnell himself. Destined to be a farmer, Bushnell had other plans. When he inherited the family farm, he sold it and sent himself to Yale, where he began (for reasons never explained in the text) to experiment with detonating gunpowder under water. Once Bushnell had created a few huge explosions, he became obsessed with the idea of attaching one of these underwater mines to British ships, thus helping the Americans to win the Revolutionary War. The Turtle was the mechanism to achieve this, and while it worked for attaching grenades, it was never successful in detonating a single ship. Following the failure of the *Turtle* to achieve its end, Bushnell retired under an alias to a teaching position at the University of Georgia. The book says that we don't know why, and that's the truth. The text leaves readers wondering.

This book is written at an extremely basic reading level, and may look too babyish for middle schoolers to pick up. A brief discussion on a teacher's or librarian's part will stimulate interest and may well have children looking the book over. There is enough material here for a report. An adult bibliography and a reasonable amount of interesting material on the beginning of underwater exploration give the book potential for stimulating interest in more involved works.

Weiss, Harvey. *Submarines and Other Underwater Craft.* New York: T.Y. Crowell, 1990. $12.95. 64p. index. ISBN 0-690-04761-4. **ER.**

Divided into 20 sections, varying in length from one to four pages, this introductory title covers the workings of submarines, the history of submersible vehicles, uses of submarines in warfare and for treasure hunting, and life aboard a submersible. The prose is easy to understand, gracefully putting terms like "collapse depth" and "bathysphere" into comprehensible English. Technology and history are given the same conversational approach.

The open format is interspersed frequently with black-and-white photographs and ink wash cartoon drawings. The latter are heavily captioned, imparting information which augments the text while injecting a bit of humor. Despite the easy-to-read text, copious illustrations, and attractive dust jacket, this book is not likely to be picked up as pleasure reading except by the select few who are submarine buffs. Parts of the book could be read aloud to incite interest in the subject—the section on "Disasters" for example—but this book is best used as a report source. Both index and contents give ready access to information, and the book does provide a source of supporting data, technical and historical, for other books like Ballard's *Exploring the Titanic* and O'Bryne-Pelham and Balcer's *The Search for the Atocha Treasure* (see entries for both, above). This volume is especially recommended for younger middle school students, competent readers put off by long books, or those needing high interest, pictorial books.

CHAPTER 10

Expanding Boundaries in a Receding Universe: The Exploration of Space

The Space Age began in 1957 with Sputnik. The first man into space was Yuri Gagarin, the first woman Valentina Tereshkova, the first space walker Aleksei Leonov. While we Americans debate the design details of Freedom, the space station we hope to put up, the Soviets make improvements to Mir, orbiting since 1986, not to mention a series of Salyut stations before that. The Soviet Union is a space-faring nation second to none....—Michael Collins, *Mission to Mars**

I was six years old when Sputnik was launched one crisp October morning in 1957. I don't remember much about it except that, being raised in Orange County in southern California, there was a bit more than the usual amount of talk about the "Communist threat." Yet what had happened, what we were watching when we looked for Sputnik to streak by in the night sky like some kind of unusually regular shooting star, was the dawn of the Space Age. Whether for economic or military reasons, both strong motivating factors, or for the satisfaction of finding new territories, men and women were beginning to reach out into the sky, expanding beyond the earthbound

---

*Collins, Michael. (1990). *Mission to Mars*. New York: Grove Weidenfeld.

horizon into uncharted and dangerous territory. In some respects this is no different from what pioneers have done for millennia. In other ways, for example, the vast amounts of money invested in any spaceward venture, it is a complete apotheosis. We have looked at the stars for centuries, speculated upon them, fantasized about what they might be like. But with Sputnik, the Soviet cosmonauts made a leap similar to that made by Columbus. They not only contemplated reaching into space, they made and then executed concrete plans to do so.

We won't ever know what the early humans thought about the stars. Given the fact that theirs was a life that was "brutish and short," we must assume their concerns to have been largely earthbound. The unidentified noise in the brush, the unusually heavy snowfall that threatened life, the pain of a childbirth, all these would certainly have had day-to-day primacy.

As technological advances made life easier and people had more time to observe, they began to develop schemes to explain their surroundings. The sun, moon, and stars all became characters in functionally universal sets of myths attempting to explain their locations and their power. In the sixth century B.C., the Greeks began to look at the motions of the heavenly bodies and created charts and tables and philosophical explanations for these changes in position. It was the beginning of the sort of methodical investigation of the cosmos that would lead not only to the understanding of the microscopic realm of subatomic particles but to the human reach into space.

Science fiction always runs ahead of science fact, and is often uncannily predictive. Writing in the first century A.D., the Greek philosopher Lucian of Somosata produced moralistic tales of heroes who got from the Earth to the moon with the help of whirlwinds and Icarus-like wings. Both Ludovico Ariosto, an Italian living in the sixteenth century, and the brilliant seventeenth-century astronomer and physicist, Johannes Kepler, wrote stories about travel to the moon. The means of ascent they proposed were hardly scientific. Ariosto employed a horse drawn chariot, and in Kepler's construct demons provided the transport. Savinien de Cyrano de Bergerac, a French adventurer and poet best known for his huge nose and difficult love life, was more scientific. In the moon travel story he composed in 1649, the protagonist tied bottles of dew to himself. He reasoned that when the sun came out, the dew would evaporate and cause his body to rise, and in Cyrano's story it did.

The literary appearance of the first technological flying machines dates from the eighteenth century, but it was Jules Verne who initially stressed the scientific angle when he wrote *From the Earth to the Moon* in 1865, followed by *Around the Moon* in 1870. Verne's swashbuckling tales had a pronounced effect on early space and rocketry pioneers worldwide. It is perhaps debatable whether we would have come as far as we have without the vision of writers such as Verne, who allowed us to believe that somehow space travel was possible. The admission of possibility allowed scientists to contemplate the means. In a chicken-and-egg sort of way, one can legitimately wonder whether science fiction follows science or the other way round.

H.G. Wells, born in 1866 in the England of the Industrial Revolution, furthered the influence of science fiction. He believed strongly in the forward march of science and technology, though he was also cautionary about its unguarded use. His best known books, *War of the Worlds*, *The First Men on the Moon*, *The Invisible Man*, and *The Time Machine*, presented the possibilities of life in space and space travel to a generation of general readers. Wells died in 1946, having witnessed tremendous strides in the development of science and technology. He had also lived through two world wars and had seen his London landscape pitted and scarred under a rain of assault rockets. It was the deadly power of these same rockets that would finally set men and women on a course into space.

Few of us have heard of Konstantin Eduardovitch Tsiolkovsky. He was born in September 1857 in a province near Moscow, the partially deaf son of a lumberjack immigrant from Poland. He was a sickly child and to pass the time became an eager reader, avidly consuming whatever he could get his hands on. The village where he lived was small and most of the books were old and out of date, but encouraged by his father, he managed to educate himself with texts on math, physics, and astronomy, while also reading any fiction that came his way. At 16 he went to Moscow and continued his education in mathematics and physics. A few years later he accepted a job teaching in a high school in Kaluga province, which he kept until his retirement in the 1920s. What import has this quiet, scholarly life for the history of space exploration? Among other fictional works Tsiolkovsky read in his youth were Jules Verne's books. He was inspired by Verne's vision and began to turn over in his mind methods by which humans might be able to approach other planets. Early on he realized that if people were ever to travel beyond the gravitational field of the Earth, they would need a strong source of propulsion. Tsiolkovsky's genius lay in the fact that he realized that this means had to be a rocket and in his ability to form a logical and practical, if visionary, approach to solving the problem. Between 1903 and 1935, he wrote dozens of papers which laid the theoretical foundations for future space flight.

"Houston, we've had a problem here." With these understated words, three astronauts, James Lovell, John Swigert, and Fred Haise, began a four-day struggle to survive in a crippled spacecraft. The Apollo 13 mission was launched on April 11, 1970, to execute a third Moon landing near the crater Fra Mauro. On April 13, an explosion on the service module Odyssey caused NASA to scrap the original plans. All energies were concentrated on getting the three astronauts safely back to earth. This was no simple matter. The service portion of the command module, the larger of the two vessels, had lost all oxygen and electric power. Accordingly, all three men climbed into the small lunar module Aquarius. The lunar module had been designed to hold two people, so the fit was tight at best. There were only enough supplies to last two men two days, not to supply three men for a four-day tenure, but the supply of oxygen was stable and there was at least a chance of survival. In order to get the crippled vessel back to Earth, it was necessary to allow the craft to orbit the moon once and then engage itself on a free-return trajectory, which is essentially a free ride resulting from the pull of the Earth's gravity. Jammed into the small lunar module which grew so cold that ice began to form, the three men waited out the lunar orbit and the ensuing trip back to the Earth's atmosphere. There, about five hours before reentry, they jettisoned the severely damaged service module and reentered the command module. Two hours later they also jettisoned their lifeboat, the lunar module. Three hours after letting the lunar module go, they splashed down safely. Their harrowing six day flight over, the astronauts were able to relate their last sight of the Odyssey service module as they cut free of it to reenter the Earth's gravitational field. One entire side had blown away, giving them a clear picture of just how close they had been to death.

No one ever said that exploration would be safe and easy. Many men and women have died in the process of settling both the New World and the Old. However, there is something about exploring the spaces around us, the invasion of a completely alien environment in which there is no safe and easy return to the familiar, that excites fear and caution. There is something about the dependence on a complex and not-always-foolproof technology which produces reactions of stress and apprehension. This is the set of conditions into which we are moving. As it becomes clearer that the environment on Earth may be seriously compromised, that our population has too nearly followed the biblical injunction to "be fruitful and multiply," that our exploratory urges still need an out, we must consider that these fears are ones which must be overcome if we are to survive.

"Moscow is go for docking; Houston is go for docking. It's up to you guys. Have fun!" Capcom Dick Truly let the Apollo 18 astronauts know that all systems were ready for the docking of the Soviet Soyuz 19 and Apollo 18 modules. The agreements, painstakingly worked out on both political and technological fronts over a several-year period, resulted in a successful joining of the two ships on July 17, 1975. In the blackness of space, 100 miles above the Earth, the two ships linked successfully; American and Soviet space explorers shook hands in an environment far removed from national borders. We may hope that this is indicative of what we will see in the future. Though the Soviet program was more advanced than the United States' program, by 1975, the United States had taken the lead in moon landings. The combined strength of both the United States and the Russian Republics will be needed as we continue to probe outward.

Our nation and the newly created republics that have emerged from the breakdown of the Soviet Union, though preoccupied with troubles at home, continue to look upward. Talk of a joint mission to Mars may well come to little until the Soviet republics settle the earthbound concerns they have as emergent nations. Though technology has reached a state where reaching Mars may now be feasible, financing such a venture may well take the combined resources of several nations. Those of us with small children look with mixed apprehension and awe at the possibility of having grandchildren who live on Mars, not just a country, but a planet away. The world is changing both at home on Earth and skyward. National boundaries change and horizons expand. We must stretch our imaginations to expand with them.

References

Spangenburg, Ray and Diane Moser. (1989). *Living and Working in Space*. New York: Facts on File.

Spangenburg, Ray and Diane Moser. (1989). *Opening the Space Frontier*. New York: Facts on File.

ANNOTATED BIBLIOGRAPHY

Nonfiction

Apfel, Necia. *Voyager to the Planets*. New York: Clarion, 1991. $15.95. 48p. bibliography. index. ISBN 0-395-55209-5.

Voyager One and Voyager Two were sent out in 1977 to "fly by" the planets of our solar system; the two satellites have now entered interstellar space, carrying with them a gold plated phonograph record of greetings from our planet. The thought of these spacecraft so far from home is almost unthinkable, yet the photographs they have sent back are stranger still.

In a clear, large type text, Apfel examines the development and travels of the two space probes and the information they have provided since they were launched 15 years ago. The text is really a gloss for the photographs, oversized and beautiful, that the satellites have sent back. Whether it's Jupiter's great red spot or the moons of Neptune, these pictures are fascinating and completely engaging. Browsers who pick the book up will find themselves staying to read the text. In the process, they will learn a great deal about our solar system, other planets, the composition thereof, and prospects for further exploration, manned or unmanned. It's a pity Apfel doesn't define gas giants, but you can't have everything.

This is an excellent title to use for introducing the exploration of the solar system or even the outer planets. Just leaving it laying about the classroom will ensure ample use. A bibliography of books about planets (not exploration) and a brief but serviceable index complete the book.

Asimov, Isaac and Frank White. *Think about Space: Where Have We Been? Where Are We Going?* New York: Walker, 1989. $14.95. 142p. index. bibliography. glossary. ISBN 0-8027-6766-4.

How rapidly will people expand outwards into space? Will our generation see the settlement of Mars? It seems certain that as we find our planet more cramped and feel the need to explore further from home, space will become the ground for this explorational thrust. Tracing the development of space exploration and policy from the fifteenth century to the present, the authors go on to discuss possibilities for the future.

The book is divided into five chapters covering introductory and overview material, early background on space exploration (i.e., Copernicus, Galileo, Newton), the Space Age from 1945 to 1988, issues of concern today, and speculations about the future. Asimov's style is polished and breezy, but his questions are sharp, and his exposition would do credit to a legal brief. Black-and-white photographs and expressive cartoon drawings break up the text. Each chapter ends with a series of review questions. Some are strictly comprehension related, but others would provide food for independent reflection or class discussion. Accordingly, this is a sound teacher resource that reads aloud well and is thought provoking. A bit sketchy for report purposes, it does give a clear overview and adds a contemplative note to supporting materials.

Baker, David. *Danger on Apollo 13*. Vero Beach, FL: Rourke, 1988. 31p. $11.89. glossary. index. ISBN 0-86592-871-1.

In clear prose, the story of the near disaster aboard Apollo 13 comes alive. In keeping with the format of The Great Adventure Series, the prose is divided into six brief chapters. The opening chapter discusses the life-threatening explosion in the spacecraft Odyssey, the living module of the two crafts that comprised the Apollo 13 mission. Succeeding chapters cover the mission of Apollo 13, how the three-man crew was kept alive, the orbiting of the moon, the long journey back to Earth, and the safe arrival home.

The index and glossary are extremely brief. The latter consists of five terms, two of which ("earth orbit" and "moon orbit") are not defined correctly. (Orbit is defined as "a circular path," when orbits are, in fact, slightly elliptical.) The index is only about three-quarters of a page long and is not particularly easy to use. Terms are flush left and all page numbers are far to the right making the term hard to align with the page number. These problems are compensated for by both the prose account, which is clear and edge-of-your-seat gripping, and the numerous color photographs, which are as dramatic and as story-extending as could be wished. A solid report source, this book is also excellent read-aloud or booktalk material. Paired with a fictional account, like Jill Paton Walsh's *The Green Book*(see entry, below), it can be used to encourage space-based creative writing.

Baker, David. *Exploring Venus and Mercury.* Vero Beach, FL: Rourke, 1989. $11.89. 47p. index. glossary. ISBN 0-86592-371-X.

————. *Living in Space.* 48p. index. ISBN 0-86592-401-5.

————. *Living on the Moon.* 48p. index. ISBN 0-86592-374-4.

Today's World in Space is a series of books dealing with exploratory discoveries about our universe. Comprising of five to eight short chapters, embellished with photos and artists' renditions of life in space and on other planets, these books can be used in the introductory/browsing category as well as for reports. Though the type font is unfortunately small, Baker's prose, which is easy and informal, enhances accessibility. It may even be used as a read aloud to get information across in a smooth, coherent fashion. The indices are vestigial, and the glossaries helpful but hardly inspired.

Exploring Venus and Mercury chronicles NASA's exploration of the two planets, describing the missions and scientific discoveries made by Mariner and Pioneer. Giving background on the solar system as a whole, the text puts Venus and Mercury into planetary perspective before giving detailed information on the discoveries of the unmanned probes. The book finishes with a consideration of the Magellan satellite and of future missions to explore these inner planets.

Living in Space is broader in scope than the title might imply. In eight chapters, Baker traces the history of manned flights from the Mercury program to the shuttle program, examining the effects of weightlessness on astronauts; the difficulties of eating, working, sleeping, and bathing on board; and future plans for a space station. A three-page chapter is devoted to the Soviet Mir station, but it hardly balances the predominantly American focus. Teachers may wish to correct the imbalance by giving students books like Spangenburg's (see entry, below), which present a more objective treatment.

More speculative in nature, *Living on the Moon* recounts NASA's efforts to explore the moon, from the photographing of the surface by the Pioneer and Ranger spacecrafts to the Apollo landings. Scientific discoveries and the possibility of setting up a moon colony are considered in the last three chapters of the five. The text allows an exploration of the possibilities and can be used to start students thinking about the potential reality of lunar living.

Bean, Alan. *My Life as an Astronaut.* New York: Pocket Books, 1988. $2.95. 107p. ISBN 0-671-63452-6..

Alan Bean has done something few of us can claim to have done—he has walked on the moon. In this chatty, open biography, Bean tells readers about his experiences as an astronaut.

Divided into eight short chapters, the book begins as Bean lands on the moon with Pete Conrad. The narrative then backtracks to discuss Bean's childhood, years in the Naval Air Reserve, experiences as a test pilot, and finally his years as an astronaut. He covers his mission in the Apollo program, time spent on Skylab, and his involvement in the shuttle program. He glosses over his familial troubles, mentions a move from active astronaut training to an administrative role, and discusses his current passion—doing paintings of the moon and the astronauts.

This is not quite gripping enough to be a successful read aloud, but middle school boys will pick it up for its story and the breezy, easy-to-read style. The numerous black- and-white photographs, though grainy, add to the book's appeal. There is, in addition, enough material here for a report.

Berger, Melvin. *If You Lived on Mars.* New York: Lodestar/Dutton, 1989. $13.95. 82p. bibliography. index. ISBN 0-525-67260-5.

Speculation about life on Mars is backed up by accurate facts on the Red Planet and research into just how humans could survive on a planet that is inhospitable to life as we know it. If you lived on Mars, Berger asserts, your home would be the equivalent of five stories underground. You could not travel outside the colony without a space suit, and your age would be calculated differently because of the longer Martian year. Yet many aspects of life would be unchanged—school, sports, and television, to mention three.

Divided into 14 brief chapters, Berger discusses the construction of the Martian colony and goes on to consider housing, history, and living in a lower gravity situation; air, water, and food; and time, weather, the planet's surface, transportation, and terraforming. Most chapters are illustrated with black-and-white photographs of Mars, and an eight-page color insert includes both actual photos and speculative drawings. The two-page bibliography is helpful, especially in pointing out periodical sources of information. The index is accurate and functional.

This volume will booktalk or read aloud well thanks to Berger's easy, conversational style. It is suitable support reading for either science buffs or science fiction fans who are ready (or need to be encouraged) to go on to nonfiction sources.

Bernstein, Joanne E. and Rose Blue, with Alan Jay Gerber. *Judith Resnick: Challenger Astronaut.* New York: Lodestar/Dutton, 1990. $14.95. 112p. index. bibliography. ISBN 0-525-67305-9.

Judith Resnick was accepted by NASA into the space exploration program in 1978. It was an historic occasion not because she was female (Sally Ride scooped her on that count), but because she was Jewish. A driven individual, one who could be prickly and charming by turns, Resnick died on January 28, 1986, in the Challenger disaster.

Ten chapters cover the life of a vigorous and determined young woman and contemplate her death and its meaning. What is more important than the factual material given here is the personal glimpse it gives of one person's involvement in the exploration of the reaches beyond earth. Resnick comes alive as a three-dimensional person, with hopes and fears. In this way, the book brings the tragedy of the Challenger home to readers.

A good reading list and index enhance the book's utility as a report source, whether for space units or for biography. Good black-and-white photographs sprinkle the text and give readers a clear picture of Resnick and of the NASA space program. Parts of it read aloud well, though there are some slow narrative stretches. Still, this book has booktalk and excerpting potential, and can be used to drum up interest in the topic.

Boyne, Walter J. *The Smithsonian Book of Flight for Young People.* New York: Aladdin Books, 1988. $9.95. 128p. bibliography. index. ISBN 0-689-71212-X.

Before the Eagle landed or was even thought of, there were other flying machines that paved its way. We can date the idea of such machines back to the myth of Icarus, but this fine book begins in 1903 with Wilbur and Orville Wright's flight at Kitty Hawk. The book also covers the hot air balloon and such modern forms of flight as the Concorde and the Rutan Voyager.

The beautiful and often historic color reprints and photographs give a panoramic history of human airborne experience. Boyne's accompanying text is informative but retains a light touch. He never bores, in part because of his judicious use of anecdotal and primary source material. Students with even a mild interest in air transportation will be caught by the pictorial aspect. Including chapters on early flight, the two world wars and the period between, the Jet Age, and the future, this book provides a nearly ideal lead-in to Ron Schick's *The View from Space* (see entry, below). Good browsing, report, or interest reading, this volume delineates the beginnings of humankind's reach into space.

Branley, Franklyn M. *From Sputnik to Space Shuttles.* New York: T.Y. Crowell, 1986. $11.95. 53p. index. bibliography. ISBN 0-690-04531-X.

This slightly older book is still useful. Branley is a veteran nonfiction writer, and his lucid prose makes this an ideal introduction. Branley traces the history of artificial satellites from the launching of Sputnik to the present day. He presents clear discussions of how the satellites have aided advances in communication, weather forecasting, and scientific experiments. He also considers how these have changed the way we live.

Seven chapters cover gravitation and orbit work; communications satellites; LandSats; military satellites; space science satellites; satellites that use space conditions for experimentation; and space stations. Frequent black-and-white photos and a four-page color insert augment the text. The bibliography is out of date now, but the index and table of contents are still useful. This book predates the launching of the Hubble Space telescope, and thus talks about what it "will do" and not what it has done (or has failed to do).

This book is good introductory material and could also be used for short reports on earlier satellites and as a source of background information.

De Old, Alan R., et al. *Space Travel; A Technological Frontier.* Worcester, MA: Davis Publications, 1989. $29.95. index. 144p. glossary. ISBN 0-87192-206-1. **Ad.**

Looking at the study of transportation in space as an emerging phase of transportation generally, this text is built on the premise that our students will need to know as much about it as they do about land transport. The emphasis throughout is on current developments in the space shuttle project and on proposed future projects, such as a space tug and manned-maneuvering system. There is also an in-depth consideration of how transportation is dependent on and related to other technological systems, drawing the analogy most closely with communication.

Following a preface and an introduction, the book is divided into two parts: "To Earth Orbit" and "Within Earth Orbit." Part One includes chapters on expendable launch vehicles (16 pages), the space shuttles (40 pages), and aerospace planes (15 pages). Part Two covers the orbital maneuvering vehicle (20 pages), the manned maneuvering unit (12 pages), and space stations (26 pages). The index is thorough.

Each chapter is followed by a succinct summary, a list of terms, a list of important ideas and events, and suggestions of related things to do. These suggestions are intended to "simulate missions and provide opportunities to 'brainstorm' lifelike situations . . . . " Some do and some don't. Many involve requests for information and hands-on design.

Containing tremendous amounts of detailed technical information on mechanical functioning as well as some "you are there" sections, this book is a solid tool for answering almost any question that arises about the engineering end of space travel. The multitudinous diagrams and drawings further explain just how space transportation does what it does. The book could certainly answer Newton's seminal question, "How does it stay up?" It reads like a text and has a necessarily complex and specialized vocabulary. Since few students will pick it up as interest reading, this volume is best used as a classroom teaching tool and reference source.

Donnelly, Judy and Sydille Kramer. *Space Junk: Pollution Beyond the Earth.* New York: Morrow Junior Books, 1990. $12.95. 106p. index. bibliography. ISBN 0-688-08678-0.

At this moment, hundreds of miles above where you sit reading, hundreds of pieces of human debris are circling our planet. These include everything from burned-out satellites to paint chips. This extraterrestrial debris is a relatively new and potentially deadly form of pollution. How did it all get there? In this brief, absorbing book, Donnelly and Kramer take a look at how "humans in space . . . leaving their garbage behind" have created a hazardous situation for those who would orbit the earth later.

The six chapters consider the history of space flight, rocketry and its associated debris, the debris from the U.S. and Soviet space programs, and the considerable dangers of debris. For example, in 1983 a paint chip hit the window of the

Challenger and left a pea-sized pit. On the Earth the chip, almost invisible, could not conceivably have caused any damage, but in space, travelling at about 14,000 miles an hour, such a tiny fleck is potentially deadly. It could have cracked the window wide open. Measures to contain space garbage and the question of who owns space are also explored.

The typeface is large and the vocabulary fairly simple. Clearly stated questions are put and answered completely. There is a sound index and excellent, comprehensive bibliography. The frequent black-and-white illustrations extend the text well, adding interest and clarity. This book is an excellent report and information source on a topic of increasing concern.

Embury, Barbara. *The Dream Is Alive: A Flight of Discovery Aboard the Space Shuttle.* New York: Harper & Row, 1990. $14.95. 64p. index. ISBN 0-06-021814-2.

This oversized pictorial treatment of shuttle flights is a nightmare to shelve and not strongly attached to its binding. But beyond that, the only quandary may be how to detach it from enthusiastic and interested students. Based on the IMAX film, *The Dream Is Alive*, which documents the activities of three 1984 shuttle missions, this volume features stunning color photography and a lucid text.

The three missions looked at are Mission 41C (April 6-13, 1984), Mission 41D (August 30-September 5, 1984), and Mission 41G (October 5-13, 1984). The first and third of these missions were flown on the Challenger, a name now shrouded in doom. It is a change to see it used in the context of successful operations. Each of these missions had a task to complete. Forty-one C repaired the Solar Max satellite, 41D unfurled the Discovery's solar-array panel, and during the course of 41G Kathryn Sullivan became the first American woman to space walk.

The book is arranged in four chapters: "Riding a Column of Fire," "Putting It All Together," "A Day in Space," and "Coming Home." There are astronaut profiles, a look at shuttle construction, discussions of take-off and landing, and a look at highly technical maneuvers as well as day-to-day life—going to the bathroom in space and eating. The Challenger tragedy is mentioned, as is the rejuvenation of the shuttle program. The index and table of contents give access to report writers, and the glorious photos make this a browser's delight as well as a great teaching tool for classroom or library introductions to the optic angle of space exploration. Added trivia information (how the orbiters got their names and space exploration as it appears on postage stamps) boosts appeal.

Fichter, George. *The Space Shuttle.* New York: Watts, 1981. $10.90. 64p. glossary. index. ISBN 0-531-04354-1.

Describing the early history of the space shuttle, our "sky truck" for transporting materials to space stations, Fichter covers prior aeronautical innovations; the debut of the Enterprise, the first shuttle, completed in 1976; some of the problems encountered (all pre-Challenger); the flight script; the interior and exterior construction and features of the orbiter (the actual shuttle vehicle); the use of Spacelab; the proposed use of the shuttle for eventual colonization purposes and construction of solar satellites; and the actual flight of the Columbia on April 12, 1981.

The 10 chapters are brief and are frequently interspersed with black-and-white photos or artists' representations of aspects of space life. The final chapter contains a higher concentration of photos depicting the Columbia's flight. These pictures capture the excitement and sense of success that the flight produced by showing the human response in the faces of astronauts Crippen and Young.

The typeface is small and dense, giving a cramped look to the text. However, students looking for historical information on the shuttle will find it here. The glossary and index are both acceptable, though not comprehensive, making this a workable report source.

It is unfortunate that the book is so dated. However, as most students associate the shuttle with the Challenger tragedy, this book will stand well as a balancing element, showing the climate of optimism and enthusiasm that characterized the shuttles' early days.

Furness, Tim. *The Exploration of Space.* Vero Beach, FL: Rourke, 1990. $11.95. 48p. bibliography. index. glossary. ISBN 0-86592-097-4.

In an interesting alternative look at space exploration, this volume in Rourke's World Issues series looks at the exploration of space, how it can benefit people, and how problems like space debris and military investment may hamper our future growth. Furness writes in an approachable manner, using a reasonably complex vocabulary and addressing fairly involved issues. For example, he covers types of orbits (low polar, geostationary, and 60 degree), uses of satellites, and costs of space research in a succinct, economical way while still managing to look at issues from several angles. The author does have a slight anti-militarist, pro-conservationist bias, but it does not infuse his text to the point of being problematic.

The book is divided into seven chapters covering satellites and orbits, benefits and costs of research, space debris and militarization, and space as the final frontier. The type font is small and quite dense. The columnar arrangement and inclusion of copious illustrations—photos, drawings, and diagrams in both black-and-white and full color—give it a newspaper-like look. The pictorial content gives this title considerable browsing appeal, as well as increasing its book talking or class sharing potential. The glossary and index are both brief but functional. A short bibliography of juvenile titles is current to within seven years. This book is a good report source, but will have to be pushed with older middle schoolers because its slimness gives it an elementary appearance. Younger middle school students may have some problems with the vocabulary, but can glean information from the illustrations.

Lauber, Patricia. *Seeing Earth from Space.* New York: Orchard, 1990. $19.95. 80p. index. bibliography. ISBN 0-531-08502-3.

In this volume, breathtaking NASA, LandSat, and Meteosat photographs of the Earth from space meld with a smooth narrative that alerts us to the problems our fragile environment faces. Whether science buffs, photography enthusiasts, or budding environmentalists, students will be stimulated by these discussion provoking images.

Lauber divides her breathtaking pictorial treatment into five chapters on "Planet Earth," "Sightseeing," "Remote Sensing," "Using Remote Sensing," and "Spaceship Earth." The rather elementary level text will not hinder middle school use. The book draws readers through the illustrative material. Though the focus is not on space exploration, the brilliant photographs speak for our abilities to see far above the surface of our planet, and to use technology to create and translate images. Explanations of concepts such as remote sensing, and of spacecraft like weather satellites, are brief and crystalline. This book is an ideal introduction or summing up for units on space exploration because it brings the focus from space to our Earth, the starting and ending place for those who would investigate the stars. A supporting bibliography and good index back up an unparalleled teaching tool.

Mason, John. *Spacecraft Technology.* New York: Bookwright, 1990. $12.40. 48p. index. bibliography. glossary. ISBN 0-531-18328-9.

In 20 two-page sections, this entry in the Technology in Action series provides an introduction to space technology, discussing the principles of rockets, various types of satellites, travel in the solar system, and space stations.

The prose style is strictly informational and, set in a rather small typeface, barely escapes being dry. The format, however, militates against putting the book down. Each double-page spread contains an equal amount of text and illustration. There are photos and artists' renditions of life in space, each type of picture equally fascinating. Diagrams are clear, colorful, and explanatory, extending and enhancing the information given in the text.

The two-page sections cover early forays into space; rocketry; communications and spy satellites; X-ray satellites and the Hubble Space Telescope; missions to Venus, Mercury, and Mars; the Voyager probes and future probes; manned spaceflight from the lunar modules to Soviet and American shuttles and space stations; mission control's function; colonization in the future; and moving outward toward the stars. It is worth noting that this book was written before the Hubble Space Telescope was launched, and thus does not mention its problems.

The book packs a lot of information in a very brief form and its browsing draw is high. Students who pick it up for the pictures will go on to the text for explanation. The index and glossary are sound, and the bibliography is current, though it reads like a paid advertisement for the publisher. This volume is good browsing, report, or interest/supplemental material.

Maurer, Richard. *The NOVA Space Explorer Guide: Where to Go and What to See.* Rev. ed. New York: Clarkson N. Potter, 1991. $20.00. 118p. index. ISBN 0-517-57758-5.

If you were to travel through the solar system, what would you find? Based on the PBS television series, this updated version of a previously published text provides an answer to that question, couched in serviceable prose. A "you are there" format adds some badly needed verve.

Divided into eight chapters, text and lovely color photos cover a voyage through the solar system from lift off, to the moon, the inner planets, the giant planets, and out beyond Pluto. Maurer's explanations of planet ecology are especially well done, and the color and black-and-white photos that pack each section speak worlds more than the competent text.

Useful for only short reports (the information given demonstrates breadth rather than depth), this book is nonetheless valuable for generating interest and a browser's delight.

Nicholson, Iain. *The Illustrated World of Space.* New York: Simon & Schuster, 1991. $12.95. 64p. index. glossary. ISBN 0-671-74127-6.

What does a galaxy look like? What happens to things drawn into a black hole? What kinds of vehicles travel in space? The basic facts about the solar system and such astral phenomena as black holes and comets, sunspots and launch vehicles, receive a pictorial browser's treatment.

The text is divided into five sections: "Studying the Planets," "The Universe," "The Solar System," "The Inner Planets," and "The Outer Planets." Each section covers various aspects of its topic in two-page sections. Copiously illustrated with drawings and photos, the text consists, for all practical purposes, of captions. There is a wealth of information presented in a digestible *hors d'oeuvre* manner. Giving facts on all the planets as well as on history and space exploration, this book is a good source of anecdotal, attention-getting material.

The glossary is excellent and the index good, though the table of contents is thorough enough to direct students to the appropriate pages.

Ressmeyer, Roger. *Space Places.* New York: Collins, 1990. $45.00. 208p. ISBN 0-00-215732-2. **Ad.**

From Stonehenge to the Xichang Satellite Launch Center in China, Ressmeyer documents "space places," where people gaze at, aim for, and contemplate the stars. Short explanatory paragraphs describe the facility under examination. For example, the entry for Stonehenge gives the history of its construction and a brief explanation of its use as an early astronomical observatory. Coverage for the Xichang Satellite Launch Center introduces Western readers to the Long March booster rocket and to the exigencies of locating a rocket launching facility next to farm land. Each entry is paired with a one-inch global map showing the location of the site under discussion.

The beginning of each chapter is composed of a double-page spread or, at the beginning and end of the book, a series of spreads matched with quotes. There are seven chapters: "Ancient Astronomy," "Great Telescopes around the World," "The Process of Discovery and Supernova 1987A," "Life in the Universe," "International Advances in Space Exploration," "Missions to the Planets," and "The Dawn of the Second Space Age." While textual coverage is good, the pictorial elements give this hugely oversized volume its value. The color photographs are clear and informative, intriguing and mysterious at once. Browsers will be glued to *Space Places* and, in reading captions, are sure to pick up information and perhaps an interest that will send them on to more textually detailed treatments. This intriguing introductory tool is good for booktalking if you can hoist the book to show the pictures without back strain.

Schick, Ron and Julia Van Haaften. *The View from Space: American Astronaut Photography, 1962-1972.* New York: Clarkson N. Potter, 1988. $30.00. 128p. bibliography. ISBN 0-517-56082-8.

A marvelous oversized pictorial tour de force, *The View from Space* reproduces some of the most spectacular color photographs taken during the heyday of U.S. space flight. Following a foreword by William Styron and a detailed introduction, the pictures are arranged chronologically with brief biographies of the 16 astronauts who took them. Camera makes and models and the histories of some of the pictures are all described in a clear, readable prose.

This book is fascinating browsing material; students who pick it up just to look will end up reading first the picture captions and then the text. Brilliant photos of the Earth from space, the lunar surface, astronauts engaged in extra-vehicular activity, and space capsules and docking adapters are sharp, beautiful, and mysterious. A brief bibliography of adult titles gives a pointer to other photo collections. This volume is an excellent support and extension tool, fascinating for introductory booktalks or classroom topic openers, especially if paired with Wayne Barlowe's fiction work on Darwin IV (see entry, below).

Spangenburg, Ray and Diane Moser. *Exploring the Reaches of the Solar System.* New York: Facts on File, 1990. $18.95. 109p. index. bibliography. glossary. ISBN 0-8160-1850-2.

————. *Living and Working in Space.* 114p. ISBN 0-8160-1849-9.

————. *Opening the Space Frontier.* 111p. ISBN 0-8160-1848-0.

————. *Space People from A to Z.* 100p. ISBN 0-8160-1851-0.

For presenting information on the history of space exploration and its current status, these four volumes in the Facts on File Space Exploration series are invaluable resources. The volumes have identical formats: between 8 and 13 chapters are followed by uniformly excellent glossaries, indices, and bibliographies which include not only books, but magazine sources. All four contain numerous black-and-white photographs and diagrams that delineate everything from the gravity assist technique used to send the Mercury Ten spacecraft toward Mercury, to the link up between the Apollo and Soyuz space modules in 1975. An eight-page color section shows plates appropriate to the topic. The authors use a conversational style that is easy to read and comprehend. Browsers are sure to pick up space facts painlessly.

Exploring the Reaches of the Solar System opens with detailed chapters on the moon and the eight other planets. Missions carried out by Mercury, Mariner, Viking, and Voyager satellites are given in detail, covering both technological and scientific aspects of the exploration process. A second section looks at Earth, asteroids, comets, the sun, and other galaxies. The color photos from the 1989 Voyager mission to Neptune are fascinating, as are other photographs included from Apollo and Viking expeditions. The book offers new perspectives on the greenhouse effect, a brief chronicle of humans on the moon, an introduction to the

Hubble Space Telescope (now slightly out of date), and plans for future fact finding missions. This volume is an unimpeachable source for reports or interest reading.

The same can be said for *Living and Working in Space*. In this volume, the focus is on space work stations. Part One, entitled "Living on a New Frontier," opens with a chapter on the original Soviet Salyut Space Station and moves on to chapters on Skylab, Apollo-Soyuz, and Salyut Six and Seven. The second part, "Making a Work Place in Space," treats satellites, the space shuttle, the Soviet Mir space station, and the exploitation of this new frontier, which covers such international groups as the European Space Agency and the U.S./E.S.A./Japanese Earth Observing System. This volume concludes with an epilogue on the human future in space and includes two appendices listing Soviet and U.S. missions in space.

Opening the Space Frontier begins by looking at visions of space travel, early rocketry to 1945, later rocket development (1945–57), and the advent of Sputnik and Explorer One (1957–60). Part Two, "Sending Humans into Space," discusses the X15, Vostok, and Mercury programs; Vosthod and Gemini, the tragedies of 1967; Apollo missions to the moon; and Soyuz missions. Part Three is concerned exclusively with Apollo missions 11 through 17, the missions to the moon. An appendix of "Pioneers in Space" lists both Soviet cosmonauts and American astronauts who flew successful missions. This book ends with the Apollo 17 mission in 1972, but the subsequent history of space exploration is picked up in *Living and Working in Space*.

Space People from A to Z gives brief (one paragraph to one and a half pages) biographies of all the men and women who have flown on Soviet or American space missions. "Spacionauts" from other countries are also included. People who have worked on equipment, aeronautics, or rocket propulsion are listed as well. A sort of "Who's Who" of the space flight world, the brief capsule biographies are extended by black-and-white photos and drawings pertinent to the entries they accompany. The Soviet biographies are noticeably briefer than those of their American counterparts. One assumes this has to do with the availability of information. The center section shows color photographs of a number of space notables, mostly astronauts and cosmonauts. Because of the brevity of the entries, this volume is best used as supporting material for reports.

Giving thorough coverage to both American and Soviet space efforts, these volumes are excellent sources for browsing, interest reading, reports, or background information.

Vogt, Gregory. *Apollo and the Moon Landing.* Brookfield, CT: Millbrook Press, 1991. $14.90. 111p. index. bibliography. sources. space flight log. glossary. ISBN 1-878841-31-9.

On May 25, 1961, President John F. Kennedy announced his intention to put a man on the moon before the end of the decade. Though he did not live to see his dream come to fruition, in July 1969 on the night of the first moon landing someone is reported to have placed a bouquet of flowers on Kennedy's grave. Attached to it was a note: "Mr. President, the Eagle has landed." A tremendous amount of work went into the achievement of that landing, and this entry in the Missions in Space series documents it in considerable detail.

Eight chapters cover the history of moon explorations from Galileo to the lunar orbiters, Project Mercury, Project Gemini, choosing a route to the moon, Saturn V and the lunar lander, early Apollo missions through the moon landing, later Apollo missions, and the lunar legacy with prospects for the future. The text is attractively set in a clear type font, and runs in a fairly narrow column down the center of the page. Frequent color and black-and-white photos increase the appeal of the volume. The moon is shown in unappealing and unrealistic shades of pink, gold, and rust, but, aside from this, the pictures are well reproduced. Vogt's prose is dry, though he does try for the anecdotal and lively.

This serviceable volume is best used as a report source; it has solid detailed information on the U.S. manned space flight program. The joint Apollo-Soyuz flight is also mentioned. The index is adequate and the brief annotated bibliography leads to other sources, though they are almost all U.S. government publications and may be hard to find. The same is also true of the source list. A "Space Flight Log" gives brief information on all U.S. unmanned and manned flights, providing an overview of our space program between 1961 and 1972.

Vogt, Gregory. *Space Explorers.* New York: Watts, 1990. $11.90. 32p. index. glossary. chronology. ISBN 0-531-10461-3.

————. *Space Stations.* ISBN 0-531-10460.

————. *Spaceships.* ISBN 0-531-10405-2.

The Watts Space Library series provides introductory and browsing fare for students interested in space exploration. All the books have identical formats. Each slightly oversized book comprises 12 two-page sections treating various aspects of the area of exploration under consideration. A chronology of important dates, glossary, and index finish each volume. The indices are serviceable but provide only minimum access. The glossaries are exemplary, with succinct and precise definitions. The books contain a range of photographs and artists' renditions of life in space that are intriguing, fascinating, and excellent for engendering contemplation and "what if" thinking. The texts are not really engaging, but coupled with the pictorial content they will be read for their explanations. The informational content is high, with both U.S. and Soviet advances considered.

Space Explorers covers historical aspects of space exploration, telescopes (whether in orbit or not), measuring the moon and moon landings, robot planetary explorers, and explorations of the other planets in our solar system. The book finishes with a consideration of possible colonies on the moon and Mars.

Space Stations begins with an intriguing account of Edward Everett Hale's 1869 story about a "brick moon," perhaps the first inkling of the space stations of the present day. This opening is a snappy attention-getter, and can be used to reinforce the notion that fiction, especially science fiction, often precedes and predicts science fact. Discussion of early orbiters is followed by information on the Soviet Salyut stations, Skylab, the Apollo-Soyuz mission, the Mir space stations, American designs for shuttle constructed stations, ESA Spacelab, the Freedom Space Station, and the possibilities for colonies in space.

Spaceships opens with Spaceship Earth, discussing the differences between this natural ship and mechanical ones made by humans. Vogt next considers the concept of rocket propulsion, early rockets, animals in orbit, and the American Mercury, Gemini, and Apollo programs. The space shuttle and (tiny) manned maneuvering unit are the focus of the next section. Commendably, Vogt devotes a two-page section to the loss of the Challenger, a setback barely mentioned and glossed over in other introductory treatments. Aside from the shuttle, other space planes, such as the French Humes and British HOTOL crafts, are examined, as are spaceships of the future.

These books are excellent, well-rounded opening materials for units on space exploration. Attractive, accessible, and useful, these volumes are useful for browsers, report writers, and teachers in need of stories and concepts to engage students' attention.

Vogt, Gregory. *The Space Shuttle.* Brookfield, CT: Millbrook Press, 1991. $14.90. 112p. index. bibliography. glossary. ISBN 1-56294-049-X.

————. *Voyager.* Brookfield, CT: Millbrook Press, 1991. $14.90. 112 p. index. bibliography. glossary. ISBN 1-56294-050-3.

Two books in the Missions in Space series share an identical format: narrow columns of dark, clear type leave wide center margins. In the first book the text is paired with photographs of views from or life in the shuttle. In the second, photographs taken by the Voyager satellite are shown.

Vogt's prose is readable. The information given is correct and accessible through either a table of contents or index. Both books contain bibliographies of predominantly adult works—mostly from NASA—and good comprehensive glossaries. These books are acceptable report sources but cannot compete visually with either Barbara Embury's *The Dream Is Alive* or Necia Apfel's *Voyager to the Planets* (see entries for both, above). In the absence of these works, however, Vogt may fill the bill.

Fiction

Barlowe, Wayne Douglas. *Expedition: Being an Account in Words and Artwork of the 2358 A.D. Voyage to Darwin IV.* New York: Workman Publishing, 1990. $18.95. 192p. ISBN 0-89480-629-7.

"My fellow expedition members and I were tucked into our sleep-pods. Once past Pluto our Yma pilots engaged the main drive, and in the blink of an eye we traversed the 6.5 light years to the Darwin system. We attained orbit above Darwin IV on January 6, 2358." Roughly three and a half centuries hence, our planet has been saved only by intercession of the benevolent Yma. As they slowly revitalize Earth's destroyed ecological system, they send young scientists to other systems to observe the flora and fauna. This is the record of one such expedition.

The book is divided into sections (the grasslands and plains, forest, amoebic sea and bittoral zone, mountains, tundra, and the air) and describes 31 different animals in detail. The verbal descriptions, clear, succinct, and marveling though they are, are no match for the tour de force artwork. Black-and-white sketches give way to large full-color paintings of strange beasts, denizens of land, sea, and air. Because the pictorial element is so strong and the verbal explanations so consistent, the reader may well come away believing that fictional Darwin IV must exist.

A superb instrument for inspiring creative writing and artwork, this book has a "what if" element that will catch the attention and hold it. Used as hook for a unit on space exploration, this book can add excitement and intrigue, and give a deeper meaning to more fact-grounded informational treatments.

Lawrence, Louise. *Moonwind.* New York: Harper & Row, 1986. $13.95. 180p. ISBN 0-06-023734-1.

Interspersed with information on what it might be like to live in a permanent base on the moon is a love story of considerable power. Gareth and Karen are two young people who have won trips to the moon. Bethkahn is an astral being who has been asleep for 10,000 years on her damaged star ship. The arrival of the two teenagers coincides with Bethkahn's awakening and her decision to risk contact with the humans at the lunar base in the hopes of repairing her ship. Needing a conduit to speak for her, she chooses the bitter Gareth and finds herself in love with him. Karen is concerned for Gareth and feels the astral presence, but can do nothing to intervene.

Strong plotting and vigorous prose make this book suitable as either recreational reading or as a read-aloud. Both the scientific elements of the story and the extraterrestrial life facet provide food for discussion and contemplation.

Paton Walsh, Jill. *The Green Book.* Illustrated by Lloyd Bloom. New York: Farrar, Straus, & Giroux, 1982. $9.95. 103p. ISBN 0-374-32778-5.

Planet Earth is dying, and the last shipload of refugees is allowed to take along a limited number of necessary supplies and a luxury—one book each. Pattie, the youngest member of the expedition, takes a blank book. While this at first seems to be a waste, it later becomes The Green Book that holds the account of the settlement on Shine, the planet on which they have landed.

A simple yet eloquent prose style and a gripping story make this an excellent book for reading aloud. The scenario is uncomfortably possible, and the new planet believably drawn. Lloyd Bloom's soft pencil drawings heighten both the sense of familiarity and strangeness that life on a new planet brings. An unusually fine discussion starter, this book could also fire students' own conceptions of other worlds.

Supplemental Adult Books

Booth, Nicholas. *Space: The Next 100 Years.* New York: Orion Books, 1990. $21.95. 128p. index. ISBN 0-517-57764-X.

There is science and there is science fiction, and though the latter often produces the former, one must be wary of predictions. They aren't always true. Nuclear power hasn't brought free power, and none of us lives in a society even slightly resembling that of the Jetsons. Progress on the technological front may not be quick but it does continue. By extrapolating from already existing technologies, Nicholas Booth explores the myriad possibilities offered to us by space—possibilities that have a fighting chance of becoming realities.

Following introductory material on space exploration to date, Booth discusses "Robot Explorers," "The High Frontier," "Extending the Frontier," and "The Far Future." Each section contains between 10 and 15 two-page sections covering everything from the exploration of planets and heavenly bodies to laser and nuclear powered space ships. The Soviet Mir station receives close scrutiny, as does the Freedom Space Station. Each section is arranged chronologically beginning with 1990 and extending in the final section to 2070+.

Booth's vocabulary and information density both rate high. His style is unfortunately humdrum, lacking the sparkle and verve of the average encyclopedia. The typeface is almost microscopic. The book's greatest draw is its many attractive illustrations. Photographs, charts, artists' extrapolations, and detailed diagrams bring our future off-world to life with an unsurpassed degree of vividness. The index is detailed and helpful and can be used to give students access to supporting material for reports. This excellent browsing book will have students poking into its dry text for explanations. The "what if" aspect also gives this title special applicability to the gifted child.

Burgess, Eric. *Return to the Red Planet.* New York: Columbia University Press, 1990. $34.95. 222p. index. glossary. bibliography. ISBN 0-231-06942-1.

It seems a fact that there is no life on Mars now, but the possibility that there may have been life in the past remains. If it existed, was it life as we know it? Recent investigation of the Martian terrain indicates that Mars is wetter and more complicated than we thought, and that it may be possible that about three billion years ago life evolved on Mars as it did on Earth. If this is the case, we are faced with two interesting possibilities: either life on Mars became extinct or it has adapted to immense climatic change and we have not yet recognized it.

Noting mythological and astrological views of Mars in passing, author Burgess turns to the wealth of scientific information gathered by the Viking and Mariner probes. Pointing out that there are seasonal changes, the author indicates that the Martian climate's closest terrain equivalent is Antarctica. He feels that much about our planet's past can be discovered by exploring Mars and analyzing what we find there.

The seven chapters into which the oversized book is divided are fairly lengthy. The text is clear and attractively set, but stylistically complex. The scientific aspects are fairly sophisticated, making this suitable only for advanced independent readers. An excellent index and bibliography add to the potential of this book for research and report writing. The glossary is a model of its kind, being both comprehensive and understandable. Frequent black-and-white photographs and diagrams, meticulously captioned, add to and extend textual information, but are not sufficiently arresting to attract browsers.

Used by a teacher as background or for raising intriguing questions, *Return to the Red Planet* can increase student understanding of how life may evolve in our universe and of the many purposes of interplanetary exploration.

Burrows, William E. *Exploring Space: Voyage in the Solar System and Beyond.* New York: Random House, 1990. $24.95. 502p. index. sources notes. ISBN 0-399-56983-0.

Burrows covers the technological, historical, and political aspects of unmanned planetary probes, such as Voyager, Mariner, and Viking, offering insight into the complex relationship between manned and military space programs. This popular-science, popular-history approach will appeal largely to better readers who will not be daunted by the book's length. For such serious students, or older middle schoolers with sufficient interest to tackle an adult source, this book will provide highly readable, informative fare.

"When you get an answer you couldn't formulate a question for, that's exploration," Merton E. Davis observed. In this lengthy book, divided into 14 chapters, many such answers are investigated. Dealing with aspects on planetary exploration from the dreaming stage through the efforts of the Jet Propulsion Lab, to prospects for the future, *Exploring Space* shows how rivalry between the superpowers drove both lunar and planetary exploration. A 16-page insert of black-and-white photos gives faces to the names mentioned in the text, as well as showing views of some of the planets photographed by unmanned investigative spacecraft. A detailed list of "Solar System Exploration Missions" outlines objective results of each. An extensive list of sources from books to magazines, anthologies to news releases, and letters to audiovisual treatments is also included.

Collins, Michael. *Mission to Mars.* New York: Grove Weidenfeld, 1990. $22.50. 307p. index. ISBN 0-8021-1160-2.

Michael Collins flew into space for the first time as the pilot of Gemini 10 in 1966. Three years later he manned the command module of the Apollo 11 moon-landing mission. In this intriguing book, he argues compellingly for a revitalization of space exploration by focusing on one goal: human exploration of Mars, with the long-range goal of establishing a permanent colony. In describing this complex undertaking, he has created a mission to Mars complete with departure and return dates, and a listing of the physical, technical, and physiological demands to be met in order to survive on the Martian surface. He also addresses issues of funding, interim space stations, and cooperative work with the Soviet authorities.

The book is divided into 25 brief chapters, but each contains a wealth of both technical and historical information in an accessible and involving style. An eight-page color insert contains photographs of the Martian surface, detailed drawings of the route to Mars, and space vehicles that will be needed to explore and colonize the Martian surface. The speculation on the Martian mission will engage science fiction enthusiasts who like science facts as well, and the large open typeface may encourage readers who might otherwise be off put by the book's length. This is a book for better independent readers, but sections from it could be read in class or in the library to ignite discussion and "what if" thinking. The table of contents and excellent index enhance access to key points in the text, making the book an unusual but effective report source.

Elias, George Henry. *Breakout into Space: Mission for a Generation.* New York: Morrow, 1990. $16.95. 213p. index. source notes. ISBN 0-688-07703-X.

That our small blue planet is in trouble is news to no one. Pharaoh's biblical plagues seem small compared to our soaring population, the greenhouse effect, ozone holes, AIDS, and the nuclear threat. George Henry Elias here presents the case for moving civilization out into space. He believes that it is the task of the gifted generation that came of age in the 1960s and 1970s to make space accessible to the greater population and to begin the construction of a trans-solar system civilization.

The book is divided into seven chapters on "The Gifted Generation"; "Manifest Destiny and the Space Frontier"; preserving democratic ideals; the opportunities afforded those of us who are adult at this time; the functions of technology, education, and business in furthering space expansion; the role of the Gifted Generation; and a rationale for breaking out into space. Detailed source notes give references to supporting arguments for the author's premise. The indexing is thorough and helpful.

This book offers an extremely right-wing solution to earth's problems. Many statements are sweeping, provocative, and open to the question: "The solar system is ours. No other form of life exists to claim the bounties of a civilization that spans the solar system . . . . " But this view is precisely the value of the book. When Elias calls students to question his values and assertions, he helps them to clarify their own. Older middle school classes will benefit from the intense debate and discussion this book engenders. It can set them to ruminating on just what our future in, and our obligation to, space may be.

Index

by Linda Webster